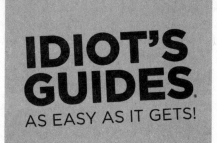

Project Management

Sixth Edition

By G. Michael Campbell, PMP

ALPHA
A member of Penguin Group (USA) Inc.

This book is dedicated to the important women in my life—Molly, Heather, Megan, and Courtney.

ALPHA BOOKS

Published by Penguin Group (USA) Inc.

Penguin Group (USA) Inc., 375 Hudson Street, New York, New York 10014, USA • Penguin Group (Canada), 90 Eglinton Avenue East, Suite 700, Toronto, Ontario M4P 2Y3, Canada (a division of Pearson Penguin Canada Inc.) • Penguin Books Ltd., 80 Strand, London WC2R 0RL, England • Penguin Ireland, 25 St. Stephen's Green, Dublin 2, Ireland (a division of Penguin Books Ltd.) • Penguin Group (Australia), 250 Camberwell Road, Camberwell, Victoria 3124, Australia (a division of Pearson Australia Group Pty. Ltd.) • Penguin Books India Pvt. Ltd., 11 Community Centre, Panchsheel Park, New Delhi—110 017, India • Penguin Group (NZ), 67 Apollo Drive, Rosedale, North Shore, Auckland 1311, New Zealand (a division of Pearson New Zealand Ltd.) • Penguin Books (South Africa) (Pty.) Ltd., 24 Sturdee Avenue, Rosebank, Johannesburg 2196, South Africa • Penguin Books Ltd., Registered Offices: 80 Strand, London WC2R 0RL, England

IDIOT'S GUIDES and Design are trademarks of Penguin Group (USA) Inc.

International Standard Book Number: 978-1-61564-442-1
Library of Congress Catalog Card Number: 2013950650

20 19 18   13 12 11 10 9 8 7 6

Interpretation of the printing code: The rightmost number of the first series of numbers is the year of the book's printing; the rightmost number of the second series of numbers is the number of the book's printing. For example, a printing code of 14-1 shows that the first printing occurred in 2014.

Printed in the United States of America

Note: This publication contains the opinions and ideas of its author. It is intended to provide helpful and informative material on the subject matter covered. It is sold with the understanding that the author and publisher are not engaged in rendering professional services in the book. If the reader requires personal assistance or advice, a competent professional should be consulted. The author and publisher specifically disclaim any responsibility for any liability, loss, or risk, personal or otherwise, which is incurred as a consequence, directly or indirectly, of the use and application of any of the contents of this book.

Most Alpha books are available at special quantity discounts for bulk purchases for sales promotions, premiums, fundraising, or educational use. Special books, or book excerpts, can also be created to fit specific needs. For details, write: Special Markets, Alpha Books, 375 Hudson Street, New York, NY 10014.

Publisher: *Mike Sanders*
Executive Managing Editor: *Billy Fields*
Senior Acquisitions Editor: *Brook Farling*
Development Editor: *Kayla Dugger*
Senior Production Editor: *Janette Lynn*

Cover Designer: *Laura Merriman*
Book Designer: *William Thomas*
Indexer: *Heather McNeil*
Layout: *Ayanna Lacey*
Proofreader: *Amy Borrelli*

Contents

Introduction

Many project managers guess as a way to estimate the level of effort for a project. However, there is a better way to manage projects, and you don't need to be a genius, or even have an MBA, to understand how. It doesn't take a special certification to manage a project (although that doesn't hurt), but it does take special knowledge and skills to bring projects in on time and within budget. Yes, careful planning and tracking is involved in moving projects from start to finish, but this book takes the practical approach to the process and puts you in control. The following pages map the road to successful project management.

Idiot's Guides: Project Management, Sixth Edition, explains in easy-to-understand language how the power of time-proven project management methods can help your projects come in on time, on budget, and on target. You learn how to point project teams, in spite of politics and personalities, in the same direction and how to manage changes, no matter how frequent, to keep projects on track. Finally, you learn that it's knowledge and skill—not luck or fancy degrees—that makes the difference in making your project a success.

How to Use This Book

The book has six parts, which I recommend you read from beginning to end. The parts work together to provide you with the steps and tools behind successful project management and offer practical advice you can adapt to the needs of today's fast-moving, ever-changing organizations.

Part 1, The Power of Project Management, explains how to link projects to the business requirements that all project managers must satisfy. I'll tell you what it means to be a project manager, and how to get started correctly so you can bring your project in on time and on budget.

Part 2, The Project Definition Phase, presents techniques to start a project off on the right foot with a clear scope and a well-defined work plan. You'll also learn how to identify and manage stakeholders while controlling project risks.

Part 3, The Project Planning Phase, explains the basic planning processes central to successful project management. You observe how to define, schedule, and budget tasks using powerful charting and analysis tools that can help you plan projects of all sorts and sizes. This is the most technical part of the book, so you might want to read it twice. Mastering the information in this part is important because no project is ever better than the plan used to manage the effort.

Part 4, The Execution Phase, presents proven techniques to transform the plan into action focused toward meeting the project's business requirements with a motivated project team. This is key to successful project management. The end result of a project is always related to the way the plan is translated into actual work in the real world.

Part 5, The Monitoring and Controlling Processes, talks about ways to monitor, track, and adjust each project so you can keep everything on schedule, within budget, and with the right quality. You also find easy-to-follow guidelines for dealing with the most common project problems and for minimizing the impact of the changes that are part of almost every project.

Part 6, The Close-Out Phase, shows you how to finish your project and reap the rewards of a job well done. This is often the most ignored part of project management, but you will readily see why it is so important.

Extras

To add to the material in the main text, a series of sidebars throughout the book highlight specific items that can help you understand and implement the material in each chapter:

WORDS FROM THE WISE

These quotes from other experts may help inspire you to greater achievements or simply motivate you to do your best.

RISK MANAGEMENT

Sometimes things just go wrong, no matter how well you plan your project. In these sidebars, you learn how to read the danger signs before you get swamped with problems.

DEFINITION

These sidebars highlight the most important definitions and concepts in project management. Use these words in meetings to impress your boss and your co-workers and demonstrate that you know what you're talking about.

TIME IS MONEY

These tips and suggestions can help you keep your schedule up to date and your budget under control.

NOTES FROM THE FIELD

These sidebars include personal experiences I and other project managers have had working on different projects.

You will also find a Review Questions section at end of each chapter. Its purpose is to prompt you to think about what you have read. If you have difficulty answering any of the questions, you can simply go back and reread the information related to that question so you can answer it confidently.

In the back of the book are appendixes to help supplement your project management knowledge. Appendix A walks you through how to build an organization, Appendix B shows you how to set up a Project Management Office, and Appendix C provides online project management resources.

Acknowledgments

Any acknowledgement would be incomplete without recognizing my wife, Molly, and her undying patience as I worked to complete this book. Her support and the love of my children is the rock upon which everything else is built.

Trademarks

All terms mentioned in this book that are known to be or are suspected of being trademarks or service marks have been appropriately capitalized. Alpha Books and Penguin Group (USA) Inc. cannot attest to the accuracy of this information. Use of a term in this book should not be regarded as affecting the validity of any trademark or service mark.

The Power of Project Management

Each year, companies launch mission-critical projects involving millions of dollars in capital investment that provide significant opportunities of project-savvy people. The processes and methods of project management provide the structure, focus, flexibility, and control to help guide these significant investments to outstanding results, on time and within budget.

In this part, you learn how companies develop a new strategy to improve performance and how projects are often the vehicle for delivering that new strategy. I also introduce you to the processes and life-cycle phases of the project management discipline and the successful techniques that experienced project managers utilize. You also learn the 10 key knowledge areas of project management, the first step to consistently bringing your projects in to meet the strategic business requirements. If you can deliver those projects, you'll be a rising star within your organization. That's the power of project management.

Linking Projects to Performance

The twenty-first century is here, along with tighter budgets, less time to get things done, and fewer resources. Sure, ships that allow faster-than-light travel are still *Avatar* fantasies, but rapid change, expanding technologies, and global marketing are real today.

To compete, you need to do more with less. Generally, projects are undertaken because they are a part of the plan to take your company to a new level of performance. However, to build the business of the future, you need to build things faster, cheaper, and better. And you need to get things done right the first time.

Projects are becoming the way of the working world. Computers and automation have eliminated many types of repetitive work, freeing people to focus on building new products, new services, and improved organizations. And where things need to be created, collected ideas are organized as projects, as I'll discuss in this chapter.

In This Chapter

- How projects meet business needs

- The four phases in a project

- A different approach to managing change

- Paying attention to the schedule, budget, and scope of a project

- What defines project success?

- Running all projects great and small

Meeting Business Needs with Projects

Projects are usually begun to address one or more demands from inside or outside the company. The drivers might be the following:

- A market demand to expand production of products

- An organizational need to train people with new skills

- A specific request from a key customer

- A legal requirement from the government or regulatory body

Projects can take many different forms. For example, there may be projects around the following:

- Technology implementations, such as automation equipment

- Information technology or systems that will change the computer system

- Business development initiatives to grow the business

- Human resource performance, such as training projects

- Strategy initiatives, such as introducing a whole new product line

- Integrating two companies after an acquisition or merger

For definitions on the relationship between project management and organizational strategy, refer to the Project Management Institute's *A Guide to the Project Management Body of Knowledge Guide* (referred to as the *PMBOK Guide*) section 1.5.2.3; for business value, refer to *PMBOK Guide* section 1.6.

Any and all of these projects usually start with a decision about what the customers will require from the company in the future and focus on meeting or exceeding these customer requirements or needs. These requirements are then put into a strategic plan that is carried out over a period of anywhere from a few months to as many as five years. In addition, to execute these requirements, various projects are created. When projects are related, they become a *program*.

The focus of program management is to manage the interdependencies among projects, and also to do the following:

- Resolve conflicts and constraint issues

- Maintain alignment with the strategic direction

- Utilize a shared governance

For more on programs and program management, refer to *PMBOK Guide* sections 1.2 and 1.3.

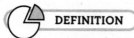

DEFINITION

A **project** is defined by the PMI as a temporary endeavor undertaken to create a unique product, service, or result. This means that a project produces something that has never existed before; has a deadline or target date when the project must be done; and has a budget that limits the amount of people, supplies, and money that can be used to complete the project.

The PMI defines a **program** as a group of related projects managed in a coordinated way to obtain benefits and control not available from managing them individually. A project may be part of a program, but a program will always be comprised of projects.

Projects and programs may have a variety of outcomes in the forecast, but one constant is the same—the need to improve performance in the future. The project manager is the person who takes overall responsibility for coordinating a project, regardless of its size, and for making sure the desired end result comes in on time and within budget. It is essential for a project manager to understand the link to the business need the project is seeking to solve. The project manager must also make sure that each key member of the project team understands the link to the future of the organization and the performance results the business is trying to achieve. Why, you may ask? The answer is relatively simple as a concept, but much harder to execute. As the project proceeds, the project manager and the project team will be making numerous decisions as they work to overcome a wide variety of technical and business problems that were unforeseen at the start of the project or program. If these people do not have an understanding of the strategy and how their project or program helps fulfill the desired performance results, the team could make decisions that would not enable the project deliverables to maximize the business value intended at the beginning of the project.

Four Classic Phases of a Project

Although each organization may use three to seven project phases, a typical life cycle might have four phases in a project: define, plan, execute, and close-out. Each phase has specific elements of work that must be completed in order for the project to deliver the expected results. And each phase has the deliverables that are depicted in the following figure. As you proceed through the book, you will learn more about each phase and the associated deliverables with the objective of delivering the expected value to the business.

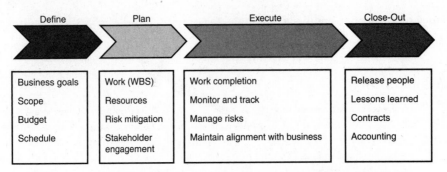

Define	Plan	Execute	Close-Out
Business goals	Work (WBS)	Work completion	Release people
Scope	Resources	Monitor and track	Lessons learned
Budget	Risk mitigation	Manage risks	Contracts
Schedule	Stakeholder engagement	Maintain alignment with business	Accounting

These are the classic phases of projects and the major work products produced in each phase.

Viewing Change from a Different Perspective

When project managers think of *change management,* they probably relate it to something an individual goes through during the course of a change. Such theories are very popular, and you may even think of change in this way. Many theories equate change with a death of something familiar and suggest that organizations and people in them experience a similar process when going through a significant change. This meshes well with theories that organizations are "living organisms" that take on a life of their own. The major problem for project managers in these theories is "How do I and my projects fit in?" Good question! I would like to propose a different approach.

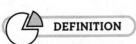

DEFINITION

When a project causes organizational changes, a project manager should view those changes as an engineering problem that requires the alteration of concrete parts of the organization. **Change management** is getting the organization prepared for those alterations effectively and efficiently.

In today's fast-paced world, project managers need to be good at handling change. The best way to control coming changes is to use a disciplined, structured approach. And that approach is to plan the project and then execute against that plan. I'll cover this more fully in Chapter 17.

For more on managing changes in a project, refer to *PMBOK Guide* section 5.6.1.1.

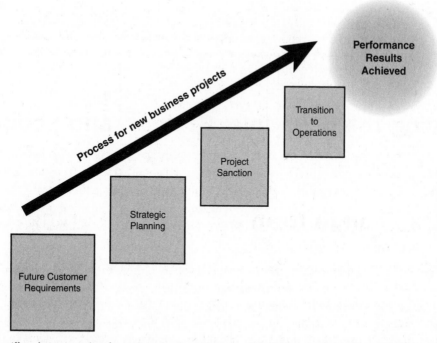

All projects are undertaken to improve the performance of the business, and they all roughly follow this path: understanding the future requirements of the customer; completing the strategic plan to address those future requirements; sanctioning projects to implement the strategic plan; and then transitioning from the project to ongoing operations.

The basic problem with the project approach most companies use is that less than 40 percent of the projects companies employ to change their business are successful. *Less than 40 percent!* That is clearly unacceptable. Those projects include mergers and acquisitions, major technology initiatives, or reengineering, to name a few. According to the research, more than 30 percent of IT projects are cancelled, more than 50 percent of projects experience cost overruns, and only about 16 percent are completed within the desired time frame and budget and achieve the desired results. Amazing!

The good news for you is that if you master the techniques in this book, your company will see you as a rising star. Why? Because you will be successful in completing a project, and the contrast of the completed project with so many other failed projects will be striking.

That's why many people see the advantage to becoming a project manager. The Project Management Institute (PMI), an international organization dedicated to the advancement of project management, has over 400,000 members at the time I am writing this book and will probably exceed that number by the time you read it. This institute has established standards and certificates to raise the knowledge and professionalism of project managers worldwide.

TIME IS MONEY

The PMI differentiates projects and operational work as follows: both have many of the same characteristics, but operations are ongoing and produce repetitive results, while projects are temporary and have a defined endpoint.

Balancing the Schedule, Budget, and Scope

One of the hardest tasks any project manager will face is balancing a project's schedule, budget, and scope. By looking at the three elements in the accompanying triangle, you can clearly see that if the schedule begins to slip (so that you may miss your deadline), this impacts the other two elements. For example, you can get the project back on track by getting more people involved (and increasing your budget), by reducing the scope that originally was designed into the project, or by asking for more time on the schedule.

A good project manager makes sure he understands which of these three elements is paramount. In other words, what is most important—the schedule, the budget, or the scope? Every project manager hears that they are all of equal importance, but I guarantee that if you ask the right questions, you will find out which is the key element and which elements are negotiable. After you establish this, you can work to keep all the elements in balance as the project progresses.

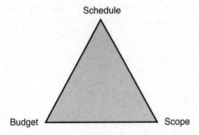

This triangle demonstrates the traditional balance between schedule, scope, and budget required to bring a project to a successful conclusion.

This brings us to the factors essential to the success of all projects:

- **Agreement among the project team and the stakeholders (which includes internal and/or external customers and management) on the goals of the project.** Without clear goals and agreement among everyone involved, the results can be devastating. No project can be a success unless everybody agrees that they want the same thing produced. In this book, you learn ways to develop clear, agreed-upon goals. You learn more about clear goals in Chapter 7.

For more on balancing time, resources, and results, refer to *PMBOK Guide* section 5.3.3.1.

- **Support from management to supply the resources and to remove organizational obstacles.** Without management support, project managers rarely have enough authority of their own to execute the decisions and policies necessary to complete a project. To get that support, you need to manage "upward" as well as manage the project team. You also learn ways to do this as you read through this book. You learn more about preparing your management in Chapter 5.

- **Communication that is effective, appropriately delivered, and ongoing throughout the project.** Almost every project management technique involves some form of communication. Without clear, concise communication, the people on a project team will never be able to agree on goals and then meet them. The project plan is one major component of this communication, but many other components are required for project success. This book not only explains how to plan a project, but it also examines the ongoing communication necessary to keep a project focused and on schedule (see Chapter 19).

Let me walk you through how the preceding list may be applied to a problem. An after-market auto parts manufacturing company has two key problems it is trying to solve:

1. The sales department is not able to access accurate customer information to determine a customer's buying patterns and if incentive discounts in the past encouraged larger orders.

2. Production management is not able to retrieve accurate information on customers' purchasing profiles to plan the correct inventory. As a result, some items ordered by customers are on back order, while other items collect dust on the shelves in the warehouse.

To correct these problems, management has sanctioned a project to implement customer management software. The goals for the project are the following:

- Allow the reporting of customer data in near real time for use by both sales representatives and senior management to drive sales revenue higher.

- Report on historical buying trends, by customer, to improve the production schedule within manufacturing and reduce inventory to nearly just-in-time delivery.

Even though the project manager has an idea about the problems which caused management to sanction the project, there is still a lot more work needed to really define the problems. For example, the problem of accessing accurate information could be caused by sales reps not entering the information correctly. That means it is not a system that is the root cause of the problem.

Also, the problem in the production department could be the result of a bad business practice in production planning. Again, just installing a new system will not necessarily fix either of these bad business practices.

In summary, a project manager's job is to really solve the problem and improve performance, not just install a new software package.

Defining Project Success

Great project managers are made, not born. They have learned to use methods that have been successful for other project managers and adapt them to their particular situations. Sometimes they were lucky and had an opportunity to watch a great project manager at work or even have one as a mentor. However, most of us are not that lucky. We can either muddle through it by trial and error, or we can use tried-and-true techniques.

Remember that the information in this book presents the most successful techniques of hundreds of project managers, not just one! And because all projects share similar features and require a balance among schedule, budget, and scope, similar formal project management techniques—the science of the great project managers—are also necessary to bring your projects to successful conclusions. Here you can learn about all these techniques.

 TIME IS MONEY

The first great project managers were those that managed the building of the pyramids in Egypt 5,000 years ago. The Romans had great project managers as they built roads across their empire 2,000 years ago. And recently, great project managers built the rockets that carried astronauts to the moon and outer space. The tools and techniques for project management were utilized by all of them, and you can learn them, too!

The tools and techniques for project management were developed to handle construction projects. However, these same methods work whether you're training a team of new employees, creating an ad campaign, developing a new software product, or reorganizing a corporation. You can also use project management tools to correct midcourse problems that would otherwise go undetected and undermine the success of any project.

In spite of their similarities, all true projects are unique. Projects involve different goals, employ different people with distinctive personalities, take place over varying time frames, and produce different results. No two projects, even projects with the same general objectives, are ever identical in planning or implementation. People who manage projects successfully quickly learn to become managers of change because there are always plenty of surprises, even in small projects. Thankfully, the project management toolbox found in this book offers techniques for identifying and managing the unique attributes of every project.

If the project manager understands the business requirements that are driving the project, the project will succeed. If not, it won't. In the long term, the project will be judged, not only on how well it met the targeted objectives, but also by whether it achieved its overall business objectives and the anticipated business value the project was supposed to capture. The project manager must seek regular feedback from the client to ensure that the project, as currently defined, still achieves the business objectives. Several things may change during the course of a project, such as the following:

- Business conditions

- Company objectives

- Management personnel

- Relative priorities

- Risk factors that materialize requiring intervention to handle them

When you master the techniques of project management, you see that the project of setting up a national sales meeting and the project of building a major freeway expansion depend on many of the same project management skills, even though the projects are on vastly different scales.

For more on defining acceptance criteria from key stakeholders, refer to *PMBOK Guide* section 5.3.3.1.

It's usually easy to identify the most complex projects in business, such as developing a new model automobile, installing a new financial reporting computer application like Enterprise Resource Planning (ERP) tools, or building an overseas manufacturing facility. But smaller and more mundane business endeavors can also be projects, even though they may not be labeled by that name.

Most people might not consider the job of hiring new people for your company as a project. Most experienced recruiting managers wouldn't consider this a project because they know how to plan and schedule all the steps in their head. They would post a position on a bulletin board, interview some people, and make a choice. But hiring and effectively and efficiently onboarding new people involves deadlines, people, money, and time because you'll probably use a team of people to interview the candidates. You will have to do the following:

- Schedule time

- Commit people to interviews

- Conduct a background check

- Follow an evaluation process

- Write an offer letter

And when you're done with the project, you'll also have something you didn't have before—a new employee.

Then there are all the steps for onboarding them:

- Going through an orientation

- Getting them a badge and security clearance

- Setting up a work space, including computers or other equipment

Good project management helps you hire the right person in the shortest period of time, which could make a big difference to your company.

Sure, it doesn't take as long to plan the project of hiring a marketing manager as it does to plan how to build a new bridge. You probably don't have to use a computer program to create the schedule or to manage the budget (although you might). But using good project management techniques is still important because the choice of a new employee that fits your needs and will "fit in" is important to your business.

You can't afford to treat even a small project, such as hiring a new employee, like ordinary work. Now would be a good time to identify two small but important projects that you have been postponing. For practice, you can apply the techniques you learn in this book.

 NOTES FROM THE FIELD

When I talk to my colleagues who are experienced project managers, we often observe that project managers are brought into the discussion about a project too late—after the project has already been vetted and approved. So experienced project managers have to dig deeper into the business problem they are charged with correcting; otherwise, we might end up implementing the project but not really solving the problem. The take-away for you, the reader, is to be very sure you understand the problem and be wary about accepting the solution (project) as it has been handed to you. Recognize that you may need to adjust the solution to address the root cause of the problem.

Running a Project Step-by-Step

In the following pages, I'll take you step-by-step through the fundamentals of planning, scheduling, tracking, and controlling the costs and resources of any project—whether it is mundane or technical or multifaceted and complex. These practical techniques are applicable to projects that people in sales, marketing, human resources, finance, and general management positions are responsible for, yet are based on the same general, accepted methods employed by engineering project managers in building skyscrapers, satellites, or software systems.

I also give you some review questions for each chapter, such as the ones in the following section, to help keep the concepts in your mind. If you can't answer these questions, please go back and reread the appropriate section in the chapter. After you read this book, you should be able to answer these questions and more for your project! And you will be able to feel comfortable that you are using the latest thinking on the practical application of project management.

Review Questions

- Do I understand the business need that my project will address?

- Do I understand how my company defines each phase of a project?

- Do I understand how the completion of my project will change the way the business operates?

- Can I explain the business value that my project should deliver?

The Least You Need to Know

- All projects meet a business need.
- The four classic project phases are define, plan, execute, and close-out.
- Use a planned, structured approach to managing changes brought on by projects.
- Balancing the schedule, budget, and scope is key to project management.
- Great project managers use the time-tested fundamentals for managing their projects.

What It Means to Be a Project Manager

Regardless of what your business card says, if you manage projects, your company is depending on you to deliver a successful project. In this chapter, you learn what it takes to be a good project manager, because your company's success depends on successful project managers.

The Business Connection

Most companies decide to begin a project for one reason and one reason only: they hope to make more money. So this means that every project is linked to the business strategy in some way, as I discussed in Chapter 1. A project is usually begun to meet the future business requirements of customers. And the final end result is better performance from the business. What does this mean for you as the project manager? It means you must understand the business context or strategy that prompted your management to hand you the project in the first place. Without that understanding, you are like an architect who is designing a building without knowing what the business to be housed in it will do!

For further information on the business value of a project, refer to *PMBOK Guide* section 1.6.

In This Chapter

- Understanding the link between project manager and business strategies
- The role of the project manager
- The knowledge areas possessed by effective project managers
- The skills of successful project managers
- Seven traits of effective project managers

What Are Your Responsibilities?

As a project manager, you are the one person assigned to lead the project management process, and in most cases, you alone are ultimately responsible for the project's success. (The project sponsor is often the person paying the bill for the project and so wants to make the project a success, too, but I talk more about that in Chapter 6.) Even if you have other work to do or if you manage the project as part of a project team, you need to make sure the project gets done as specified.

For more information on a project manager's role, refer to *PMBOK Guide* **section 1.7.1.**

So how does a project manager go about doing this? First of all, she must work with the customer to determine the *requirements*. When I use the term "customer," I am not necessarily referring to someone outside the company who will buy the product or service. If I am the project manager for a project that is designed to reconfigure the warehouse to get the products boxed and shipped faster, my "customer" may well be my company's manufacturing general manager. And I want to make sure that I have a steering committee of all the potential customers (or stakeholders) so that I can confirm they all approve of my plan. (I talk more about steering committees and stakeholders and how to define them in Chapter 6.)

 **DEFINITION**

According to the Project Management Institute (PMI), a management **requirement** is a condition or capability that must be met by the project to satisfy a contract, standard, or other formal specification.

As project manager, after you have the requirements from the customer, you must make sure the steering committee is on board with those requirements.

What Do You Need to Do?

Being a successful project manager means that you must master two very different skills. First, you must be very creative in solving problems because all projects, by definition, are unique. However, you also must be very self-disciplined in your approach and employ technology, charting techniques, and budgeting tools to monitor the project. The bottom line is that to be truly successful as a "project" manager, you must first establish yourself as a competent manager.

Learn to Plan and Act

Project management as a discipline evolved because of a need to coordinate resources and technology to secure predictable results. The common project management tasks include establishing objectives, breaking work into well-defined tasks, charting the sequence of tasks, scheduling, budgeting, coordinating a team, reporting, and communicating throughout the project. These tasks involve two general types of activities: planning and definition activities, and implementation and control activities.

During the course of the project, you are asked to develop various plans, such as a risk management plan, that all add up to the project management plan. You also need to develop a set of project documents, such as the charter, which assist you in managing the project, but are not part of the project plan. While that may seem a little confusing now, as you go through this book, you look at each of these areas in more detail so you will know exactly how to plan and act at each stage in the project.

 WORDS FROM THE WISE

The world will belong to passionate, driven leaders—people who not only have an enormous amount of energy but who can energize those whom they lead.

—Jack Welch, former CEO of General Electric

Focus on the Project's End

In the 1990s, Stephen Covey's *The 7 Habits of Highly Effective People* became a best-selling book. Covey wrote that one key to success was keeping the end result in mind as you decide what to do and how to do it. Successful project managers should develop this essential habit. Instead of looking at a project as 250 tasks, always keep the end result in mind. That way, the project is less likely to stall midstream. It also makes you a stronger project leader. If you have a clear vision in your mind about how the product will look upon completion, you can steer your project through difficult times and still succeed.

Be a Manager and a Leader

Good project managers can handle both the authority and the responsibility necessary to guide the project (you'll learn more about leading a project in Chapter 17). Management of the project and leadership go hand in hand. Your team members expect their leader to be honest, competent, and inspirational as well as skilled in the use of project management techniques. On the individual level, you need to motivate, delegate, mentor, and coach at various times. So having those skills plus the ability to help your team members resolve conflicts are critical elements to your success (and the success of the project).

For more information on leadership skills, refer to *PMBOK Guide* section 1.7.2.

You must develop administrative procedures for ensuring that work is getting done on time and within budget (more on that in Chapter 18), but more importantly, you must gain the trust and respect of the project team so that people feel comfortable taking your direction.

Most of all, to be an effective project manager, you need to lead the project with energy and a positive attitude that make you the catalyst for moving your project forward. Never put the techniques of project management above your attitude. Your attitude gives you power!

Let's take a closer look at project managers as leaders.

 TIME IS MONEY

A project manager who views the responsibility of managing a project as one of guiding, facilitating, negotiating, and coordinating will do better than one who views the project management responsibility as one of ordering, dictating, and coercing.

The Leadership Roles of the Project Manager

As part of your responsibility for leading the various phases of the project, you need to assume a variety of roles with other people. Accomplished leaders move effortlessly among these various roles.

Interpersonal Roles

To be perceived as a leader, you must be regarded as honest, capable, and dependable—as well as personable. In your interpersonal roles, you need to do these kinds of things:

- Deal effectively with people from various professional backgrounds.

- Solve team disputes and create team unity.

- Focus and motivate team members to achieve milestones on the way to achieving the project goal.

- Build positive relationships with project stakeholders.

- Be sure to listen carefully to others' opinions when making decisions.

Informational Roles

You need to assume informational roles to keep people up to date and on track. When you do so, you need to accomplish these sorts of tasks:

- Arrange and lead team meetings.
- Create and maintain work schedules for other people.
- Communicate the project vision to upper management.
- Provide feedback regarding results, quality, and project deliverables.

Decisional Roles

To move forward, projects demand that countless decisions be made, ranging from trivial to critical, at every phase of the project. When a decisional role is required, you need the expertise to do the following without alienating the people who may be affected by your choices:

- Distinguish between features and benefits.
- Appropriately allocate resources if a project falls behind schedule.
- Strike a balance between cost, time, and results.
- Prevent *scope creep* and budget "slippage" (when the money starts running out).

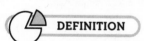
DEFINITION

Scope creep is the process of adding work to a project, little by little, until the original schedule and cost estimates are completely meaningless.

The Other Business Management Roles

In addition to the roles detailed already, project managers need all the general skills required of any competent business manager. Human resource management is one of the most critical of these.

Seven Traits of Good Project Managers

In addition to having knowledge of project management processes and an understanding of your various roles as a project manager and leader, research and experience point to seven traits that can help you become a successful project manager. The following figure shows these seven success traits, each of which are discussed in this section.

As project managers gain experience, the successful ones develop these traits to make their work easier and more satisfying.

Enthusiasm for the Project

Good project managers want to do a good job. Your enthusiasm for the project spreads to other people on the team, making it easier to keep people motivated and involved.

Ability to Manage Change Effectively

Change is inevitable in projects. Customers change their minds about the end results. Managers decide to make changes to the scope of the project. Team members need to change their schedules. People who manage projects successfully learn to become managers of exceptions because surprises will occur, even in small projects.

NOTES FROM THE FIELD

One of the best project managers I ever got to see in action had all the characteristics a project manager needs. First, he understood the link between his project and what the commercial business was trying to accomplish. He also built a great team with exactly the right skills and experience. He communicated effectively with both his stakeholders and his team members to keep everyone engaged. Finally, he managed changes to the project by effectively negotiating with key stakeholders.

I can imagine that you might be thinking he is Superman, but he is not. He followed the steps outlined in this book, and he is now a senior executive with a global company. All that project knowledge and skill has translated into the executive suite within his company.

Tolerant Attitude Toward Ambiguity

Project managers often have ambiguous authority because people may have other bosses to report to during the project and may not consider you a manager (unless you earn their respect as a leader). In fact, many of the roles in large projects are not clear-cut.

Some of the team members may make more money or have more senior jobs than the project manager; customers may get involved as team members; other departments may have a stake in the project. A good project manager must feel comfortable with these ambiguous roles and expectations and must learn how to manage them to see the project to a successful conclusion. If you need clear authority and an absolute plan, your project management days are numbered.

Talk to experienced project managers. They'll tell you (if they admit it) that at least one of their first projects was a dismal failure. If a project fails for you, don't kick yourself. Instead, pick up the pieces, learn from your mistakes, and move on.

Team-Building and Negotiating Skills

A project manager needs to build coalitions among the various stakeholders in a project: management, customers, the project team, and suppliers. Power is granted only to a project manager who builds these relationships. Project managers must negotiate authority to move the project forward, so the success of any project depends on the project manager's ability to build a strong team among internal and external players.

Customer-First Orientation

In projects that involve customers or clients (and most do), a good project manager puts the customer first and understands the customer's perspective regarding the project. After all, the ultimate measure of the project's success is the customer's satisfaction with the results. In a partnership with a customer or client, a skilled project manager crafts a vision for the project that she can communicate to the rest of the project team. Through alliances, team building, and empathy with the customer or client, the project manager is ultimately able to turn changing expectations into satisfaction with the completed project.

Adherence to Business Priorities

Earlier we talked about the project's connection to the overall business strategy. You also hear this called a "bottom-line" orientation, but paying attention to the budget and costs is only part of the business equation. Other business priorities involve maintaining a competitive advantage, integrating the project into the culture of the organization, managing stakeholder issues, and ensuring both productivity and excellence as the project proceeds. However the business connection is served up, never lose sight of it during the project. Make it your compass point that tells you that you are heading in the right direction.

 WORDS FROM THE WISE

The elevator to success is out of order. You have to use the stairs and climb one step at a time.

—Joe Girard, listed in the *Guinness Book of Records* as the world's greatest salesman

Knowledge of the Industry or Technology

Even though most project management skills are industry-independent, as a project manager, you need to have both project management skills and some experience or specific knowledge relevant to the industry you're working in. For example, if you're managing software projects, you need experience with programming concepts. If you're managing the development of a new shopping mall, you need a background in construction. However, you don't need to be an expert in the field because you shouldn't be doing the work, but managing it. I once worked with a project manager who insisted on supervising every move his project team made because he knew so much about the topic. However, he was actually a hindrance to the projects he managed because, for all practical purposes, he was doing everything himself!

Sometimes, all you need is your experience at project management; you don't necessarily need to be an expert with that technology or industry. For example, an energy pipeline company decided to install a new automation control system for optimizing the pipelines and reducing the risks of an accident or leak. Due to a weakness in project management, the company hired a very experienced project manager to handle the job. This project manager did not have much experience in these types of systems, but understood how to manage and execute a project.

While it might seem strange for the company to make the choice they did, all of the technical knowledge for automation systems was in the company already. What they needed, and what they got, was someone who could manage all that technical know-how to deliver a project. And it was successful!

Review Questions

- Do I understand my role in decision making on this project?

- Am I enthusiastic about this project?

- Do I have the skills and experience for team building and negotiating? If I don't, should I get some training, or can I bring someone to the team who does have those skills?

- Do I have a customer-first attitude within the team?

The Least You Need to Know

- The responsibility of the project manager is to lead and manage the project.
- You must be familiar with key knowledge areas before starting a project.
- You need people skills, communication skills, business skills, and technical skills to be an effective project manager.
- Seven traits define the successful project manager.
- Being a good project manager takes ongoing, enthusiastic effort.

The Rules of the Project Game

I know you just can't wait to get started managing your projects. But before you become convinced that project management is more about process than substance, you need to know that all the ingredients that make up the project management recipe for success boil down to only 12 rules.

All kinds of project managers responsible for all types of projects in diverse managerial and political environments have honed these 12 golden rules from years of experience. So whether your projects involve building spaceships or building ships in bottles, you'll get better results by following these rules from the project definition phase to the project closing phase. This chapter goes over those rules, as well as ways you can avoid a project failing.

In This Chapter

- Universal project success criteria revisited

- The seven causes of project failure—and how to avoid them

- The 12 golden rules of project management success

- Simple ways to help you follow the rules for success

Universal Project Success Criteria

For almost all projects, success is defined as meeting three criteria:

1. Finishing the project on schedule

2. Keeping costs within budget

3. Meeting quality outcomes (or goals) that have been agreed upon by the project stake-holders and the project team

Quality may be difficult to define in some cases, but in project management, quality is always defined as meeting the requirements of the customer. If your project is to design a container that can hold an internal pressure of 500 pounds per square inch (psi), then a quality container will meet that expectation. A container will not meet the quality standard if it holds 400 psi or 600 psi.

 WORDS FROM THE WISE

Most people think of success and failure as opposites, but they are actually both the products of the same process.

—From *A Whack on the Side of the Head* by Roger von Oech

Project Failure: The Reasons Are Simple

According to research done by the Project Management Institute (PMI), projects fail for seven key reasons. The problems and solutions are as follows:

- **Poor project and program management discipline.** To avoid this problem, develop a well-defined project plan using a proven methodology and use project management tools to track and control your project.

- **Lack of executive-level support.** This is an all-too-frequent project killer. To avoid this problem, you must enlist the executive leadership (I talk more about this in Chapter 5). Provide the executive team with regular communications, and constantly reinforce the need for their involvement at the appropriate times.

- **No linkage to the business strategy.** Provide a clear business direction understood by everyone who is impacted by the project. Make sure everyone knows *why* this project is important, *what* it will mean when it is complete, and *how* you plan to implement that finished product.

- **The wrong team members.** Sometimes people are selected for a project because they "have the time." This should be the last criteria for choosing someone for the team. Pick the best players and give their day-to-day workload to those who "are available." If the right people aren't available, hire contractors or consultants who do have the knowledge and experience. You'll be glad you did!

- **No measures for evaluating the success of the project.** Too often, no one has developed the acceptance criteria to determine exactly how the team will know whether the project is a success. These measures should be contained in the business case for the project (I discuss the scope of the project in Chapter 7). If you haven't been given those measures, then develop them yourself and get the project sponsor and the steering committee to agree to them before you get too far into the project plan.

- **Lack of a robust risk strategy.** All good projects have a well-defined risk plan. Identify as many potential risks as possible and develop a plan for mitigating them.

- **Inability to manage change.** All too frequently, the organization is simply not prepared to accept the changes a project might entail. For example, if the project is to install a new software system to capture orders and schedule delivery, you likely will meet with major resistance to this change. You will need to develop a robust communications and change-management plan to get the organization ready to use the new system.

People don't start a project hoping it will fail, yet projects fail all too often because project managers disregard the 12 basic project management rules that can help avoid the seven reasons for failure.

Twelve Golden Rules of Project Management Success

The 12 basic rules of project management define the focus you need to get things done on time, within budget, and to the expectations of the stakeholders. As you read this book, you see how project management techniques are designed to help project managers put the 12 golden rules into action over and over again.

In the sections that follow, I guide you to the chapters of this book that offer specific advice related to the rule being discussed. Of course, if you consistently break or ignore the rules of project management—regardless of your diligent use of my recommended charts, plans, and reports—you'll probably doom your project to failure anyway, or at least cause a lot of problems you otherwise might have avoided.

You'd be wise to keep the following list of rules in front of you throughout your projects:

1. Gain consensus on project outcomes.

2. Build the best team you can.

3. Develop a plan and keep it up to date.

4. Determine what you really need to get things done.

5. Have a realistic schedule.

6. Don't try to do too much.

7. Remember that people count.

8. Gain the support of management and stakeholders.

9. Be willing to change.

10. Keep others informed of what you are doing.

11. Be willing to try new things.

12. Become a leader.

Let's look at each of these rules in more detail.

NOTES FROM THE FIELD

I still remember the conversation I had with a project manager who was very upset and confused. After talking for a while, I discovered the source of both his anger and his confusion. He and his team had worked for nearly two years on a project to deliver a new production SCADA (Supervisory Control and Data Acquisition) system into his energy company's onshore assets. They had delivered exactly to the requirements. However, the charter for the project was two years old and never updated—the business had changed, but the project had not. Therefore, the project was not labeled a success—not because the project manager and his team had not delivered, but what operations needed at the end was different. Another project was required to upgrade the SCADA system with additional time and money. The moral of the story is to continuously engage key stakeholders during the course of a project—particularly one of long duration.

Gain Consensus on Project Outcomes

If you don't know what you intend to accomplish, you likely won't accomplish anything of value. A project without clear expectations is really just a bunch of work without a purpose. To be considered a success, a project must have clearly defined goals that specify the results the project is to achieve when it's finished.

However, for you to know exactly what you want to do is not enough. You also have to reach consensus with the stakeholders and team members on the project that the goals and expectations are the right ones. In Chapter 7, you learn how to set clear project goals and expectations, and you get tips for gaining the consensus required to ensure the project you finally finish is the project people wanted to get done.

Build the Best Team You Can

A willing, skilled, appropriately organized project team is the key to success. You have to develop this group of people because the perfect team almost never starts out that way. A good team starts with good choices on your part; however, sometimes the people you pick may turn out to be total dummies or uncooperative blockheads. You'll learn about building your team in Chapter 13 and organizing your team in Chapter 18.

Your challenge is to make sure the project team gets smart very quickly and stays ambitious in spite of inadequate experience and training, family problems, or conflicting priorities. If people must be trained to get things done right, that's one of your responsibilities as project manager. Of course, the people must also be willing to work on the project and learn the new skills. That means you have to use your best management skills and motivational tactics to guide them in the right direction. (That's the direction you want them to go!)

TIME IS MONEY

Review the 12 golden rules at least once a week, and you'll have a much better chance of getting things done the right way: on time; within budget; and to the specifications agreed upon by customers, management, and other stakeholders. Of course, the schedule and budget may change over time, but as long as people agree on the changes, you're still getting things done the right way. A review of the rules reminds you of that.

Develop a Plan and Keep It Up to Date

A complete, appropriately detailed project plan is central to the successful completion of any project. The plan helps you guide the project. This document communicates the overall intentions, tasks, resource requirements, and schedule for the project. Without a plan, it's almost impossible to lead a group to achieve a common goal. You learn about creating the various parts of the project plan in Part 3.

Of course, creating a plan isn't enough. Because you can't see into the future any better than a fortune teller with a broken crystal ball, the plan you develop and get approved will probably change many times from project initiation to project completion. As you gain more information about the realities of the project and as the stakeholders change their minds about what they need, your plan will have to be reevaluated. Be forewarned: if you don't update the project plan and negotiate these changes with the stakeholders, you will be responsible for the budget and schedule of the original plan (you hear about this again in Chapter 22).

RISK MANAGEMENT

Consider a project in Boston, Massachusetts, nicknamed "the Big Dig." The project, started in 1991, was designed to replace the six-lane highway called the Central Artery that runs through the center of downtown Boston with an underground expressway of 8 to 10 lanes. At the time of the project initiation, the budget was $11 billion, and the project was scheduled to be completed before the end of the decade. The budget grew to $22 billion and didn't finish until 2007. This project is similar in scale to the building of the Panama Canal or the English Channel Tunnel (dubbed the Chunnel). However, for the poor citizens of the Boston area, this was an expensive, inconvenient project that must have seemed like it took forever to finish.

Determine What You Really Need to Get Things Done

No matter what your boss says, you can't squeeze blood from a turnip. Without adequate people, capital, and equipment to complete a project, there is no way you can make it happen. You must get sufficient resources allocated to the project, or you must renegotiate what can be done so that fewer resources are required (refer to Rule 1). In most companies, getting sufficient resources (including equipment, people, and supplies) for a project is an ongoing problem and one of the most important responsibilities for all project managers. In Chapter 14, you learn how to scope out what you really need to get a project done. In Chapter 22, you discover some techniques for negotiating when you don't get everything you need the first time around.

Have a Realistic Schedule

Without a realistic schedule, you never succeed, and you run out of time before you get to try again. You may be able to bring more people on board and buy more supplies, but you can't produce more time no matter what you do. There's no faster way to lose credibility as a project manager than to change the schedule without a really good reason. Then again, if you follow Rules 1 and 8, you can get more time for yourself by getting a new schedule approved. In Chapters 10 and 11, you learn how to develop a schedule you can meet and how to change it when necessary.

Don't Try to Do Too Much

You must have an appropriate scope for the project. The scope of the project involves more than goals. For example, the goal could be to build a two-story building on the location of the back parking lot by next December. But the scope of the project could range from putting up a prefabricated metal building with a cement floor to building a miniature Taj Mahal for the chairman of the board. While the first scope is feasible, the second is not. Make sure that the objectives and the scope of the project are clear to everyone if you want to be considered a success when the project is done. Although *gold plating* the project might score you bonus points, don't make it one of your primary goals.

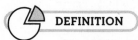 **DEFINITION**

In project management jargon, doing more than the project requirements call for is called **gold plating** the project.

Remember That People Count

Learning to work with people takes a lifetime, and at the end, you'll still be wondering how people really work. Even with all the good advice in this book, people will surprise you in mysterious and wonderful ways. That's what keeps project management interesting.

Sometimes, in focusing on the process of project management, you may forget that projects are mostly about people. Project success depends on people, not on reports or charts or even computers. To be a successful project manager, you must accommodate people's needs and priorities. People manage the project. People do most of the work. People enjoy (or curse) the end results. Projects also put stresses on these people because projects almost always involve new group structures, deadlines, and extra work. If a project's end results don't serve people, then the project has failed.

Another way of stating Rule 7 is this: Do no damage to the people on the project! Don't overwork the staff; don't demand the impossible; never lie to anyone even if it does seem like a way out of a tight situation.

Projects almost always incorporate built-in priority conflicts between ordinary work and project work. The bad news is that you must eventually satisfy people's needs, priorities, and conflicts for the project to come to a happy ending. The good news is that, in Chapter 21, I show you some techniques to help you prepare operations for the deliverables of your projects.

Gain the Support of Management and Stakeholders

It's obvious (or at least it should be) that you must have approval from management and the key stakeholders before you initiate a project. This involves not only communication skills but also negotiation skills. This rule is much like Rule 1, except that it means you must add a formal approval stage to the general consensus you gained in keeping Rule 1. You need to get everyone who has to contribute resources (time or money) or who may be impacted by a project (if it will change his job or life) to formally endorse your project and to agree that the project is worth doing. From the stakeholders, you also need to get formal agreement on some basic rules for dealing with issues of authority, changes in project scope, and the handling of basic communications.

For many of the stakeholders, support requires signed approval, but it doesn't stop with a signature. Keeping this rule also demands you ensure the stakeholders' ongoing interest in your project. If you start a project for your boss who has no real interest in the project even after he has signed on the dotted line, it's unlikely you'll get any praise for finishing the feat. Remember to review Chapters 6, 19, and 22 whenever support wanes for your projects.

Be Willing to Change

This rule goes along with Rule 3. You must be willing to adapt the project plan and implementation to guide the project where it needs to go. Sometimes things change for justifiable reasons, such as a rainstorm that stops the work on a construction project. Sometimes things change because you get new information. Sometimes changes are simply the result of peoples' whims, like the advertising agency's customer who now wants a TV commercial instead of a brochure to promote his new product, even though the brochure is almost ready to go to the printer.

You also learn in Chapter 22 that change is an important part of controlling a project. The main thing to remember here is that it is *not* the project manager's job to say "no" to a change; rather, it is his job to inform the stakeholders of the impact the change will have on the time, cost, and quality of the project and to let them make the decision about the change.

 WORDS FROM THE WISE

Graham's Law: If they know nothing of what you are doing, they suspect you are doing nothing.

—From *Understanding Project Management* by Robert J. Graham

Keep Others Informed of What You Are Doing

You must keep all the relevant stakeholders informed of your progress, problems, and changes. The way to obey this rule is simple: communicate, communicate, communicate. As things change on the project, and they always do, you'll find through your communications that the stakeholders may want or need to introduce their own changes into the project. Several specific techniques for communications are discussed in Chapter 19. While adhering to Rule 10, refer frequently to Rule 9.

Be Willing to Try New Things

Because every project is different, with different people, goals, and challenges involved, using the exact same methods, software, charts, graphs, or other aids on every project would simply be inappropriate. You can use the standard methods and tools with all projects, but not all projects involve the same risk or complexity. Thus, not all the techniques in this book should be used on all projects.

Large, complex projects likely use more methods or tools than smaller projects. Too many methods *or* too few tools can doom a project. You must adapt the processes, technologies, tools, and techniques to the needs of the project at hand. For example, you obviously need to put more detail into the network diagram (see Chapter 11 for more on these) for building a new corporate headquarters from scratch than you would for setting up a new sales office in a rented building.

Become a Leader

Leadership is an art that comes naturally to some, but the rest of us have to work at it. Chances are, you have to work on your leadership role, too. Reading management books won't be enough to bring your projects in on time and within budget. As a project manager, you must put what you read into action. You need to become a leader as well as a team member. You must not only plan, track, and control the project, but you must also be a source of wisdom and motivation for the team members and stakeholders.

Without leadership, even a well-coordinated project can fail to meet its goals if people in the project don't feel they have the support or guidance they need to make things happen. For example, a project manager and his team were asked to develop a new set of management reports to allow operations management to make decisions and manage their facilities safely. While the scope of the project was clear in the minds of management and the project team, both made assumptions that the other side was not aware of. And complicating the situation was the poor communications on the part of the project team. At the end of the project, the reports were incorrect and the project team had several months of rework to produce the new reports.

As you can see from this example, you should always check with your key stakeholders regarding assumptions and make sure your assumptions and theirs are aligned. Finally, you should make sure you plan and watch the project closely. For the managerial reports, the project manager might have developed interim reports for review by key stakeholders.

Chapter 2 details the skills and traits of a good project manager, and Chapter 17 expands on leadership.

Review Questions

- How do I know that I have consensus on the project?

- Can I be sure my project team has the right skills to deliver the project?

- Is my schedule realistic, or have I put too much pressure on the team?

- How do I know that management will support the project?

- Do I have a good plan for keeping people informed about what I am doing?

The Least You Need to Know

- When projects fail, it is usually due to one or more identifiable reasons.
- Follow the 12 golden rules of project management to help guide projects of all sizes and complexity to more successful conclusions.
- Your first loyalty is to your project, even though you may be pressured from all sides for change.
- Keep a list of the 12 golden rules of project management on your desk or office wall to keep you focused on the success factors during the tough times of a project.
- Remember that the success of a project always depends more on people than on process, but the processes and structures are important in helping people stay on track.

The 10 Knowledge Areas

Based on their best practice research on projects worldwide, the Project Management Institute (PMI) has established a guide for managing projects called *A Guide to the Project Management Body of Knowledge* or *PMBOK* (pronounced *pim bock*) *Guide,* which is what you've probably already seen cross-referenced in earlier chapters. In the *PMBOK Guide,* the PMI has defined the fundamental areas a project manager should address during the course of a project. I introduce each of these 10 knowledge areas in this chapter and elaborate on each of them in the chapters that follow.

The *PMBOK Guide* is important for many reasons. First, the definitions given in the *PMBOK Guide* are used universally in the project management field. As you know, using the right terms identifies us immediately as insiders within a given community, and the project management field is no different. Second, although much of the material in the *PMBOK Guide* is theoretical (unlike this book, which was designed to be much more practical), its framework is still very useful for planning and managing projects. It provides a comprehensive picture of what a project manager should be working to achieve as she delivers a project.

In This Chapter

- The 10 knowledge areas of project management
- Project time management and the triple constraints—time, cost, and quality
- The importance of integrating all knowledge areas

Project Integration Management

As you read in Chapter 1, all projects are meant to address some business need. Otherwise, the project would not have been approved in the first place. When the project begins, you have several people working on a variety of things, often at the same time and only occasionally together.

For more information on project integration management, refer to *PMBOK Guide* section 4.

Eventually, someone will have to bring all this work together in a coherent way, and that is the job of the project manager. In many ways, the project manager can be described as the conductor of an orchestra. Many different types of instruments are playing music at the same time. However, everyone in the orchestra is watching the conductor for her cues that keep the musicians together to produce the beautiful sounds. So think of yourself as the conductor! You need to make sure all the work fits together to produce the results that were promised by the project in its business case.

Finally, when the project is completed (successfully!), the product or service produced by the project needs to be integrated into the company's ongoing operations. That is your job, too! (I'll cover that in Chapter 21.)

Integration Management as Part of Planning

Much of the work around successful project management is planning your project. The next part of the book covers planning in detail. Your planning considers how the people in the team work together and particularly where coordination will be important. For example, often team members require information from other people, some inside the project team and others outside the team, to complete their work. Planning for this type of integration is important as you develop your plans. After you have completed the planning, you will save your plan as a baseline. That baseline plan allows you to see how the project changed over the course of the project and should provide you with valuable information for your lessons learned at project close-out.

 WORDS FROM THE WISE

Luck is a matter of preparation meeting opportunity.

—Oprah Winfrey, TV personality and humanitarian

Integration Management During Project Execution

Here, the focus changes from planning to managing the processes. During project execution, the project manager works to ensure that the product or service the project produces will be acceptable to the customers by carefully managing the written plan and following the outlined procedures.

One of the key procedures, which I present in Chapter 18, is the work authorization system, a formal process for approving project work that makes sure the right work is being done at the right time in the right way. The other key is maintaining a control system that is visible through a reporting system that identifies the status of the project.

Integration Management of Project Changes

During the course of a project, things always change. A project manager's job is not to prevent change, but to manage it effectively. In Chapter 22, you see how to manage changes by pulling together a change control plan.

Sometimes you can almost predict which changes will be requested. In those situations, the process you put into place becomes a lifesaver and a face-saver. You need to include specific steps, one of which is an impact analysis of the change on the project.

Finally, when you do follow the process, the last step is to revise your project plan. The new plan reflects the change and the corrections to schedule and budget. You also need to keep a record of changes made so you can document them at the conclusion of the project.

 WORDS FROM THE WISE

Most bold change is the result of a hundred thousand tiny changes that culminate in a bold product or procedures or structure.

—Tom Peters, author and business guru

Project Scope Management

During the project, managing the scope of the project is extremely important as one of the leading causes of project failure is the problem of "scope creep," when the project keeps getting bigger and more complex.

For more information on project scope management, refer to *PMBOK Guide* section 5.

One of the first planning exercises in any project is to define the project scope. You need to clarify what is included in the project as well as what is *not* included in the project. Project managers can get into trouble if they make assumptions about what is not included in the project but never confirm those assumptions.

It is good practice to write a clear, definitive scope statement and to have your sponsor and the key customers review it. If any adjustments need to be made, it is best to know that earlier rather than later.

During the planning phase, you begin to define the scope in great detail as you plan for all the tasks that need to be completed to finish the project.

When you finish the project, you will want to verify that you have indeed completed the scope and your sponsor and your key customers accept it as completed. (See Chapter 6 for more on the role of the project sponsor.)

Project Time Management

Many people often refer to project management as a detailed time management exercise. However, time is only one component you must control during a project. Time management is one of three elements referred to as the triple constraints (the other two are cost and scope, which are coming up soon!).

For more information on project time management, refer to *PMBOK Guide* section 6.

Sometimes time management, as defined by the project schedule, is the key driver for a project. For example, if you are developing a new product, time may be of the essence since there is always the fear a competitor will move into the market ahead of you. On other occasions, time is important but not the key driver. For example, I had a customer for a software installation project state he was willing to sacrifice the schedule if the software worked when finished. In other words, quality was more important to him, and he was willing to make some concessions on the schedule.

Just remember, even if time is not the key driver, extending the time on a project usually means costs also will increase.

Time and the Schedule

In simple terms, you manage time during a project if you develop an accurate schedule and manage the project to that schedule. You may also set *milestones* for your project as a way to track how well you are doing in meeting the schedule.

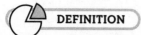

DEFINITION

A **milestone** is a clearly definable point in a project that summarizes the completion of a related or important set of activities. Milestones often are used to summarize important events in a project and help key customers keep track of the project when they don't want to know all the details.

Controlling the Schedule During Execution

You spend important time developing and establishing the schedule for completing that work. However, all that time and effort goes to waste if you don't manage the time your team uses as they execute the work. Most project managers use a baseline schedule as a way to manage the time. By comparing the way the schedule is progressing versus the baseline schedule, the project manager can see trends and make course corrections before things get out of hand.

Project Cost Management

One of the key questions a project manager is always addressing is "So, how are you doing against the budget?" You always are asked to report on how much money you are spending to complete the project.

For more information on project cost management, refer to *PMBOK Guide* section 7.

Financial Issues Outside of Your Control

Sometimes the project manager can't control all the factors that influence her project. For example, a project manager in Houston budgeted a certain amount of money for renting generators as part of the project plan. Then a series of hurricanes hit (Katrina and Rita), and all the generators became much more expensive to rent (if any could be found). You should build contingency funds into the budget, but be careful you don't burn that money up too quickly. As any manager knows, asking senior management for more money is never fun!

Competing for Funds with Other Projects

Most companies have a limited amount of funds to invest in projects and other investments, such as new equipment. Remember that you are always in competition with these other initiatives for money. If you need more money, you will need to make the case because you may be taking money from another project or initiative. And if your project is perceived as not well managed, don't be surprised if your budget shrinks unexpectedly.

Project Quality Management

Quality is a key component in any project. We have all seen projects that were completed, but the results were disappointing because the quality of the product or service was poor.

For more information on project quality management, refer to *PMBOK Guide* section 8.

The processes for quality in a project are the following:

- Determining what the quality objectives need to be and how you are going to achieve them

- Enforcing quality assurance to measure that the project is producing against the requirements

- Checking quality control to ensure quality standards are met and that any deviations are identified and corrected

As you will see in Chapter 23, defining the scope of your project correctly is *the* key ingredient in developing a quality plan. I give you several ideas for managing quality.

 TIME IS MONEY

> The PMI has a professional designation, the Project Management Professional (PMP), for those who have the right experience and knowledge and can pass the test on the information contained in the *PMBOK Guide*.

Project Human Resource Management

In a large project, and even some smaller projects, managing human resources over the course of the project is one of the most important aspects of a successful project. If you think about it, this makes sense. People do all the work on the project, whether they are under your direct control (as part of the project team itself) or not (as contract labor or workers for one of your vendors). I devote Chapter 6 to stakeholders of your project; that discussion emphasizes the broad impact people will have on your project.

For more information on project human resource management, refer to *PMBOK Guide* section 9.

Organizational Planning

Depending on the size of your project, you probably want to develop an organization chart that shows who reports to whom and the teams or groups that sit in across the project. A chart certainly helps clarify reporting relationships, and you begin to have some vision of the span of control your different team leaders have to contend with.

You also want to clarify role definitions for the team since you often are "borrowing" people from operations to fill out parts of your project team. These people have a clear understanding of their roles as part of their departments or functions, but that same intuitive clarity may not be there for the project. And you may need to think about how you will do performance appraisals for a project team. That brings us to where and how you get the people to staff your project.

Staff Acquisition

Getting the people you need is always a challenge—as is keeping them for the duration of a long project. In Chapter 13, I show you how to think through the types of people you want (their skills, knowledge, and experience), but you also need to understand how to acquire them if you are hiring consultants or contract workers. To do this, you need to be familiar with the procurement policies and procedures within your company. If you want to hire consultants, for example, you need to know how to make that happen within the time frame you have available (see "Project Procurement Management" later in this chapter).

Making Them a Team

Finally, as part of your human resource management for the project, you need to mold this group of people into a team. You want to consider broad topics, such as operating procedures within the team, as outlined in Chapter 18. I knew one excellent project manager who developed a specific seating chart so he could determine who he wanted to sit next to whom and why to help promote teamwork.

Project Communication Management

Communication is a key success factor in all projects. You can predict how successful a project will be by assessing how well the project team members communicate with each other and how well the project manager communicates with the key stakeholders. If strong communication is evident, you can be sure that success will follow, and poor communication almost always leads to a failed project. The PMI has determined that more than 89 percent of a project manager's time may be spent in various forms of communications, from meetings to emails and progress reports.

In Chapter 19, I tell you how to build a communication plan that will help you with this important aspect of project management.

For more information on project communication management, refer to *PMBOK Guide* **section 10.**

Project Risk Management

Many people think project management is all about managing risks, and risk management is one of the key areas of focus for a project manager. While you can never control everything around your projects, using a strong project management methodology, such as *PRINCE2,* helps you to manage risks effectively.

For more information on project risk management, refer to *PMBOK Guide* **section 11.**

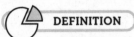 **DEFINITION**

> **PRINCE2** was originally a methodology for managing projects developed by the British government to handle their large information technology projects. Many companies in the United Kingdom and the United States have since adopted it as their methodology of choice. The official website is www.prince-officialsite.com.

In handling risks, you must think about what may go wrong during a project and develop a strategy to either prevent it from happening at all or reduce the negative impact on the project if it does happen. I identify risks and give you tips on how to address them in Chapter 8.

Project Procurement Management

Almost all projects need to buy goods or services from outside the company. This usually includes negotiating contracts and payment schedules and can potentially involve locations all over the world.

For more information on project procurement management, refer to *PMBOK Guide* **section 12.**

So you must know how to get the help you need to buy necessary materials. If you have a procurement department in your company, start talking to them as soon as you begin planning your project. You will want to develop a good relationship with them so they can assist you through some of the more difficult procurement aspects.

Debates always arise about whether it is cheaper to make or buy a product and whether to use an inside source for a service or go outside to get it. There are no easy answers to these questions. As you plan your project, you want to do a cost-benefit analysis of the options available to you and decide which one makes sense in the light of your budget and schedule.

Project Stakeholder Management

This is an extremely important part of project management. It is so important, in fact, that the PMI recently added it to the knowledge areas for all project managers. Before the fifth edition of the *PMBOK Guide* was released, stakeholders were part of the communication knowledge area. However, identifying and managing the stakeholders is paramount to success. Only if the key stakeholders are satisfied with the deliverables produced by your project can the project be declared a success. And managing stakeholder expectations is more than communications—it includes meetings, handling problems effectively, and leadership skills to engage stakeholders.

For more information on project stakeholder management, refer to *PMBOK Guide* section 13.

 NOTES FROM THE FIELD

The 10 knowledge areas developed by the PMI represent the best practices established by project managers from all over the world. New project managers sometimes try to find shortcuts around these standards, but they are fooling themselves. You can use the practical application of these best practices based on the size and risk involved. However, practical application assumes that 1) you know these knowledge areas very well, and 2) you have enough experience to understand how rigorous you need to be in applying them.

So shortcuts are not impossible, but in order to employ shortcuts, you must be so familiar with the territory that you can take shortcuts safely and without putting the entire journey in jeopardy.

Review Questions

- Do I understand the practical application of the knowledge areas?

- Should I read the *PMBOK Guide* sections to learn more about the technical details of a knowledge area?

- Do I recognize which chapters in the book will help me learn more about these knowledge areas?

The Least You Need to Know

- Become familiar with the *Project Management Body of Knowledge (PMBOK) Guide.*

- As a project manager, you are expected to manage your time, the costs, the scope, and the quality of the work.

- To manage a project effectively, you need to manage risks, people, communications, and procurement.

- To be a successful project manager, you are expected to integrate all the knowledge areas.

Starting Off on the Right Foot

No matter how big or how small a project is, the simple fact is that as a project manager you are operating within a larger context. That context is the environment and corporate culture that exist within the organization where you work. Any project manager who doesn't recognize how significant these things can be is in for a rude awakening. In this chapter, you take a look at how to organize the project and factor in the environment, too!

The Project Life Cycle

You can break all projects into distinct phases. Taken together, these phases comprise the project life cycle.

Since every project is unique by definition, each has a large degree of uncertainty associated with it. Remember you are often creating something that has never existed before. One of the techniques that can help you develop your project plans effectively is to use the project life cycle as a guide.

In This Chapter

- Learning the project life cycle
- Differences between a project life cycle and a product life cycle
- Project life cycle phase one: defining your project

Project Phases and the Project Life Cycle

Four phases can be used to define the project life cycle, as you can see in the following diagram. For this book, I have labeled the four phases according to what occurs in them.

> **NOTES FROM THE FIELD**
>
> Within a company, there may be more or fewer phases, and they may have different names than the ones I have chosen for this book. For example, if a company was in the business of building facilities, the phases might be labeled Design, Build, Commission, and Operate.
>
> The Project Management Institute (PMI) and project managers in general don't believe that universal names for the phases of the project are important. However, what is important is that each phase be clearly defined with a set of activities and deliverables.

For more information on project life cycles, refer to *PMBOK Guide* sections 2.4 and 2.4.2.

- **Phase 1: Project Definition Phase.** This phase of the project defines what the project will attempt to accomplish when it is finished.

- **Phase 2: Project Planning Phase.** In its simplest form, during this phase, the project manager and key project team members are planning all the work they must finish to make the project successful.

- **Phase 3: Project Execution Phase.** During this phase, the greatest amount of effort, time, and money are expended to complete all the activities defined during the planning phase.

- **Phase 4: Project Close-Out Phase.** After a project has been successfully completed, the project manager and sometimes key team members capture what they have learned and complete all the administrative tasks that officially end the project.

In each phase, a *stage gate* marks the end of the current phase and gives the project manager authority to continue. You can use it to follow through the four phases of the project life cycle.

> **DEFINITION**
>
> The conclusion of a project phase is generally marked by a review of both key deliverables and project performance to date, to determine whether the project should continue. These phase-end reviews are usually called **stage gates.**

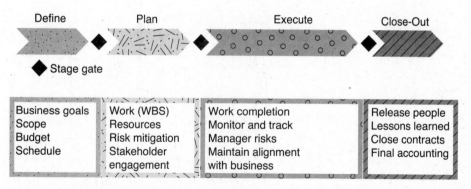

A more detailed view of the four phases of the project life cycle. Note the stage gate at the end of each phase.

Project Life Cycle vs. Product Life Cycle

As you can see in the following two diagrams, a distinct difference exists between a project life cycle and a product life cycle. In a product life cycle, there is a natural progression from the introduction of a new product as it goes through growth and maturity and into decline. In a project life cycle, you can see the majority of the money and time is spent during the execution phase of the project. As you go through these chapters, you will see why that is the case.

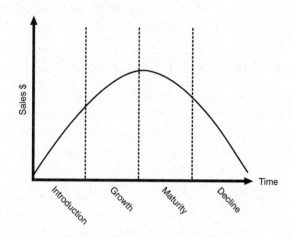

The classic model of a product life cycle.

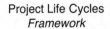

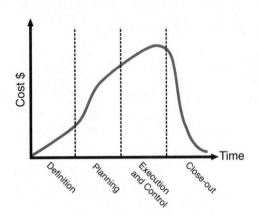

- Four Phases of a Project:
  - Definition
  - Planning
  - Execution and Control
  - Close-out

There are four phases in the project, and it takes time and money to accomplish each phase.

NOTES FROM THE FIELD

As part of my consulting work, I have been asked by clients to assist a project manager whose project is in danger of failing, and see if we can work together to put the project back on the right path. The most common problem that I have seen in those situations is that the project was poorly defined. The project manager and his team are working hard, but that lack of direction in the project definition phase means they are doomed right from the beginning. So my strategy in those situations is to stop and do the definition work that was missing at the beginning and that leads to a successful project after all.

The Project Manager (That's You)

Sometimes when a project has been proposed, senior management may want you to conduct a feasibility study and determine what this project might cost to roll out and if it is technically feasible to complete. The objective is to provide predictable results for a specific project. After acceptance by the executive committee, the project will start. They will often have a rough idea of how quickly they want to deliver the project and what they estimate it will cost. With a feasibility study, they are either looking for confirmation of their assumptions or a more realistic estimate of time and money involved.

Project Definition Phase

In the definition phase of the project, you will need to collect information and also develop some of your own. Here are some concepts for defining your project; they will be detailed in the chapters that follow:

- Identify stakeholders that will be interested in the outcome of the project.

- Analyze the business problem or problems that this project is trying to solve.

- Review the business case that was developed as part of sanctioning this project to understand the expected benefits achieved by this project.

- Clearly define the scope of the project. Develop the goals for the project and complete a charter that summarizes the project succinctly. (In Chapter 7, I recommend that you work with your project sponsor on this activity.)

- Identify all the risks and constraints that are apparent at this early stage of the project.

- List and challenge all the assumptions being made as the project is defined.

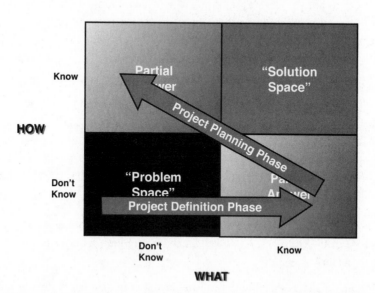

The definition phase of the project moves from the space where you don't know what you will do or how you will do it, to the space where you have defined what you will do. In the planning phase of the project, you will move to the space where you know what you will do to how you will do it. During the execution phase, you move the project into the space where the solution resides.

Preparing the Leadership

For any project manager to be successful on a project that will change the way the business will operate, the project manager needs to get the leadership of the organization involved. The PMI has done several studies on the factors involved in executing a successful project. Nearly all these studies have concluded that management leadership and support are critical success factors. Why? Because people respond to the agenda their "boss" feels is important. And how do they determine what is important to their boss? They notice what he talks about and pays attention to on a day-to-day basis. If you consider your own situation, you probably use this primary technique as well. Even if you have top management support for your project, you will have to work hard to keep them engaged and supportive, particularly if the project is fairly long. I'll detail more about that in Chapter 6 on stakeholders.

How Involved Should the Leadership Be?

While the leadership team seldom has the time to be "in on the details" concerning the project, the project manager needs to develop specific roles and responsibilities for them. The project manager must make clear to the leadership team that at certain times during the project, he will call upon them to assist in delivering the project. My experience has been that leaders are more than willing to participate if they understand how they can contribute and why. For example, if you need a leader to deliver an important message to the organization, he should be willing to do that. However, this usually means that you, or someone from the project team, will craft the message the executive will deliver.

 RISK MANAGEMENT

In most cases, the leader will want to review and edit the message so that it sounds more like the way he would deliver it. There's nothing wrong with that, as long as the basic message stays intact. If he begins to edit it in such a way that it loses the core message, you may need to do a better job of explaining what you are trying to accomplish with the message and educate him on the risks and possible consequences if the message is not delivered as you developed it.

If a communication specialist within the project team developed the message, you may need to get him involved in the conversation as well since he may have a better chance of explaining his words and approach than you do.

Also, many project managers deal with multiple layers of management during the course of planning and executing their projects. Midlevel managers are notoriously difficult to deal with in times of change. Navigating these political waters may require the help of the senior executives, who can assist as various issues occur during the project.

For example, in one manufacturing project I worked on, an issue arose about how the project would handle a customer's request for special orders. The sales department wanted to cut through the red tape and get the order filled quickly to meet the customer's need and build goodwill by showing quick responsiveness to the requests. However, the shipping department insisted the right paperwork be completed within the existing policies before they would authorize and ship the order. Clearly, I needed the help of senior management to resolve this conflict. As I explained to the leadership team, the project team could deliver either solution, but I needed their guidance to know which way to go. The issue involved different departments and would require a change in policy if the sales option was selected. I felt this kind of decision, to change policy, was inappropriate for the project team to make without direction. The leadership team needed to help me resolve this type of situation. The executive team worked through the situation and came up with a compromise that ensured a quick response, but also provided the shipping department with documentation and authorization assurance.

Focusing on the Project Team

Now that you have some idea of *what* you are going to do, you need to begin to think about *how* you will do it and with *whom*. In other words, you need to start thinking about the people you'll need who can do the work and make the project a reality. You need to consider people's technical skills—perhaps the experience they have in the industry or within the company—and determine whether you need resources not available inside the company, such as consultants or contractors. You'll take a closer look at the people involved on projects in Chapters 13 and 14.

Review Questions

- Am I clear that phases may have any name as long as they are defined?

- Am I clear on the difference between a project life cycle and a product life cycle?

- Do I recognize how critical the definition phase of the project is to success?

- Have I thought about how I need the leadership to support me as part of this project?

The Least You Need to Know

- Since you are working on something that is new and unique, use the project life cycle to get organized.

- You need to know the difference between a project life cycle and a product life cycle to properly define the project.

- Stage gates are part of every project phase and determine whether you can move on to the next phase or not.

- Fully understanding the project and beginning to define it is a critical step to success.

- Get the leadership team involved at the early stages so they are ready to act when you need them.

The Project Definition Phase

You may think it's easy to get a project started, but starting a project off right takes some hard thinking and rigorous planning and involves some tough decisions.

First, you need to identify who the players are; these people are the stakeholders who'll help you define the project and whom you must ultimately please if the project is to be considered a success. Next, you begin the process of defining what to include and what not to include in the project you have been assigned in order to meet the business goals. After that, you need to define the specific requirements for your project and identify all the risks and constraints that may cause problems for the project after you get it started. You then need to create and get approval for a project charter, which defines the project you're going to deliver and the rules by which you're going to play. This part walks you through this phase step-by-step.

Identifying and Analyzing Stakeholders

Always remember that projects are successful when the stakeholders on the project are satisfied. Thus, identifying a complete list of stakeholders must be the first step in getting your project moving and should be an ongoing responsibility throughout the project. Some stakeholders are key, and they will make many of the important decisions during the project. In this chapter, I tell you how to identify the key stakeholders—those people who, as you proceed, will have the greatest influence and authority in defining and planning your project.

In This Chapter

- Identifying key project stakeholders
- Understanding the roles of project stakeholders
- Learning to work together with the stakeholders
- Communicating and managing the expectations of key stakeholders
- Using a stakeholder analysis tool

Identifying Stakeholders

The first *stakeholders* you need to identify are those who will make a meaningful contribution to a project. Thus, beyond you, the stakeholder list includes the following:

- Your project sponsor
- The managers in your company involved with approvals
- The customer (whether internal or external)
- The project team

 DEFINITION

A **stakeholder** is someone who has a vested interest in the success of a project. The Project Management Institute (PMI) identifies stakeholders as individuals and organizations who affect, are affected by, or perceive to be affected by a decision or outcome of the project.

For more information about stakeholders, refer to *PMBOK Guide* section 13.

There may be other stakeholders as well. For example, when the project involves building a chemical plant, government regulators at the local, state, and national levels are stakeholders. Environmental action groups, community and neighborhood groups, labor unions, and a variety of other groups might also be stakeholders.

Key Stakeholders and Their Contributions

Sponsor (may be a customer representative or functional partnership manager)	Provides authority for project to proceed and provides the financial resources for the project; guides and monitors the project engagement or selection process and plays a significant role in the development of the initial scope and development of the charter. Typically, the sponsor will approve the project charter.
Core Project Team	Provides skills, expertise, and effort to perform the work defined for the project; not necessarily involved with the management of the project.
Program Managers	Responsible for related projects.
Customer (may be internal or external)	The individual or organization that will use the product created by the project. Establishes the requirements for the project; provides funding; reviews the project as milestones and deliverables are met. Ultimately accepts the finished product.

Functional Managers	Establish company policy; provide people as subject matter experts; some may provide review and approval authority.
Operational Managers	Manage the core business areas of the company, such as design, manufacturing, and testing of the products that the company sells into the marketplace.
Vendors/Sellers	External companies that supply equipment or services necessary for the project to succeed.

Organizational Stakeholders

Potential stakeholders for any project.

Sometimes the roles of various stakeholders overlap, such as when an engineering firm provides the financing for a plant it is designing.

Your job is to manage the stakeholders by keeping them informed of any key decisions that are made. You must also communicate with them regularly on the status of the project. As a rule of thumb, stakeholders should never be surprised by any key decisions or the project status. However, not every customer representative or manager in the company is or should be considered a stakeholder.

Classifying Stakeholders

The latest thinking about stakeholders is to analyze the power they can have on the project and/or decisions affecting the project. The classification generally breaks down into four groups:

- **Authority** they have in the organization and how that authority can allow them to impose their ideas on the project

- **Influence** (particularly technical expertise) they have in the planning or execution of the project, or even veto power regarding certain decisions

- **Involvement** in the project, which could include people seconded to the project or participation in the steering committee

- **Level of concern** or interest in the outcomes of the project

The output of your identification and classification will become input into your communication and engagement plan.

Stakeholder	Roles	Approvals
Project Manager: Joel Baker	Defines, plans, controls, monitors, and leads the project.	Makes recommendations for approval; signature authority for any purchase over $1,500.
Sponsor: Joe Macdonald, Director of Engineering	Authority for most operational project decisions; helps guide the project; assists project manager with planning and approvals by other stakeholders.	Approves personnel requests and hiring decisions; signs off on SOW and project plans before submitting to the customer; signature authority for any purchase over $15,000.
Customer: Managers Sarah Goodwin, Vice President Fred Catwalk, Director of Finance	Helps define the project; authority for all major project plans and changes; budget approvals.	Final approval for SOW and all project plans; initial budget approval; signatures required for any nonplanned purchase of $5,000 or more.
Customer: Experts Allen Strange Jell Elsewhere	Experts who help define the project and develop product specifications.	Works with project manager and team; makes recommendations; not formal signature authorities.

A simple chart like this can help you identify the roles and authorities of the key stakeholders on your project.

The Customer

The customer is the person or organization who will use the product or service delivered by the project. In some cases, the customer may be a department or division of your own company. In other cases, the customer is external. In either case, the customer contributes both funding and project requirements. When defining the customer stakeholders, remember to distinguish between the people with final authority for project approvals and changes and those whom you must simply keep informed.

The Project Sponsor

The project sponsor is your most important ally in the project. This person shares responsibility for project success and helps everyone on the project team be successful. If the project is internal to your organization, usually a senior manager within the organization is the sponsor. If the project is for an external customer, the sponsor is usually someone from the customer organization who has authority to make decisions and provide money for the project.

This authority and the person's support are the sponsor's primary contributions to the project. The sponsor supports the project through approving the project charter, advising you as the project manager, assisting you in the development of the scope of the project and the scope of work (see Chapter 7), helping to secure the people needed to complete the project, and consulting on the development of other project documentation.

A good sponsor also assists you in overcoming organizational and political obstacles. Navigating the political waters within an organization often requires the help of the project sponsor. You usually need a senior executive to assist in the various issues that occur during the project and require someone who can help with the political aspects of a project.

 NOTES FROM THE FIELD

As project managers, we usually think of ourselves as the person "on the hot seat" for the project. However, never underestimate the pressure on the sponsor to deliver on the project. At the highest levels of corporations, it all comes down to politics. The perception about an executive's strength or weakness carries great weight at this level. If a sponsor does not appear to be in control, or there is a negative perception about the project, there is a political price to pay within this group. Your sponsor will help you as much as she can, but if she is surprised by developments and/or there is a perception of failure, don't be surprised if the sponsor begins to distance herself from you.

If you are working on a project outside of your company, the sponsor may also help you with the corporate culture. The culture is required for you to understand the protocol for decision making and how to get things done. Sometimes the sponsor may be your direct manager, but other times a person from another department or a customer representative with a primary interest and assigned authority for the project is the sponsor. Developing and maintaining your relationship with the project sponsor is key to making the overall project and its implementation successful; in many ways it's a partnership. The sponsor should always be the first person you confide in when you need help or think you're in trouble.

Here is a typical checklist of the project sponsor's role for a project:

- Holds the ultimate authority, responsibility, and accountability for the success of the project

- Resolves cross-functional organizational issues

- Promotes innovation to achieve the project goals

- Provides guidance, support, and direction to the project

- Signs project charter and business case

- Signs project plan and scope of work

- Certifies quality of the implementation

- Contributes to and approves the responsibility *matrix*

- Assists in developing project policies and procedures

- Approves project deliverables

- Approves changes to project scope and provides additional funds for those changes as required

- Monitors the progress of the project, the project budget, and schedule

- Works with the steering committee (see the following section)

- Makes business decisions for the project

- Provides user resources to the project as needed

- Shields the project from corporate politics

- Works to resolve conflicts

When it comes to working with a sponsor, always have a process for escalating issues to that person that are beyond your authority or ability to handle. Prepare the sponsor by letting her know about potential solutions you are working on. And when you present those potential solutions, explain how they may impact the schedule, cost, or quality of your project.

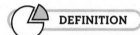

DEFINITION

It's common for people to devote only a percentage of their time to projects. This is usually identified as a **matrixed** organization, which means people may work on projects part time and have dedicated duties in a functional group while they work on your project. In these cases, it's very important that you work with these people's functional managers to ensure their support of the project.

The Steering Committee or Governance Board

The steering committee (sometimes called the project governance board or the review and approval team) is the group of stakeholders who must approve and agree on project scope, schedule, budgets, plans, and changes.

Obviously, you should include one or more key customer representatives—either internal or external—in this group, but you also are likely to include selected functional managers and executives from your own organization who must approve aspects of the project. The key is to keep this team limited in size to those people who really do need to approve project documents. On a large project, you need to develop an approval process that describes the people who will have a say in, review, and approve each type of document and project change.

The steering committee for a typical project is expected to perform the following roles:

- Advises on the business processes
- Monitors the project and maintains priority relative to other projects
- Settles priorities between related/competing projects
- Provides organizational support
- Provides timely decisions
- Resolves major issues of significant risk to the enterprise
- Disposes of issues and change requests that impact the organization beyond the commercial area
- Executes formal reviews and management reviews
- Approves changes in scope, budget, and/or schedule
- Provides feedback to the project sponsor and the project managers
- Manages environmental factors beyond the control of the project

Functional Management

Company officials with an interest in your project make up functional management, also known as line management. These people may include department supervisors, managers, or vice presidents. With the exception of companies that are organized around projects, these managers are responsible for organizational units within the company, such as engineering, marketing, or finance. Often, they supply the people who will be working on your project team, so you must work closely with these people to ensure you get the best people for your project. You also need their commitment to *continue* to support the project with resources. Too often, functional managers cut back the time they allow their people to spend on a project.

Therefore, as the project proceeds, you must keep the relevant functional managers informed of project progress and personnel performance issues. These managers can help you out of personnel jams if you let them; but if you don't keep them informed, they can derail a project from underneath you.

The Working Committee

Now you've come to the hard part—getting the business involved. Remember from the earlier discussion that a critical success factor is for the business to "own" the project. You want to implement a working committee of people from the commercial parts to develop the business case for the project since they are the ones responsible for delivering business results after the project is completed. These people need to come from all areas of the business. For any given project, the working committee might come from sales, marketing, information technology, accounting, and so on. After you have completed your stakeholder analysis, you may want to invite key stakeholders to nominate a member for the working committee. Based on the stakeholder analysis mentioned earlier, you would want to attract as many working committee members as possible from the "influencer" category who also have credibility with the "authority" category.

 TIME IS MONEY

On large projects, you can also identify different stakeholder types. A *champion* is powerful, with a high level of interest and a positive attitude—pay attention to this person at all times. A *friend* has low power but a high level of interest and positivity—use her as a sounding board. A *sleeping giant* is someone powerful who supports the project by displaying low levels of interest or enthusiasm—you need to raise her level of interest. An *acquaintance* is someone with low power and low interest who just needs to be informed from time to time. A *time bomb* is powerful with a high level of interest but has a negative attitude—she must be actively engaged and diffused to prevent a major disruption to the project.

After identifying the obvious functional authorities for your project, you need to identify those people who have informal veto authority on decisions affecting the project. Many of these managers are involved in approval processes even if they don't have a formal stake (such as required signatures) in the project. For instance, if you have a contract administration function within the organization, the members are not really involved in a direct way with the project. However, they control the process you will use to manage procurement activities. It's your job to identify these people and make sure they are included at strategic points in the project initiation, development, and execution.

Let me give you an example of a working committee in action. An energy trading company sanctioned a project for implementing a new software program for entering deals and delivering natural gas to its customers. The application of the working committee concept required that the project have a knowledgeable representative from the following:

- Gas traders

- Risk management

- Controls

- Information technology

- Accounting

- Scheduling and transportation

- Credit

- Marketing

This group worked with the project team to assess various technical options for the project as well as the business impact of what was being delivered. One of the greatest benefits in this process was that each function learned much more about what the others did. As is usually the case in large companies, they worked in silos and had only a passing idea of what others did. However, the detailed analysis and decision-making process allowed them to be far more knowledgeable about how the entire company made money and how each function contributed.

Working Together: The Magic Success Formula

As project manager, you are responsible for ensuring that the stakeholders on the project work together and gain consensus on project decisions. Not only at the beginning of the project but also as it progresses through its phases, the project manager must continue to review who the key stakeholders are and what roles they will play.

Many of the stakeholders—including the sponsor, the functional managers in your company, and the customers—will have more formal authority than you, but even so, you need to lead them.

Your leadership will be embodied in the tough questions you ask, the facts you provide, the ideas you inspire, and the enthusiasm you convey for the project. (I talk more about that in Chapter 17.) You need to coordinate the stakeholders and guide them through the various project stages. Some experts call this "managing upward." Your ability to do this is at the heart of successful project management.

Stakeholder Analysis Tool

As you begin to think about key stakeholders, consider the questions posed in the following table and how you might answer them in the "Response" column.

Question	Response
Who are the key individuals who care about the work that will be affected by the project? For example: • Sales • Customer Relations • Manufacturing • Vendor management and contracts • Marketing • Senior Management Team	
What are their responsibilities related to the project?	
What do they know about the project already?	
What authority level do they have related to the project?	
Who can influence the project and how will they exert that influence?	
What involvement would I like to have from this stakeholder?	
What level of concerns do they have about the impact of the project on their area of responsibility?	
What information and techniques are most likely to be accepted by these stakeholders?	
How will I best manage their expectations for the project?	
How will I receive feedback from key stakeholders?	

Review Questions

- Have I identified each stakeholder and the type of stakeholder they are?

- Do I have a spreadsheet with all of the stakeholders identified?

- Have I classified each stakeholder?

- Do I understand why they are interested in my project?

- Can I use the stakeholder analysis tool to identify potential members of the working committee?

The Least You Need to Know

- The identification of primary stakeholders on your project is an ongoing process and is key to the implementation, planning, and execution of the project.

- At the very least, the project stakeholders include you (the project manager), the customer, the project sponsor, company functional managers, and the implementation team members.

- Coordinating and communicating with the stakeholders is a primary role of the project manager.

- As a project manager, you need to "manage upward" to guide the key stakeholders through the project phases.

- Use the stakeholder analysis tool to help prepare for dealing with key stakeholders.

Scoping Out Project Success

Even a good idea can turn into a bad project if its goals (also called objectives by some project managers) and scope are not clearly defined before major resources are committed to it. SMART project goals identify *s*pecific, *m*easurable, *a*greed upon, *r*ealistic, and *t*imely results. Different people can interpret fuzzy goals in different ways; thus, stakeholders may never agree on whether you're finished or whether you've succeeded or failed. It's not enough to say you're going to build the next version of a software product; you need to establish what the new version will do, how much it will cost to build, and how long it will take to design it, among other goals for the project.

In this chapter, I explain why you need to get very specific about what you expect to accomplish on your project. I also tell you how to set goals for your project that no one can argue with.

In This Chapter

- Why specific requirements are important to project success
- Six criteria of all good project goals
- Steps for establishing project goals
- Choosing a scope for a project that meets the project goals
- Creating the project charter

Starting with the Business Case

In Chapter 1, I talked about the need to align the project with the business needs and requirements since it's the only reason companies undertake a project in the first place! So you must start with the business case. Most important, it should include the expected savings or revenue increases that will occur after the project is completed.

Companies format their business case templates in many ways, but most include these items:

- Reasons why the company undertook the project—typically the need it is trying to address or the increase in performance it is trying to achieve.

- Options that were considered in addressing the need or performance requirements (there is rarely one way to address the issue).

- Benefits that the company hopes to achieve as the result of the successful project. As you move into the goal section later in the chapter, you see that these benefits need to be clearly measurable and feasible.

- Analysis of the high-level risks. (There is much more in-depth discussion of risks in Chapter 8.)

- A study of the costs and schedule, again at the highest level (upcoming chapters discuss building the detailed cost estimates and schedule, but this is the basic target).

- Assumptions that were used to develop the business case and those used to build the project plan.

- The business case for most projects includes a cost/benefit analysis. As a rule of thumb, if a project depends on only one key benefit to justify it, your project is very risky. Why? Because most projects have several benefits so if one is not achieved, others still make the project worthwhile. Generally the assumption for this analysis is to maintain the status quo and then work through the potential options referred to earlier.

Understanding the Requirements

A good business case or contract is a great starting point for understanding the *requirements* on a project. However, there are more areas to investigate as you develop the true scope of your project.

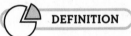 **DEFINITION**

A **requirement** is a condition that must be present at the end of the project in order to meet the contract or customer expectation.

The first place to begin is meeting with stakeholders to understand their requirements. You may do the following:

- Conduct meetings

- Schedule one-on-one interviews

- Facilitate workshops

You can also use a variety of other techniques to gather more detailed information.

Facts of Life—Why Are Requirements So Important?

Within companies today, whether they are publically traded or not, senior management is relentlessly pushed to do the following:

- Increase profits

- Minimize headcount

- Increase efficiency

- Improve effectiveness

At the same time, customers are pushing for the following:

- Reduced costs

- Improved products and services

In this type of climate, senior management really must handle two important tasks simultaneously:

1. Manage the business day-to-day to get the products and services to the customers and get paid.

2. Prepare the business to meet the future customer requirements so the business can competitive in the future. This is where your projects usually come in.

When senior management decides to sanction a project, they have been considering it over an extended period of time. The business has a certain amount of capital (money) that the company is prepared to invest to meet future customer requirements. After they review all the options, they place their bets (your project!). Each executive represents their function in the company and has an idea about why this project is important. However, since they are considering it at a very high level, they can all agree. But when you begin to discuss the details with managers who report to them, you will find these individuals have a much different view, because they are the managers who actually supervise the work that runs the company. This is where you are likely to run into disagreements over what the project must deliver to be acceptable.

For the most part, this group of senior managers will not think much about these projects again, except for one: the sponsor. The sponsor is usually one of these senior managers tasked by the management team to deliver the project.

Acceptance Criteria

During the requirements gathering, as project manager, you are really trying to gauge the acceptance criteria for key stakeholders. The business case will often sum up the concerns of stakeholders, but you are seeking more details so you can manage expectations as you work to deliver the solution.

Your goal in these activities is to make sure your customers will agree that your team has delivered what was promised at the end of the project. If you identify a conflict between stakeholder groups on acceptance requirements, it is much better to know that early on. It will allow you to work with your sponsor to get it sorted out before you begin work. In all probability, that conflict will not go away later on—in fact, it may intensify.

    TIME IS MONEY

Whenever you have meetings with key stakeholders, be sure to take notes on the topics that were discussed, key agreements or decisions, and any next-steps that were discussed. You should immediately write up these notes and send them to the people involved—whether individuals or groups—by email.

Passing along these notes may be important later on, because I can almost guarantee that some people will forget what was discussed and agreed upon. Too often, stakeholders will say later "I didn't say that," "I didn't agree to that," or "We never discussed that." Therefore, you want to have actual "evidence" in the form of emails or other documents to prove your point. And if the topic or decision is really important, you may even ask them to sign a copy of the document.

For more on collecting requirements as part of the scope, refer to *PMBOK Guide* section 5.2.

Conducting a Feasibility Study

The company may ask you to conduct a *feasibility study* to see whether the project makes sense, from an economic or business point of view. The purpose of a feasibility study is to identify any make-or-break issues that might prevent the project from being successful—in other words, to decide whether the project makes good business sense. The information developed in the feasibility study provides good input into the building of the business case.

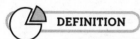

DEFINITION

A **feasibility study** is a general estimate used to make a decision about whether to pursue a particular project.

Normally, you develop the business case that outlines the information listed earlier so that decision makers can determine whether it makes sense to go forward with the project. This is especially useful if you are not the person who decides whether to go forward—if, for example, you have a steering committee or governance board that oversees the project.

Examples abound of companies that initiated major projects and then flushed millions of dollars down the drain because of poor project planning. The city of Denver spent millions of dollars on a state-of-the-art baggage handling system at its airport. When the system was finally tested, it not only failed to deliver baggage to the right places, but it shredded and mangled the luggage en route! The project was over a year late and millions of dollars over budget. Pity the poor taxpayers in that city!

Or consider Dell, the large computer manufacturer that spent more than $50 million for a computer software program that promised to provide instant access to all the information managers would need to run their business. They tried and tried to make the system work to their customized requirements. Finally, they gave up and abandoned a project in which they had more than $50 million invested!

If you want to avoid similar mistakes, you need to clearly define some points before you commit to a project:

- Clarify the goals, including the need for the project and the measurable benefits to the stakeholders and users.

- Define the scope.

- Create the time needed to carry out the project.

- Generate a rough estimate of your timeline, resource requirements, and costs.

Doing this work up front gives your project more credibility and manageability.

WORDS FROM THE WISE

The project should be stopped if the viability of the business case disappears for any reason.

—*Managing Successful Projects with PRINCE2* (UK government publication from the Office of Government Commerce)

Clear Project Requirements That Make Sense

The Dell story illustrates an important concept about setting appropriate goals for your projects. Of course, you can use project management techniques on projects with poorly defined requirements and still accomplish something, but you may fail to do anything useful. For example, one of the biggest complaints about information technology (IT) projects is that end-users perceive them as a waste of time. Often, the IT department is totally baffled by such claims. In a software application project (as a typical example) they point out, usually quite correctly, that the software works just as advertised. The problem often centers on the fact that people don't know how to use the software to get their job done. As a result, the software is not utilized by the target users. Was the project a success? Maybe from a technical point of view, you could argue that it was. However, from a practical point of view, it was a failure. If your key customers don't like the product you have produced for them, then the project is a failure regardless of whether it works or not.

The Primary Goals of Every Project

Every project has three primary goals:

1. To create something (such as a product, procedure, organization, building, or other deliverable)

2. To complete it within a specific budgetary framework

3. To finish it within an agreed-upon schedule

Beyond these goals are other goals that must be specified and that actually define the project. For example, it's not enough to have the goal of building a midpriced sports car. A more appropriate set of goals would be to build a midpriced, convertible sports car that will do the following:

- Use both gas and electric power

- Be of a quality comparable to the Volvo C70

- Sell for 10 percent less than all comparable cars

- Offer specific features to meet competitive demand, such as antilock brakes, a geo-navigational system, onboard internet access, and an electrically powered convertible top

- Be available for the 2014 sales year

- Be manufactured by a factory in Japan but designed by engineers in the United States

To differentiate primary goals from other project goals, other books often refer to these other goals as "objectives," but "goals" and "objectives" are really just different words for the same thing. Whether you call the ideas goals or objectives, they should meet the criteria outlined in the following section.

 WORDS FROM THE WISE

It concerns us to know the purpose we seek in life, for then, like archers aiming at a definite mark, we shall be more likely to attain what we want.

—Aristotle

Six Criteria for Setting Great Goals

As you and the key project stakeholders begin setting goals, be aware that project goals should meet six general criteria to ensure the project will accomplish something of perceived value.

Goals Must Be Specific

Your goals must be adequately clear so that another, equally competent manager could take over your responsibilities and guide the project to completion. If your goals meet this criterion, you're pointed in the right direction. Ask co-workers to read your goals and determine what has been stated and what the project will look like when it's done. Confused, surprising, or conflicting responses mean they require more refinement.

Goals Must Be Realistic

Your goals must be possible or at least be within the realm of possibility. For example, if you have a project to implement a software application that costs $5.7 million and you only have $2 million available in cash and credit, you obviously have little chance of getting the project done. In this case, perhaps you should consider a preliminary project to build up your cash reserves before you draw up plans for the installation.

The Six Criteria for Good Project Goals

If you write goals for your projects that always meet these
six criteria, you'll be working on projects with a purpose.

Goals Must Have a Time Component

Projects must have a definite finish date, or they may never be completed. Projects with no defined endpoint are in danger of never finishing. And projects with unrealistically short dates blow up like an overloaded circuit breaker. I had an energy company as a client that needed to overhaul the trading software they used to maximize their power generation assets. When I launched the project in January, the original target was for completion in October, a pretty aggressive target, but doable. Suddenly, in February, the deadline was moved up to an April launch! That project was doomed to failure no matter what the project manager and the project team did.

Goals Must Be Measurable

You must be able to measure your success at meeting your goals. I refer to the clearly defined results, goods, or services produced during the project or at its outcome as *deliverables*. Projects can have interim deliverables that don't reflect the final product. For example, you might need to build a model of the strip mall that you are building (the finished product) early in the project cycle so that more work can be completed later on. The strip mall itself is the final deliverable, but the model may be a deliverable for the design phase of the project.

Deliverables, like projects, are evaluated not only by the fact that something is produced but by their quality as well. Don't confuse quality with grade. Quality is how well the product satisfies the business performance needs of the customer; grade is the number of features a product may have. (I'll talk more about quality in a project in Chapter 23.) For example, consider cell phones. The basic purpose of the cell phone, of course, is to send and receive telephone calls. A cell phone that does what it is supposed to do—send and receive calls with few "drops"—is a high-quality cell phone. However, new cell phones have internet capabilities, and some can handle music and multiple applications like an iPhone. The cell phone with all these features is a high-grade cell phone. However, if it drops calls regularly, then it may be high grade, but it is low quality. Low quality is always a problem. Judging the grade that a customer wants and is willing to pay for is quite another issue. Determining and then delivering both the quality and grade of the finished product is a key element in defining the scope of your project.

Goals Must Be Agreed Upon

At the outset of a project, you, as the project manager, and the other initiators of the project (for example, your boss, the customer, or the steering committee) must agree upon the goals before you take any further steps toward planning the project. If you don't reach consensus, there's no point in beginning the project; it's doomed from the start because the stakeholders can't agree on the outcomes that will make the project a success. In a large project that crosses many departments or other organizations, gaining consensus can be a long and thankless process. (See the section "Seeing Eye to Eye" later in this chapter.)

 RISK MANAGEMENT

> For any project, the key to success is that stakeholders believe the project has deliverable value. However, various functional groups might define that value differently. Therefore, it is critical to get consensus on the goals from all the key stakeholders. Remember, consensus means that all agree with the goals even if they are not exactly what they had hoped for.

Eventually, all the team members as well as the stakeholders must agree to support the project goals if you're going to manage the project effectively. Without consensus on the goals, the project faces a bumpy road to completion. Remember that consensus doesn't mean that everyone gets what they want; it means they will support the goals of the project as defined. Projects started with misunderstood goals often have team members working at cross-purposes or occasionally duplicating each other's efforts.

Responsibility for Achieving Goals Must Be Identified

Although you, the project manager, bear the brunt of responsibility for the overall success of the project, others may be responsible for pieces of the goals. Like agreeing on the goals, you must identify the people responsible for the goals, and they must be willing to accept responsibility before the project proceeds further.

After you identify all the major players who will be making decisions and contributing major pieces to the project, get them to sign off up front. For example, if a project is going to choose and implement a new CRM software that allows the billing department to input customer requests for changes in services, you need to get an agreement from your accounting group and the information technology group that will support the new software after it is installed.

Establishing Goals Step-by-Step

It's easy to establish goals for your project. In fact, it's so easy that you'll find yourself with more goals than you can handle. (You'll have time to develop goals for specific activities later in the planning cycle.)

Here's how to establish good overall project goals:

1. Make a list of the project's goals. At this point, don't rule anything out. Just make a list and check it twice.

2. Study the list and eliminate anything that has no direct bearing on the project.

3. Do away with anything that is really a step in meeting the goals and is not a goal for the end result of the project. Now you should have a "pure" list of project goals, so it's time for the final step in goal setting.

4. Study the list again and make sure each goal meets all the relevant six criteria. Now determine whether all these goals are doable within one project. Look for goals that really belong to a separate project or are not directly germane to the project at hand. Cross them out. Leaving them in your current project will confuse team members and eat resources you need for this project to succeed.

5. If the items you deleted from the list are important, consider alerting your management to them so they can decide what, if any, action to take. This may require explanation on your part as to why you can't take on the extra work and how each item really deserves a project world of its own.

TIME IS MONEY

Often, in setting goals, you think about what you want the final product to do. However, another key to establishing your goals is to consider what the project *will not* do.

Successful projects must meet their goals with a minimum of changes and without disturbing the main workflow of the organization. If a project derails for one reason or another, you may have to use additional resources in an attempt to meet dates. This can cause serious organizational problems as other important work is put aside to accommodate the problem project. Your task is to run the project as smoothly as possible with no requirement for additional time, bodies, or money that interferes with other projects or day-to-day operations.

The goals are important and help you to develop two key documents: the charter and the scope statement.

Developing the Project Charter

The project's *charter* is a critical document between the project manager and the customer and/ or sponsor. The formal definition states that the charter authorizes the project to begin and sets the stage for all the planning that will follow. However, I would recommend that you think of the charter as a communication document. It allows you and your sponsor to get on the same page with the additional benefits of allowing you to communicate effectively with other key stakeholders.

 **DEFINITION**

The **charter** is an integrated document that describes the alignment of the project with the business strategy, project description, high-level requirements, summary schedule, budget, and approval requirements. It officially sanctions the project manager to spend money and recruit people to work on the project.

Creating a charter requires you to find facts and data from a number of sources. The following figure shows most of the people or documents that can provide you with the information you need.

In Chapter 1, you looked at the link between the business strategy and the performance outcomes the project is tasked to improve. In the charter, the project manager wants to provide more detail on the business outcomes the project will solve. Let's look at each of these elements in more detail and see how they might look for implementing a new CRM application.

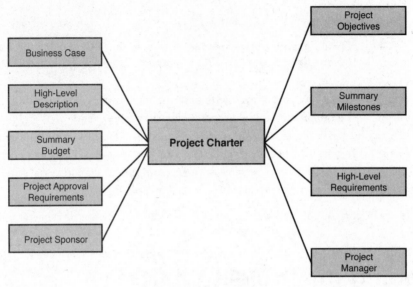

Inputs into the project charter.

Working with the Sponsor on a Case for Change

In order to effectively begin writing a charter, I have found it quite helpful to start working with the sponsor on the case for change. When this document is finished, you will have the basis for your communication plan as well as the charter.

The case for change is the way the project answers the fundamental question on everyone's mind as the project is launched: "Why are we doing this?"

In most cases, you, as project manager, have not been involved in the senior management deliberations on why they chose your project and rejected others. Working with the sponsor to answer these questions will provide you with background context. It also has the added benefit of allowing you to "get inside the head" of your sponsor to understand what he thinks is important.

Here are some general guidelines for developing a case for change. First of all, work with your sponsor to answer the following questions:

1. Why are we doing this project from a business perspective?

2. Why are we doing the project now? In most cases, the problem has existed before, so what changed to make this a priority now?

3. What will happen if we don't complete this project successfully?

4. What are the benefits of doing this project to us and the business?

5. What will we need to do differently?

Feel free to edit these questions as appropriate for your project and your situation. Just remember what you are trying to accomplish with the exercise. Remember to use words that will resonate with the people the project impacts. Nothing will turn them off faster than using language that is "project speak" or other jargon. That is where your business sponsor or business working committee members can help.

The project team should develop a first draft, and then the business or end-users can edit it. When you need to draft this document, I recommend that you start with the business case that was developed to justify the project. Of course, the audience for the case for change is not interested in all the gory details like cost/benefit analysis, return on investment, net present value, and the like. However, if you have a well-drafted business case, you can usually glean many of the answers to the questions posed earlier—at least enough to provide the draft for the business people or working committee to edit.

Putting It in Writing

For developing a charter, I strongly recommend you work with your sponsor. The audience for a charter may include all the project stakeholders, but especially the sponsor. Remember that just like you, the sponsor is accountable for a successful project. When a project is produced for the company alone (the sponsor and the project team work for the same company), the charter may be the only project agreement required. When the sponsor and the project manager work for different companies, both a contract and a charter are advisable because the charter specifies project details typically outside the scope of a contract, and the contract specifies legal agreements outside the scope of the charter. In some cases, the contract refers to a charter as the official definition of the work to be completed.

 RISK MANAGEMENT

The terms "project charter" and "statement of work" (SOW) are often used interchangeably. As a project manager, you need to understand the difference. The charter is a written document that allows the project manager to begin the project and apply money and people to it. This is the way the Project Management Institute (PMI) uses the term. The SOW, also called the scope statement, is the formal project definition document that describes in detail the products or services the project will deliver. Both uses of the term "charter" will likely continue; just be clear on how the word is used within your organization and your customer's organization.

The Components of the Charter

A charter lists and defines the goals, constraints, scope, communication guidelines, and success criteria for a project. The initial charter, once written, becomes a document subject to negotiation and modification by the stakeholders. When the charter is finally approved, it becomes the "official rules" for the project.

In size, the charter can range from a one- or two-page memo on a small project to a 100-page document of understandings for a major technical endeavor.

The usual minimum content of a charter includes the following:

Project purpose or justification. Clearly answer the basic question of "Why are we doing this project?" in this section. In addition, reference the business case for the project but don't necessarily detail it.

Project objectives and success criteria. This section defines the criteria for success. Not only specify the on-time and within-budget criteria, but also list all the other goals created for the project.

Project approval requirements. This section defines who decides success, who signs off on what, and who has authority to make certain decisions. Another useful tool is the written responsibility matrix (which you see more about in Chapter 13), the table that defines the project's important roles and responsibilities. This section of the charter is particularly important because projects often cross organizational boundaries; thus, projects have their own reporting structure that is outside the functional reporting structure of the overall organization. If project roles and reporting requirements aren't defined and agreed to in the charter, conflicts about decision-making roles and authority may derail a project midcourse. A good example might be decisions the working committee is authorized to make versus those that must be approved by the sponsor.

Basic reports. This section also details the basic reports that will be produced and any meetings that will be held during the detailed planning phase of the project. At this point, specify the frequency and audience of the status reports and basic meetings for the project planning phase. On large projects, you will produce a more detailed communication plan later in the planning cycle or during the project implementation phase(s). These later communication plans will add more information about the author, content, and frequency of reports to be produced and meetings to be held during the later phases of the project. On small projects, these more detailed communication plans probably won't be required if the charter is sufficiently detailed. You'll look at the communication plan in more detail in Chapter 19.

Benefits and risks in the early evaluations. Here the initial benefits and risks to the project are identified. They are probably more qualitative than quantitative at this stage and must be filled out more completely later. For example, a new data entry system will eliminate the need to duplicate data entry, which clearly saves time. However, how much time is probably too detailed at this point. In some projects, the benefits and risks are clearly linked. For example, the benefit of moving into this new system is providing the products and services to allow the company to grow their customer base. However, a clear risk is that if the system is not successfully implemented, the company may be left with systems that will be difficult to maintain and less and less reliable.

High-level cost and schedule estimates. This section provides the rough but well-researched estimates of both the cost and the schedule for the project. (You learn more about cost and schedule in Chapters 11 and 12.) For example, the management team might have asked the project team to complete the project within 18 months with a budget of $15 million. More complete planning is required to see whether both of these targets are realistic.

Seeing Eye to Eye

Gaining consensus is the all-important process of getting honest buy-in from the people involved that all aspects of the project are understood and agreed upon. Further, consensus implies that people chosen for certain roles will accept them and that the goals are SMART (meaning they're specific, measurable, agreed upon, realistic, and timely). Before you proceed with the project, consensus must be reached on the charter. After you and the sponsor have developed the charter, give the stakeholders plenty of time to provide their input. It may take multiple meetings and multiple iterations of the charter to get it right.

 NOTES FROM THE FIELD

As project managers, we often think of ourselves as "on the hot seat" to deliver a project—and we are. But never underestimate the pressure to deliver faced by your sponsor.

In one energy trading company, a very expensive, business-critical project failed to deliver. As you can probably guess, the project manager for that project lost his job. However, the failed project also cost the CFO and the CIO their jobs because they were the co-sponsors of the project. Their senior management colleagues decided they were no longer welcome in the executive team. The lesson is if your project begins to look like a failure, don't be surprised to see your sponsor begin to distance himself from you.

After the charter is agreed upon by all the key stakeholders, the final step in initial consensus might be a signed agreement on the charter from the sponsor and key stakeholders. The signatures provide evidence that everyone agreed to the project as defined in the charter. At this point, the charter establishes the baseline for the detailed planning activities and establishes a high-level schedule and budget for the project.

As time goes on in the project, the charter will likely need to be amended and agreed to again. Making changes to the charter becomes an important way to manage stakeholders throughout the project life cycle. The charter at the end of a large project might be quite different from the charter you agree to at the beginning of the initiative. But the difference is not important. The only things that matter are that everyone has been informed and all changes have been agreed to by key stakeholders and always put into writing. Thus, consensus building is an ongoing activity during the project, especially when project changes are necessary.

Whereas the charter is a document for capturing the business reason for a project, the scope statement is focused on defining exactly what the project will deliver. It will usually include the following:

- **Project scope.** The scope statement clearly defines what the project will and won't do. Mention the relationship of the project to other priorities or business endeavors here as well, especially when the project is a subproject.

- **Project deliverables.** This section defines what the project is supposed to produce and helps focus the team on creating outcomes. List by name the intermediate deliverables as well as the final deliverables. For example, "scale model" is an intermediate deliverable on the way to a final deliverable of "a completely built refinery." It's important to write the project management deliverables as well as the project deliverables into the scope statement; this practice ensures that the basic communications within the project are clearly understood. It is also important to detail what is *not* in scope.

- **Assumptions and constraints.** Detail any assumptions that limit the project or agreements that form the basis of interactions here. Don't leave anything out that could affect the future management of the project. If you want the project to be considered a success, all "side" or "off-line" agreements must be agreed to in the scope statement.

- **User acceptance criteria.** In this section, introduce all the key project influencers, managers, and users. Use your list of stakeholders (see the list of stakeholders from Chapter 6) and the requirements gathering I discussed earlier to determine how the project deliverables will be accepted at completion.

Review Questions

- Am I clear on why requirements are so important to project success?

- Do I understand the reason for collaborating with my sponsor on writing the project charter?

- Am I clear on the differences between the charter and the scope statement?

- Do I recognize what information should be included in the charter? The scope statement?

The Least You Need to Know

- Gather requirements to understand exactly what your customers are asking for.

- Work with your sponsor to develop the charter by using the business case for change questions.

- When planning a project, stakeholders must specify and agree upon its scope.

- Write the charter and scope statement to document the goals, scope, deliverables, cost and schedule estimates, stakeholder roles, chain of command, assumptions, risks, and communication guidelines for a project.

- The charter and scope statement becomes the basis for the detailed project plan.

Managing Risks and Constraints

A good project manager evaluates risks right from the beginning of the project. Even with clear goals, you need to assess the probability that something will go wrong and keep you from completing the project successfully. On a small project, this step may take only a few moments to ponder, but on a larger project, risk assessment can be a substantial effort. The goal of the risk and constraint analysis is to establish the feasibility of the project within the budget, schedule, politics, laws, and organizational structure that limit your project. This risk and constraint analysis accounts for the project scope you just defined in Chapter 7 and how you might address them. The major risks and constraints should also be documented in the charter as you work with your sponsor.

A project that moves beyond the initiation phase without taking risks and constraints, including the organizational and business risks, into account will be buffeted by the surrounding internal and external forces and will be more likely to fail. Bad weather? A delay. Your main supplier goes bankrupt? A delay. A strike? A delay. Waffling among senior management regarding a decision? A delay. This chapter walks you through how to evaluate and plan for these types of risks and constraints.

In This Chapter

- Understanding how risks involve uncertainty and loss
- Handling risks of all kinds
- Maintaining a risk register
- Constraints that bind you

The Three Common Types of Risk

As you might assume, the kinds of *risks* you'll encounter vary with the project. Team members may fail at their tasks; sunspots may blow away your satellite uplink in the middle of an important transmission; and the concrete rebar used in your new corporate headquarters may start to rust about one month after installation.

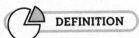

> **DEFINITION**
>
> The Project Management Institute (PMI) defines **risk** as an uncertain event or condition that, if it occurs, has an effect on at least one project objective, such as the scope, schedule, cost, or quality. And a risk always lurks in the future.

Ultimately, all the risks in a project boil down to these:

- **The known risks.** These are risks you can identify after reviewing the project scope within the context of the business and/or technical environment. You must draw on your experience and that of the key stakeholders in defining risks of this nature.

- **The predictable risks.** These risks may occur. They are also anticipated risks based on work with similar projects. They have to do with things, such as staff turnover or economic changes, that can have an anticipated impact. Instinct, rather than concrete evidence, tells us to be wary of these risks.

- **The unpredictable risks.** These are the things that go bump in the night or the "stuff that just happens" beyond the control of the project manager or team. You simply can't predict everything!

Risk Areas

You can further break risks down into areas that may impact delivery of the defined product or service. The primary among these include the following:

- **Budget.** You may not have the full amount of funding that your project needs.

- **Schedule.** You may find that things are taking longer than originally planned. Thus, you risk running out of time and missing your schedule for release.

- **Staffing.** As work on the project begins, you might realize that you can't find the right staff in the marketplace or don't have the requisite experience or skill set available in the company to meet objectives.

- **Stakeholders.** If your stakeholders don't have the time to work with the project team and assist in developing the solution to project problems, you risk having a dissatisfied customer as the project proceeds.

- **Project size and/or complexity.** The project is so large or so complex that there are just too many factors to attempt to control them all, especially given the time or budget restrictions.

- **Corporate politics.** Because of political decisions, competing work groups share responsibility for certain activities, potentially creating a situation where no one is assuming accountability for decisions you require.

- **Organizational resistance.** The project makes business sense, but key stakeholder groups are resisting the changes the project deliverables require.

- **External factors.** External risk factors hover outside your control, such as new government regulations or shifting technologies.

Don't Forget Business Risks

Business risks also may have an impact on the acceptance of a product or service. These risks include the following for developing a new product or service:

- **Market acceptance.** The product is a good one, but customers won't buy it.

- **Time-to-market.** It will be a good product, and customers will want it, but only if you can deliver it within a specific time frame.

- **Cost of production.** It will be a good product, and customers will want it, but due to the cost of producing it, customers won't be able to afford it.

- **Difficult-to-support.** It's a great product, but who's going to support it? The operations group doesn't have the people and skills to support the product once it is in the marketplace.

- **Loss of political support.** A project loses support from executive management because the sponsor has moved to a new position and the new sponsor assigned to the project knows little about it.

The Ultimate Risk: Acts of God

As humans, we can do little to prevent acts of God from affecting projects, but we can take steps to avoid the most likely problems. With this in mind, insure your project against hurricanes, floods, earthquakes, and other predictable acts of God. (Check your policy to verify that it covers such events and does not prohibit any exclusively, as is common in most commercial policies.) Don't forget to include the cost of insurance in your project budget!

Developing a Risk Breakdown Structure

One way of analyzing risk is to use a risk breakdown structure to recognize and deal with risks. A risk breakdown structure is a systematic way to put risks in the form of a hierarchy so you can identify the risks by category and subcategory. It provides a pictorial view of risks by area and potential causes. The following figure is an example of a diagram of your risks. You may want to create a chart like this one and determine, with your project team and key stakeholders, where the risks are. That will help you determine how to proceed with a risk management plan.

To learn about a variety of risk analysis tools, refer to *PMBOK Guide* **section 11.4.**

While it's important to identify risks, the real secret is to be creative by either reducing the like-lihood that a risk event will occur or reducing the impact to the project if it does happen. Here are some ideas for seeking solutions:

- Identify potential problems early in the planning cycle (the proactive approach) and provide input into management decisions regarding resource allocation.

- Involve team members at all levels of the project; focus their attention on how to identify risks or prevent them from happening.

- Avoid the problem by eliminating the cause of the threat. For example, if you feel the loss of a key team member during the project might be a significant risk, you could avoid that problem by simply finding someone else to fill that role.

- Use a mitigation strategy to reduce the impact of the risk by reducing the probability of the risk occurring. Using the same example, you might add another person to your team who has similar knowledge and experience so that if you end up losing a key team member, you have someone who is capable of stepping in to fill the role.

- Use a retention strategy. This simply means that you accept the risk as possible, and you will develop a plan for dealing with it if it occurs. This usually occurs for risks you and the project team think are relatively unlikely to occur.

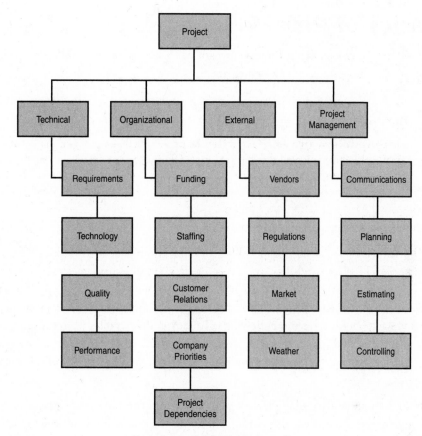

Example of a risk breakdown structure.

Risk Tolerance

Before you begin to make decisions about how to plan for risks, you need to consider the amount of risk (the risk appetite) you and your project sponsor (or your steering committee) are willing to tolerate. You might be willing to accept more tolerance for risks in some areas and less in other aspects. For example, for the management team, the project schedule may be very important as they are very concerned about the competition and losing market share. Therefore, the project manager and the steering committee might be less tolerant of risks that would impact the schedule. However, they might be far more tolerant in accepting risks to the budget.

The Basics of Risk Management

You can reduce the risks on your project through *risk management*. Some folks even refer to project management as "the practice of risk management."

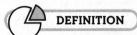

DEFINITION

In basic **risk management,** you plan for the possibility that a problem will occur by estimating the probability of the problem arising during the project, evaluating the impact if the problem does arise, and preparing solutions in advance to keep the risks at an acceptable level.

Here are the steps I suggest using on your projects:

1. Identify the risks by listing them and describing their potential impact on the project. Identifying risks involves careful analysis. Assume that anything can go wrong. Learn from past projects—the failures of the past are often the best source of risk-control information. You can also anticipate problems by looking at critical relationships or resources in the project and anticipating what could occur if these change. To look at deliverables from different points of view, interview the staff, subcontractors, vendors, suppliers, service providers, management, and customers. Also evaluate the environment, labor practices, and availability of raw materials or technologies.

2. Analyze the probability that the risk will occur and the potential impact of the risk. When you consider the impact, also consider whether the risk will impact your schedule, budget, quality, or people. Then assign a number on a scale from 1 (lowest impact) to 5 (highest impact) to quantify the potential impact of the risk to your project. Next, determine how likely you think this event will occur using the same 1-to-5 scale.

3. Determine the overall severity or importance of the risk. You do this by multiplying the probability number by the impact number (each on a scale of 1 to 5) to come up with a measure of severity.

4. Determine which risks are most important for further action. You usually establish a "risk threshold" that determines all those that are high in both impact and likelihood get the most attention (a 25). Risks with less severity are considered for further analysis. You can use whatever number seems appropriate for your situation and risk tolerance; the key is to come up with a risk threshold that establishes the risks that require further attention throughout the project.

5. Document a response plan for the risks. The project sponsor should approve this plan as part of the scope statement or project plan. You have four basic options for dealing with the risks on your list:

- Accept the risk. This means you intend to do nothing special at this point. If and when the risk emerges, the team will deal with it. This is an appropriate strategy when the consequences for the risk are cheaper than a program to eliminate or reduce the risk.

- Avoid the risk. This means you'll delete the part of the project that contains the risk or break the project into smaller subprojects that reduce the risk overall. Be aware that reducing or avoiding the risk in this way may also change the business case for the project. Sometimes you'll want to take on more risk to earn more return. This option is similar to the sentiment of "no pain, no gain" in the athletic world.

- Monitor the risk and develop a contingency plan in case the risk becomes imminent. If the best offense is a good defense, then when you encounter problems, having a contingency plan (popularly called a Plan B) in place is vital to ensuring continued success of the project. Developing contingency plans for key risks is one of the most important aspects of risk management. These contingencies are alternative plans and strategies to be put into place when necessary. The whole concept of contingency planning is based on the assumption that you can develop more effective and efficient scenarios if you do so proactively—before things happen—rather than reactively when you are under the stress of a slipping schedule or a cash shortage.

- Transfer the risk. Insurance is the most obvious, although often expensive, way of transferring risk. Risks including theft, fire, and flood are effectively transferred to the insurance company. Another way of transferring risk involves hiring someone else to implement a part of the project. For example, with a fixed-price contract with a vendor, you transfer the risk of cost increases to the vendor. Of course, fixed-price contracts aren't always possible, but when they are, they can reduce a substantial amount of a project's budgetary risk.

NOTES FROM THE FIELD

When you need to utilize experts to analyze risks, it can sometimes be difficult to reach consensus. The Delphi technique is useful here. To do this, you first summarize risks after speaking to experts individually and then circulate the summary. Next, ask the experts for comments and have them return the document to you. After a few iterations, you can often get the consensus you were hoping for. Plus, it reduces the bias and keeps one person from having too much influence on your risk analysis.

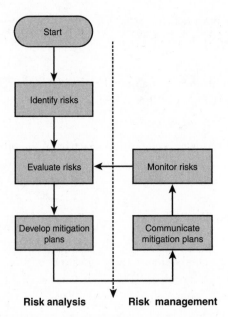

Risk analysis   **Risk management**

Identifying and managing risks is an ongoing process throughout the project.

Remember that risk management and response planning are ongoing processes. You must regularly reevaluate. Every project encounters problems neither planned for nor desired that require some type of resolution or action before the project can continue. Depending on the size and type of problem, various resources may be required to solve it. Note that, in some cases, no action is required! Project managers get to live long, productive lives by properly recognizing which is which.

There is always a balance between the costs associated with mitigating risks and the impact and likelihood that they will happen. For example, you could actually order extra equipment for a construction project to make sure you have enough when you need it. However, there would be a considerable increase in your costs. You would need to weigh those increased costs against the impact and likelihood of not having enough equipment when you need it.

 TIME IS MONEY

Ultimately, the key to managing risk is to be aware of everything that can negatively affect the project. Be suspicious. Look for problems. Persistence in analysis reveals risk, and new risks bring new plans for dealing with them. Although risk management starts at the beginning of the project by identifying the problems and constraints that are known, it will continue as you identify and contend with the unanticipated sources of risk that inevitably emerge until the project is finished. If you were a project manager running a project in New Jersey in fall 2012, think of the impact Hurricane Sandy would have had on the completion of your project if you didn't have all your work backed up in another location!

Tracking Risks with a Risk Register

Maintaining a risk register allows you to track information about the risks to the project, their analysis, their status, and the plans to deal with them if they occur. Many project managers track risks in a spreadsheet; others use a database, depending on the size of the project. Some project management software programs also have risk registers as part of their features.

Always review and update your risk register regularly. Some risks will disappear as the project progresses, and others will appear. For example, in a project, one risk identified early in the project might be the rumor of a reorganization of the sales department. However, after it is clear that the sales organization will not shrink but will actually grow, that risk disappears. But a new risk—the strain on the project resources due to an increase in the number of sales representatives that will require training—might now appear as something to be tracked and planned for.

It's also important to identify who owns the various risks, both from a monitoring and tracking perspective, but also for developing plans for handling them. If someone is not specifically assigned to a particular risk, don't be surprised if no one handles it!

During the project close-out phase discussed in Part 6, I will talk about reporting on the lessons learned during the project. It is important to recognize that your risk register will be a key tool as you develop your lessons learned at the end of the project.

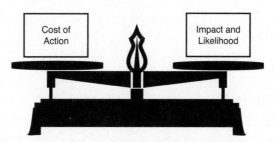

Managing risks is a balancing act between the costs associated with planning and managing risks and the likelihood and impact of a risk occurring.
(Adapted from PRINCE2)

Constraints vs. Risks

Unlike risks, *constraints* can be identified in advance. Constraints are the real-world limits on the possibilities for your projects. A typical constraint is budget. You will receive only a certain amount of money to finish the project, and to get more, you'll likely have to negotiate long and hard. If you ignore the constraints in defining your project, it will fail in some way. Your job as project manager is to make sure that you understand the constraints of your project and work within their limits.

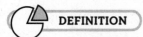

DEFINITION

A **constraint** is any restriction that affects the performance of the project or any factor that can affect when an activity can be scheduled.

Constraints to Consider

Project constraints, along with risks, are a major factor when establishing the project plan and getting the project underway. The constraints that bring a grandiose project down to Earth include answers to questions like these:

- How much money is really available and when?

- By what date must the project be completed?

- What inside resources are required?

- What outside resources are required, and can you afford them?

- Can you get consensus among project stakeholders and executives that the project is important and deserves your time and effort?

- What are you willing to settle for that will still meet your needs?

- Is there a way to do it using less expensive or fewer resources? (If there is, your problem may be solved.)

The process of answering these questions provides a modicum of reality. Use them as a tool to fine-tune a project as well as to brush off extravagant suggestions.

Project constraints are quite broad. Similar to the restrictions every manager faces when confronted with any task, you must identify constraints, like risks, beforehand, or an expensive project may fail (along with its manager) after bogging down in an avoidable quagmire.

The Budget

The budget is both a constraint and a risk. Most projects suck up money more quickly than you may realize. Whether you're opening a new sales office or developing a new product, the budget will constrain your efforts. Many companies may charge your project budget for the employees you borrow and any company-provided services you may require. Depending on the charge-back service, you may find it less expensive to bring in outsiders because you can choose exactly the skill set you require without dealing with the corporate baggage that comes with insiders from some functional groups. Be aware of the danger of agreeing to a budget to please the boss, management, or the customer when you know in advance the funds will be inadequate. See Chapter 12 for more information on project budgeting.

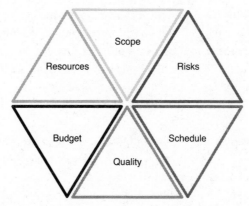

This diagram represents all of the constraints to a project beyond the classic triple constraints you read about in Chapter 1.

The Schedule

Time waits for no one. In addition to being a risk, the schedule is always a constraint, even if a project's due date is not that critical. If it rambles on after the predicted end date, the budget will expand, and team members may be pulled off to handle other responsibilities. Missing an end date may cause serious marketing consequences. A new but late-to-market product may arrive at the market window only to find it closed and firmly locked.

The People

I explain how to deal with people issues as you build your project team in Chapter 13. For now, keep in mind that people's skills, as well as their conflicts, are always a project manager's most pressing concern. You can argue for more money and time, but the people really make the project. If the right ones aren't available or are unaffordable, you will have to make do with the team that's available, no matter how inexperienced. The availability of the right people is both a risk to anticipate and a constraint you must deal with as the project proceeds.

For example, one of my customers has a policy of rotating managers about every 18 to 20 months. What it means to me and other project managers in the company is that we are always at risk of having our projects become "orphaned" through the loss of our sponsor. Along with the usual risk mitigation planning around technical risks, we have to plan on how to mitigate the loss of a sponsor.

My strategy has been to prepare a slide presentation on my project and update it about every three to four weeks. The presentation summarizes the scope of the project and its current status, along with any risks a sponsor should be aware of. That way, if I am suddenly faced with the loss of a sponsor, I am prepared to brief the new sponsor as soon as I can arrange a meeting.

The Real World

When a project is underway, reality has an ugly habit of settling in. One of the biggest reasons projects run into difficulty is that too often people underestimate the amount of time and effort it takes to complete all the work undertaken in a project.

Facilities and Equipment

Every project assumes that required equipment will be available within the project's time. Whether it's a 20-ton grader, an electron microscope, or a simple freight elevator, the right tools must be available for their period in the spotlight. Just like people, equipment resources are key to completion. If a project slips its dates, that critical piece of equipment might be tied up on another project somewhere else.

The constraints for your project should be well documented in the charter as part of the scope statement (review Chapter 7 for more on the charter). These constraints and the budget limit what you can do in the project.

Risky Business

Identifying risks and constraints beforehand provides you with time to mitigate those you can fix or to notify the stakeholders (both verbally and in writing) that the project may be in jeopardy before it even begins. A critical analysis of the project is crucial to get it off to an acceptable and workable start.

Going into a project with a "we can do anything" attitude may support team spirit at the onset, but when things come unglued and reality sets in, your team will become frustrated; management will complain; and you will kick yourself for not identifying the potential problems up front.

Review Questions

- Do I understand the types of risks that might impact my project?

- Do I understand the importance of tracking risks over time?

- Do I understand how to evaluate the impact and likelihood of a risk occurring?

- Can I define the constraints that limit what I can do during my project?

- Am I confident I know how to develop mitigation plans for risks?

The Least You Need to Know

- Project risks and constraints are known roadblocks you need to account for as you plan the project.

- Remember that you won't be able to predict everything that might happen. However, that does not absolve you of your responsibility to analyze and plan for risks.

- The impossible remains impossible, no matter how enthusiastic your team is.

- Focus on the most likely risks and plan for dealing with them in advance. The best defense against "losing your head" is to have a plan for dealing with it!

- The risk management process can help you identify, quantify, and ultimately reduce the risks (problems) that may affect your project.

The Project Planning Phase

Congratulations! You've made it through the definition phase, reviewed the project for potential risks, and identified how success will be defined for your project. Now you can start planning the key elements for successful projects, such as the tasks and activities, schedule, and budget. You will also learn how to choose the people for your team—the people who can help you deliver the project because they have the right skills and experience.

The plan is a road map for your project that helps you guide the work from start to finish. Not only does it detail the work that will be done, but it also serves as a tool for communicating with both stakeholders and the project team.

In addition to the charter, the scope of work, and the risks and constraints, project plans contain three standard components: the work breakdown structure (WBS), the schedule, and the budget. In this part, you learn how to integrate these elements as a complete plan for projects both large and small.

The Breakdown of Work

Project managers use a tool called a work breakdown structure (WBS) to break larger activities into smaller, more manageable components. Only after you've established the basic milestones for a project can the real work breakdown begin: putting together a WBS. This chapter shows you how to do so.

Breaking Your Project into Bite-Sized Pieces

Often taking the form of a tree diagram or an outline, a WBS is a hierarchical chart used to organize the project's required activities into related areas. You can also use the completed WBS for budgeting and personnel-selection purposes as well as scheduling (see Chapter 10). Organization is crucial in the WBS. On a larger project, organizing related areas into milestones or by deliverables makes it easier to visualize the overall project without getting into the details.

In This Chapter

- Understanding the work breakdown structure (WBS)
- Reasons you should break a project into work packages
- The right WBS levels for your project
- Identifying the dependencies for task completion

In a WBS, a project breaks down into the following levels:

- The total project

- Major deliverables

- Milestones that summarize the completion of an important set of activities or the completion of an important event in a project such as a subproject, which is just a smaller portion of the overall project

- Major activities (also called summary tasks)

- *Work packages*

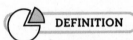

DEFINITION

A **work package** represents the lowest level of project activity where an estimate of both time and cost associated with it can be accurately estimated. A work package should have a unique deliverable associated with it.

You can have as many subprojects, milestones, major activities, and work packages in your WBS as you need. As a project manager, the levels in your WBS will help you control work at each level. An appropriately organized WBS can help identify the right time to ask and answer resource and staffing questions.

The WBS and Your Project

The WBS document organizes and summarizes the work necessary to complete the project. Every WBS starts with a summary of high-level project areas and milestones. In a major systems upgrade, those areas might be customer requirements, design and plan systems, tests, data migration, organizational readiness, and reports. For most larger projects, however, organize the activities you list into some kind of hierarchy (which you'll learn about in a moment) and then understand the dependencies among and between activities or tasks. Once a WBS is complete, the tasks can be scheduled (see Chapters 10 and 11), and a list of resources required to complete each task can be created.

The WBS should be able to help you do all of the following:

- Identify the major parts of the project so all the work needing to be done is clearly indicated.

- Organize the work in the most logical sequence so the work packages can be efficiently scheduled.

- Identify work packages you need to assign to various team members.

- Identify the resources (including equipment) necessary to complete each work package so you can develop a budget.

- Communicate the work to be done in a clear-cut way so team members understand their assigned jobs and responsibilities for completing the project.

- Organize related work packages using logical milestones.

Your WBS is the underpinning of a successful project because the need for resources and the schedule come from the WBS and the way you sequence activities. On larger projects, the WBS will likely undergo several revisions before you get it right. If you are new to project management, you should have the core team members or other key stakeholders review the completed WBS and sequences to ensure that they include all the work necessary to get things done.

 TIME IS MONEY

When you believe you have a credible draft of a WBS, put it away for a while and then revisit it. This gives you a chance to get an objective view of the various parts. You might see something you forgot to consider, or you might notice a better way to organize the work.

Take a look at the following tree-style outline WBS for a sample project. You can also use the outline method for projects that have too many layers to conveniently lay out in the tree format.

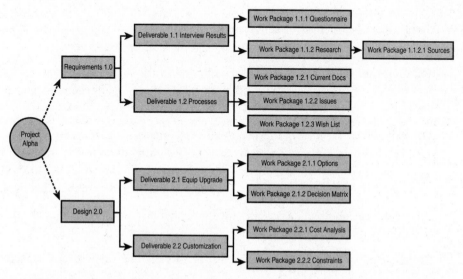

This is a small sample of a tree diagram for a project called Project Alpha that illustrates how deliverables and work packages are connected.

You can choose to focus on whatever level of the project is germane to your current management needs. Generally, most project managers find that working top-down is the easiest way to decompose the work. However, you can employ a bottom-up approach if it is more practical for a given project. Either way you choose, the smallest unit in your WBS should be the smallest unit of work you must track in your project; this is the work package. Only the work package level is actually assigned a time estimate and a cost; everything else in the WBS is simply an organizational tool for summarizing how the work packages combine to complete components of the project.

Most project managers use the 8/80 rule as a guideline for determining whether an activity qualifies as a work package. That rule states that any work package that takes less than one day to complete (8 hours) is probably too small, and you should consider combining it with something else. On the other end of the spectrum, if a work package takes longer than two weeks (80 hours), it is probably too large, and you should consider breaking it into smaller work packages. Of course, the overall length of the project will have a huge bearing on the decision about work packages. If the project will take 18 to 24 months or longer to complete, you might consider work packages that are one month.

Don't allow the lowest level in your WBS to reach the level of absurdity, but do track everything that could affect something else in the plan. While doing this, you must remember that not everything in life can be planned down to the minute; if it could, nothing would ever go wrong. You'll need to make your best guess about the detail and sequence of most project tasks.

Organizing the WBS

There's no magic formula for organizing a WBS. In the project example in the previous figure, the WBS is based on the category of deliverables. Although I'm sure you can think of other ways as well, you could base your organization on any of the following:

- **Phase of the project.** Decide what is required in each phase of the project. If you are building a facility, you could create a WBS for the design, build, commission, and operate phases.

- **Organizational structure.** In a clearly divided organization or a cooperating set of separate divisions, you can establish the WBS according to reporting structure. So you would have sales, accounting, operations, and so on with different deliverables and work packages. If outside vendors are involved, they can be included in this kind of planning.

- **Physical location.** If you are working with separate facilities, it might make sense to build the WBS based on the geographical locations instead of the people.

- **Systems and subsystems.** If there is clear demarcation between several aspects of a project, assemble the WBS to reflect this. As an example, you might have data systems, communication systems, control systems, and so on to break down the work.

You might want to consider these few other suggestions when creating a WBS. They are especially important for assembling a complex WBS:

- Each activity (also known as an element of work) should be assigned to only one level of effort. Never repeat an activity in another part of the tree or outline.

- A narrative may accompany the WBS. You may want to label certain boxes or lines with a number that references a page in an overview narrative document to provide more detail than "Get CEO approval for expansion plan." Software tools such as Microsoft Project allow you to attach "notes" to as many tasks as you like.

- Clearly identify related work packages in the WBS. A great way to show the linkage is by using the same color for related tasks.

- At all levels, the WBS should provide measurable deliverables for each aspect of the project. There are deliverables for the project itself, such as customer-required documentation, and there are deliverables for work packages, such as building the issues list for the current processes used within Pinnacle.

- Assemble the WBS in a format that allows changes if and when the project shifts slightly in direction. Computers are ideal, but a carefully protected whiteboard (you might wrap it loosely with plastic wrap) can fit the bill for a simple project. Use lots of sticky notes as well so things are easy to move around as you make changes.

 TIME IS MONEY

When maintaining a WBS for a large project, you need version control in place. This means that each version, no matter how preliminary or final, should be date- and time-stamped. That way, older plans can be relegated to the file, and everyone works with the most current document. Save each iteration separately by date so you can be sure you're using the latest and greatest plan. Also, save the older versions in an archive file, electronically, so you can use them to track project history and to serve as a learning tool to evaluate what (if anything) went wrong during your lessons learned exercise at the end of the project.

Five Steps to the WBS

You must complete five steps to develop a WBS that meets all of its goals:

1. Break the work into independent work packages that you can sequence, assign, schedule, and monitor.

2. Define the work packages at a level of detail appropriate for the length and complexity of the project.

3. Integrate the work packages into a total system with a beginning and an end. This may involve combining tasks and then creating milestones.

4. Present the work packages in a format you can easily communicate to people assigned to complete them during the project. Remember that each work package should have a deliverable and a time for completing that deliverable.

5. Verify that completion of the work packages will result in attainment of all the project goals and objectives.

For most large projects, assembling and organizing a WBS takes time, but a carefully assembled WBS goes a long way toward streamlining a project after the work begins.

Identifying Dependencies

A dependency is a logical relationship between tasks or activities. Once you develop the work packages, it is time to understand the dependencies that exist. For illustration purposes, I'll use the example of building a house.

- **Finish-to-start:** The most common dependency that occurs when you must complete one task to start the next one. If I have two tasks, "dig foundation" and "pour concrete," the pour-concrete task can't begin until the dig-foundation task is complete.

- **Finish-to-finish:** In this situation, one task must finish before the other can finish. For example, if I have two tasks, "add wiring" and "inspect electrical," the inspect-electrical task can't be completed until the add-wiring task is completed.

- **Start-to-start:** Here, one task must start before the other task can start. For example, if I have two tasks, "pour concrete" and "level concrete," the level-concrete task can't begin until the pour-concrete task has begun.

- **Start-to-finish:** This is a very rare dependency, but it does occasionally happen. For example, if the roof trusses for the homebuilding project are being built offsite, then I have two tasks, "truss delivery" and "assemble roof." The assemble-roof task can't be completed until the truss-delivery task begins.

As you begin to identify the dependencies between and among projects, it will be apparent how a project can be seriously delayed if a key task is not completed on time.

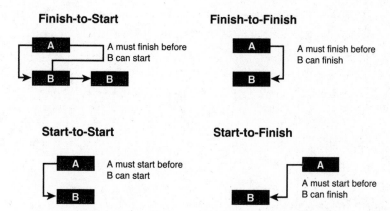

This shows the four different dependencies that could happen in a project.

In managing dependencies, you must also identify lead time and lag time. Lead time is used to accelerate the project. For example, for my homebuilding project, I will start delivery of supplies a week before construction starts to ensure the crews can work as fast as possible once construction begins. Lag time usually puts a hard constraint on my tasks. For example, if I have two tasks, "pour the foundation" and "frame the house," framing the house must be delayed by 5 days to allow the concrete to cure before the framing can begin. Therefore, I build that lag time into my project schedule.

In working to build the schedule, these dependencies influence when various work can be done and/or completed. The project may have mandatory dependencies, which involve a hard logic. However, the dependencies may also be discretionary, in that I may prefer to do tasks in a certain order based on experience or some other rationale.

Making Sure You Have Identified All the Work

Building a WBS for a complex project takes time. The WBS is a way to take the requirements the stakeholder(s) gave us (from Chapter 6) and turn them into the work that will need to be completed for the project to be delivered. Identify work so you can assess the overall amount of work there is and sequence it in the most logical fashion. A list of activities can be short and simple or long and detailed, depending on the size and goals of the project. Don't try to sequence the tasks or estimate time and budget during WBS definition. Those steps come later (see Part 3). Finally, don't try to do it all yourself, unless you are working on the project all by yourself. Enlist the members of your project team to help you think through all the required work.

The WBS makes communication among core project team members easier. And, as I've emphasized throughout this book, forgetting to list an important task can have a very negative effect on the project's bottom line and its schedule. Therefore, it's a good idea to have the members of your project team help you in developing the WBS. Generally, you have chosen them for their knowledge and experience, so rely on that expertise to build the WBS. As project manager, you may take the high-level pass at the various activities, but rely on people who are more experienced in particular areas to finish it. You will be glad you did. The WBS should account for the production of every deliverable contained in the charter that was approved for the project. Use the goals and deliverables in the charter as a starting point for developing the tasks.

RISK MANAGEMENT

In dealing with vendors, allow more time in the WBS for them to deliver than you may need. Some vendors have a nasty habit of overpromising and underdelivering.

Defining the Deliverable in the Work Package

Developing work-sense takes time. "Do I lump all these procedures into one work package? Or are they actually two, five, or nine separate ones?" Correctly defining the level of effort in a project provides an easier way to control the project and keep it in the groove.

For more technical detail about defining your deliverables, refer to *PMBOK Guide* section 5.4.3.

For you as the project manager, the important principle is that you need to know whether a work package is being completed on time. If it is not, you want to have enough time to recover and keep the project on schedule. If you wait too long, you may not have the flexibility to put some extra people on the package to get it finished in time to save the schedule.

Another way to judge the lowest-level activity you should accommodate in your WBS is to consider budget or time criteria. You also can use segments, such as half or full days, to define the smallest task levels. These approaches may appear initially imprecise, but they establish a general guideline for the lowest-level activities in your project.

A third option is to use the reporting period rule to determine the work packages. This rule states that no work package should be longer than a standard reporting period. Thus, if you make weekly status reports, no work package should be longer than a week in length. This helps eliminate work package statuses that are 73 percent or 38 percent done; work packages are only reported as started (50 percent done), not started, or complete (100 percent). If a work package using this rule is started and is on the not-complete list for more than two reporting periods, you have a problem to solve.

When you start building the WBS, you need to consider all of the required deliverables, including any drawings, designs, documents, and schematics, for example. Here are some other tips regarding your project's deliverables:

A deliverable should be clearly stated. The "design the button layout on the hand-held remote control" task is much clearer than the "design the TV control system" task, which may be really 5 to 10 separate work packages. The latter is so unclear that you can't schedule it because there are too many elements; team members won't know where one work package starts or stops. ("Do we complete the remote control and the TV's receiver side of the system as well as the power controls? Or do we just do the remote control?") But "design the TV control system" could be a milestone—one that includes activities for the remote control, primary power system, and television receiver.

All work within the same work package should occur within a sequential or parallel time frame without gaps for possible other work in between. Thus, "framing and plumbing the bathroom" is not a well-formed work package in your bathroom remodeling project because plumbing the bathroom is not necessarily related to framing the bathroom, and other tasks, such as adding insulation, could come after the framing task. It's better to define the tasks as separate work packages, "framing" and "plumbing," in the project plan rather than to risk confusion about the sequence or priority of events. Also, don't confuse work packages with milestones, which are a significant event within the project such as the completion of a major deliverable.

A work package should include only related work elements. When washing your car, for example, the work package "get soapy water" wouldn't fit with "polish the car" because there's no relationship between the procedures and they occur at different times in the project cycle. (At least they do when I wash my car!) Therefore, a work package called "get soapy water and polish the car" is not a well-formed work package because it involves unrelated steps.

 TIME IS MONEY

> Remember, work packages are tracked in the plan, but elements and activities are not; elements and activities still need to be accounted for, however, in the overall time allocated for the work packages.

Sometimes it is easier to write a listing of the work packages that you may need to do and then work on rolling them up into the WBS. Use a brainstorming technique to capture all the information and then develop a more detailed diagram, as shown in Chapter 11, to see how they will relate to each other.

Refining the WBS

As you progress through the project, you gather more information and learn more, which should allow you to refine your plan to greater accuracy and predictability. Project managers refer to this refinement as *progressive elaboration*. It is one of the key reasons for keeping your project plan accurate and current.

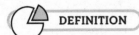

> **DEFINITION**
>
> **Progressive elaboration** is defined as continuously improving the plan as more information becomes available as the project progresses.

For example, when a project team begins to analyze the work in the WBS—and especially when it starts to identify the dependencies—the team may realize it has forgotten a stakeholder! Usually this stakeholder is someone who impacts a business process touched by the project; for example, they need to provide the team with information or data and their input creates a dependency within the WBS. The good news is that the team can go back to the stakeholder analysis and add the appropriate information for this key stakeholder. Plus, the team now has a good idea about how it needs to engage and communicate with the stakeholder to successfully complete the work involved.

That's a wrap! Now you know how the work breaks down in your project. You've taken all the project goals developed in the charter and broken them into specific work packages. But that's just one important step in planning. Now, let's take a look at sequencing the work in a network diagram.

Review Questions

- Am I clear on the five steps for completing the work breakdown structure (WBS)?

- How do I best organize the WBS?

- How will identifying the dependencies help me schedule the project later on?

- How concrete are the deliverables for my project?

The Least You Need to Know

- A work breakdown structure (WBS) organizes the tasks of a project into hierarchies and milestones.

- A cohesive work package contains a unique, measurable deliverable you can monitor and track.

- Milestones divide the project into logical, measurable segments. When you complete all the milestones, the project should be finished.

- After you create a complete activity list and WBS, you can plan the schedule and resources for the project.

- Make sure you identify the dependencies so you know what needs to be completed and when to keep a project on track.

CHAPTER 1

Establishing the Schedule of Work

As you would assume from reading earlier chapters in this book, the schedule is intertwined with the work breakdown structure (WBS), the risk assessment, and eventually, the budget. Change one, and you invariably influence the others. I have separated the schedule and the budget between this and the next chapter, but in reality, you need to work on both at the same time. The schedule and the budget work together like a pair of outboard motors on a boat to propel a project toward success.

The *PMBOK Guide* calls this "Project Time Management," and it is knowledge area 6 in their guidelines.

In This Chapter

- Scheduling based on the work to be completed
- Building reliable estimates using experienced people with a variety of perspectives
- Using Gantt charts to manage the schedule

The Schedule or the Budget: Which Is First?

Some new project managers are inclined to start with the budget first, but I don't recommend it. Because time is money, the schedule will affect the final budget in many ways. That's why I have decided to discuss scheduling first. The best project managers establish the schedule before finalizing the budget, even if everyone doesn't always understand the logic. It's best to try to determine how much time is really required to complete a project before you start worrying about the money required.

The experienced project manager can appear to assess an activity, understand what's required, and provide a reasonably realistic estimate of the time requirement as if pulling the number from the air. You will get to that point someday with the help of this book and with a few projects under your belt. But until you get that experience, you can establish a reasonable schedule using this and the subsequent chapter's advice as a process guide. And maybe more important, in the following pages, you also learn how to deal with external pressures (such as bosses and customers) that demand unrealistic dates.

Building a schedule also verifies the project's viability. If, when assembling the schedule, time is not on your side, you may need to work out an extension with management or an increase in resources. Working on the schedule might also reveal missing activities. Remember, everything is interrelated, so expect to adjust the WBS and budget as you adapt the schedule.

 TIME IS MONEY

> If you have a person with unique knowledge, skills, or experience, you must wrap the schedule around this person's availability—especially if she is only seconded to the project and not full time. The same might be true for other resources, such as specific equipment that has high demands.

The Schedule Synchronizes the Project

Accurate, realistic, and workable scheduling is what makes a project tick. The schedule shows who is doing what and when they are supposed to be doing it. Scheduling involves converting the well-organized and sequenced tasks in your WBS—as well as the list of resources and vendors you develop in Chapter 14—into an achievable timetable with start dates, finish dates, and assigned responsibilities for each activity.

For more information about the technical elements of scheduling, refer to *PMBOK Guide* section 6.6.

Carry out the steps in creating a schedule sequentially, as follows:

1. Establish the scheduling assumptions. From earlier chapters, you already know why it's important to clarify goals and requirements before the project plan reaches its final stages. For the same reasons, it's important to specify scheduling assumptions before the schedule is completed. Answering the following questions should help in this process. I've also included a simple diagram (see Chapter 11) to assist you in determining the assumptions germane to your project.

- Are there a fixed number of resources (remember that resources include people, time, technology, and money) you can use on the project? Or can you add them to meet the schedule priorities?

- Is there an absolute date by which the project must be completed or the entire effort is lost? (An example would be designing a new trade show booth for the big July show. If the booth never arrives, then the time and money used to design and build it as well as the cost of the trade show floor space is lost.)

- Can you negotiate the completion date if you have resource constraints that will hurt the quality of the final product?

- Will people work standard workdays, or will overtime be allowed or expected? Watch for holidays and expect to pay extra for having people work on holidays!

- Are all resources currently trained and available? Or will your project require hiring additional people and acquiring new equipment? If training or hiring is required, you need to schedule it.

Here are some examples of assumptions for a major systems implementation: A network expert from inside the company will be available from August through October to work on the project; there will be no customization of the software, and it will be installed "out of the box"; no major changes in the sales and marketing departments will occur within the next six months. Assumptions protect the project from being severely impacted by planned change in other parts of the organization, change the project manager may not be aware of. Assumptions can also reveal risks and limitations and then enable you to build contingencies for them into your plan.

Large projects require you to document your assumptions in writing. That way, you are less likely to forget something. Also, when you review those plans with your project sponsor or the project steering committee, they may alert you to incorrect assumptions you are making. Simple projects don't always require documentation of the assumptions, but you should have a verbal agreement on them among your team and outside resources.

2. Estimate the number of resources, the activity *effort*, and the work package *duration* based on the resources you have on hand or can afford. Remember that these estimates are all constrained by your personnel and equipment resources. The more resources you have, the less time may be required to complete a package of work, in most but not all cases. Here, you need to estimate the duration of an activity over a number of days.

Sometimes duration and effort are the same. If it takes seven hours of effort for a team member to prepare a survey during the course of one day, then the effort is one workday, and the duration of the work package is one workday. Sometimes duration and effort are very different. It may take only four hours of meeting time to get the building inspector's approval of a building's wiring, but these meetings happen over a period of two weeks. Thus, the effort for getting the wiring approved is four hours, but the duration of the work package is two weeks. And remember to consider the people you have working on the project. Some of them may be more experienced and just plain faster at completing the work than others.

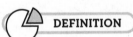 **DEFINITION**

Effort (also called *labor estimates*) is the time it takes, usually in hours or days, to work on an activity or work package. **Duration** is the time, usually in days, that it takes to complete the activity within the WBS, not including holidays or weekends. It is sometimes confused with elapsed time.

To create both an accurate schedule and a detailed budget for a project, it is important to know both the effort and the duration required to complete a work package. It's also important to know that you can often, but not always, shorten the duration of an activity by adding more people to complete the labor. Thus, estimating the number of people and resources that will perform an activity is an important consideration in estimating duration.

Duration stands out in project management terms because the accumulated duration of activities along the critical path in the project plan directly affects all the subsequent activities in the project. (I explain the importance of critical path in Chapter 11.) It is the duration of the activities that, when added together, establish the time required to complete the project.

3. **Determine calendar dates for each activity and create a master schedule.** For a complex project network, you also will need to determine how much flexibility you have to complete various activities (called *float* or *slack* in project management circles; see Chapter 11).

4. **Adjust the individual resource assignments as necessary to optimize the schedule.** This is called the resource-leveling process. (You also learn about this in Chapter 11.)

5. **Chart the final schedule.** In most cases, a computer program makes all of these scheduling steps easier, as long as you enter all the information correctly.

Estimating Time: Your Best Guess at Effort and Duration

Of all the steps in scheduling, estimating the duration of tasks is the most important. Unfortunately, this is like trying to predict the future. You can only guess, but there are better ways to guess than others. Without accurate activity duration estimates, the entire plan and project might crumble around you.

When estimating the duration of activities, you can use these five options to make the estimates (guesses) as good as possible:

- Get an objective expert's opinion (for example, from someone who isn't working on the project).

- Find a similar task in a completed project plan to see how long it took to get done. This is called an *analogous estimate*.

- When you know the relationship between a certain activity and time, use that estimate. For example, most programmers can tell you how many lines of code they can develop per hour or per day. This is called a *parametric estimate*.

- Make your best educated guess. This is the last resort when you're under pressure, so make sure the guess is more educated than it is arbitrary. If possible, instead of guessing, try the preceding options.

Some Other Options

To get reliable estimates on the duration of tasks and the effort required, you likely need to ask other people about the time it will take them to get things done. The following sections present some of the people you can ask to help determine the task duration and the effort estimates for your schedule.

TIME IS MONEY

Four tips for outstanding estimating are 1) only use actual information if at all possible, 2) develop a network of experts (often called subject matter experts [SMEs]) who can provide a sanity check on estimates, 3) recognize when an estimate is coming from an optimist or a pessimist (it will make a difference!), and 4) use lessons learned from similar projects if available.

Representative Team Members for Each Part of the Project

Seek out the most experienced team members who will be completing work on your project. (I give you ideas for choosing your project team in Chapter 13.) If they have worked on similar projects in the past, they can use what are called *historical estimates,* or how much time it took them last time. Again, I typically ask them for the level of effort, not the duration. Some team members pad their estimates a little or a lot, and some are overconfident about their abilities to accomplish miracles. You must adjust the duration in the final plan to account for these idiosyncrasies if you want to come up with the optimum schedule.

To sit down with all the key team members to estimate activity durations is often useful. Even if nothing useful (to you) comes of the sessions, they still serve to build team relationships and to give you a better understanding of the project from the team members' points of view. It's also an excellent technique for assembling a rough-cut schedule in a hurry.

Outside Vendors and Service Agencies

You must get estimates directly from any outside service providers and consultants who will work on your project. Never estimate their time for them. You can negotiate their estimates, but if you dictate a vendor's schedule without her input, you'll never get the schedule you demand. You should politely request a written estimate that fixes the cost and commits them to a schedule (unless the project runs off the rails or changes in scope, of course). Shop both price and time!

Experienced Project Managers

People in your organization who have handled similar projects can provide excellent advice and can study cost estimates for problems. They also might be able to provide exact estimates if they worked on a project that had elements common to yours. Or they may be much more experienced project managers and be willing to help. If no such experts exist within your company, you could get advice from a consultant or a colleague in another company who can help verify your work and duration estimates.

Management and Other Project Stakeholders

If you want your managers and stakeholders (such as the steering committee members) to buy into your schedule, you need to give them an opportunity to help plan the schedule or at least review it before you submit the project plan for approval. By bringing stakeholders into the process, they'll see that you will efficiently use your time and wisely spend their money. Their involvement will assist you in getting the final plan approved because they'll already have a grasp on the realities of the schedule.

Weighing the Risks

After getting information on the labor requirements and activity durations from various sources, you need to use your judgment to determine the duration you'll actually assign to the schedule. Each of these durations has a risk associated with it. It's often useful to come up with a best-case schedule and a worst-case schedule based on these risks. For example, the project manager for a project may estimate it will take the team one month to design and build the various reports the company will require after the new CRM software is implemented. However, if the project manager only has one person with the skills to complete the design, there is risk. What if the developer gets sick, or is involved in an automobile accident and hospitalized for a while? The project manager must always plan for these kinds of risks.

A Compromise Between Best and Worst Case

In estimating every activity, assume that the actual time required will fall somewhere between flawless execution and major disaster. The best approach is to establish a compromise between the two. Some project management methodologies, such as Program Evaluation and Review Technique (PERT), provide the mechanics for estimating all three. These include the following:

- **The optimistic estimate.** Everything goes like clockwork and without problems.

- **The most likely estimate.** A few problems crop up, and normal delays compromise the optimistic estimate.

- **The pessimistic estimate.** Allowances are made for many elements to go wrong, substantially delaying or jeopardizing the activity. The pessimistic estimate assumes the project is still going ahead.

Ultimately, you will use these three estimates in combination with each other to come up with a "most likely" schedule based on your confidence in the estimates. Sometimes people just go with the pessimistic estimate; at other times, the most likely estimate wins out. If you use the optimistic estimate, you're just looking for trouble.

Many managers of large, high-risk, big-money projects use these estimates and feed them into a formula to determine the most likely duration. The approach that's best for you depends on the project, your experience with similar work, and your organization's culture.

 TIME IS MONEY

In the standard PERT methodology, the accepted formula for coming up with the "most likely" estimate of a task's duration is the following:

Expected duration = [OD + 4(MLD) + PD] ÷ 6

OD = Optimistic duration

MLD = Most likely duration

PD = Pessimistic duration

The Confidence Factor

For the duration of each activity on your list, you'll have varying degrees of confidence. The tasks with the highest degree of confidence are usually those you've performed previously or those you'll do yourself. The tasks you aren't sure of usually are those with which you have either no direct experience or very little control.

The degree of confidence is also influenced by the complexity (or simplicity) of the task and how much the task is dependent on the completion of preceding (and possibly complex) tasks.

Remember that if you do the estimates alone, your team members may not buy into them. You might create and sell a schedule to management that team members cannot or will not support or deliver on. Remember to involve key team members in task estimating.

If many of the estimates have low confidence associated with them, move your schedule dates toward the worst-case scenario. If most of the estimates are high confidence, a schedule closer to the best-case estimate is the best choice. The more complex and interdependent the tasks, the more you might want to lean toward a worst-case scenario.

RISK MANAGEMENT

Don't pad the schedule just to cover your uncertainties. Too much padding is as bad as agreeing to complete the impossible in no time at all. A little padding (called *contingency planning*) is standard practice in all project plans because no one can foresee the future; however, padding adds expenses and time to your project. Most experienced project managers include a 10 to 15 percent contingency in the budget to cover unexpected delays to the schedule.

Scheduling a large project to the hour from the beginning of the project would produce silly schedules and mounds of useless paper. On the other hand, inadequate schedule detail at the beginning of a small project might leave team members thinking they have more time to get things done than they really have. As you develop your schedule, remember to evaluate the dependencies your project has on other projects for success. If you add a little protection to your schedule for risky tasks, never make your padded time estimates too obvious, because this tactic won't win you any popularity contests with management. Such obvious protection schemes will have management sniffing through the entire project for inflationary tactics at all levels, including in the budget. Ultimately, you'll not only lose credibility, but potentially the real resources and time you need to get things done.

If your schedule starts looking like it will take too long to get things done, try adding more people or resources to the plan. This impacts the budget, however, and sometimes tasks suffer because just too many people are working on the same activities. Just having more people doesn't always mean you'll get things done faster. Adding people always has unforeseen costs in management time and coordination, so make sure this idea is really a good solution to adjusting the schedule before you do it.

Details, Details ...

After estimating the task duration and making a judgment on the estimates, you must decide on the level of detail you want to put in the initial schedule. Usually, the scheduling level should relate to the levels in your WBS or network diagram (see Chapter 11 for more about network diagrams). For example, you can probably schedule a small project down to the day on the first go-around, but you won't be able to schedule a larger project any finer than by the week or the month.

For planning purposes, you may produce the schedule at the weekly or monthly level. As work on the project proceeds, you can schedule the work at finer levels (remember progressive elaboration in Chapter 9?). Many large projects are scheduled phase by phase instead of scheduling the entire project from the beginning.

Applying Calendars to a Resource

Every resource will have dates and times when it will be available for use on your project. These dates and times are called the *calendar* for that resource. For people resources, create calendars that include their work hours, workdays, holidays, and vacation days. Remember the details!

NOTES FROM THE FIELD

Don't forget holidays and vacation time when scheduling project duration. One project manager thought he was going to get a lot accomplished between December 10 and the end of the year. Unfortunately, several people on the customer side of his project team had vacation time coming and took the last three weeks of the year off! Also, if you are working on a project with an international team, remember to check on the dates of holidays in those countries and schedule accordingly.

You also need to specify how many overtime hours will be allowed, if any. Sometimes you may want to assign a different person to a task based on her calendar availability instead of paying overtime.

For equipment resources, you need to indicate any special restrictions on availability. For example, if you have only one electron microscope available and three different research projects are using it, you need to specify when this resource will be available for your project. (Or vice versa, you need to tell the other projects when you'll need it if your project has priority.) As you develop the schedule for tasks, you need to take the calendar into consideration as you write out the dates.

On a complex project, dealing with the calendars of all the resources can get very complex. Thank heavens for computerized project management programs that enable you to define calendars for all the resources, including working days, hours, and nonworking periods (such as holidays and vacations). The computer can then do the complex scheduling for you.

Keep in mind that although computer programs will allow you to establish the workday and the work week, on some global projects that is not so simple to define. For example, one project I led from Houston, Texas, involved people in Australia, the United Kingdom, and the Middle East. The work week is Saturday through Wednesday in the Middle East, while the others had a Monday through Friday work week. As you can imagine, that complicated things even with a computer program!

Developing the Initial Schedule

After you nail down the assumptions for the schedule (that is, the number of people and the activity sequences) and the activity effort, you can begin assembling a reasonable schedule. For a simple project with few dependencies, you can simply list activity effort. For more complex projects, use the WBS and a diagram project management software package to schedule your project.

Scheduling with software is conceptually simple. Plug in the estimated activity duration for each activity in the program and then add their durations to get the total time required to complete the project. Just lay the days out on a calendar, and voilà!—you have a schedule. To show you how it's done, I've provided the following example of a network diagram with task duration and dates added.

Of course, nothing is ever as simple as it sounds. You need to take into account workdays, holidays, vacations, parallel tasks, and other special circumstances. That's why scheduling a large project is easier with a software program designed for the job. You also need to level the resource utilization on a large project if you're overworking some of the resources (or under-working others). You learn more about making these schedule adjustments in the next chapter.

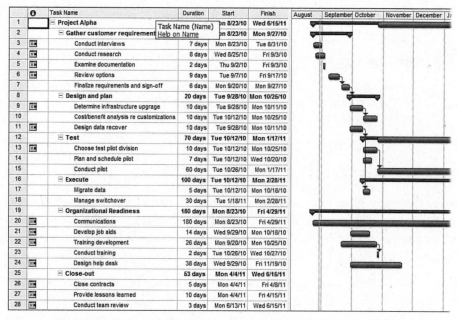

This partial Gantt chart from Microsoft Project illustrates a project and includes the duration of each activity in the project.

Schedule Charting Pros and Cons

You should be aware of several schedule-charting formats. The trick is choosing the format that best suits your project. Here are some of your options:

- **Calendar charts.** Annotated calendars can be extremely useful for keeping track of schedules for many small projects. You can enter multiple projects or different team member tasks in various colors. Calendars are a good communication tool when displayed in a central location where many team members can see the dates. Large display calendars with reusable, washable surfaces are available at many business supply stores for this purpose.

- *Gantt charts.* You can best use Gantt charts as a visual overview of project timelines; however, don't necessarily think of them as a substitute for a network diagram or master schedule listing. Gantt charts can be very useful in initial schedule planning, for simple projects, or for individual timelines on a complex project involving many people. These charts also are good for comparing project progress to the original schedule.

- **Milestone schedules.** You can also use milestones to chart an overall project schedule. A milestone schedule doesn't have enough information to help you manage a project, but it can be useful for communicating an overall schedule on a large project to upper management or other people who need an overview of the project without task details.

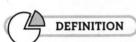 **DEFINITION**

Named after Henry Gantt, who developed it in the late 1800s, a **Gantt chart** is a special bar chart that lists activities on the left side of the chart, dates across the top, and activity duration as a date-based horizontal bar running across the page.

More on Gantt Charts

Simple Gantt charts, sometimes referred to as project timelines, are the most commonly used scheduling charts in business because they're easy to produce and easy to understand. A line on the Gantt chart shows the date each task begins and ends based on its precedence and duration.

The time periods you use on the top of your Gantt charts will determine the level of scheduling detail you display: daily, weekly, monthly, or whatever is appropriate for your project. If a project takes a year or more to complete, you may want to use a monthly or weekly Gantt chart. If your project takes 30 days or fewer, a daily Gantt chart will provide more useful information. Gantt charts are most effective if you can present the whole chart on one document.

In a Gantt chart like the one shown in the following figure, you can see the activities and their numbers to the left of the activities. The small icons let the project manager know that additional notes are attached to those activities. To the right of the activity, you will see the names of the people who will be working on that activity. The percentages indicate the percentage of their time they will devote to that activity. This is also a time-scaled diagram. This combines the timeline approach of the traditional Gantt chart with the precedence relationships of the network diagram (see Chapter 11). For example, if you look on the chart at activity #13, *Choose test pilot division,* you will notice an arrow coming out and down to activity #15, *Conduct pilot.* That arrow illustrates the dependency relationship between the two activities. For obvious reasons, you must choose where the pilot will occur before you can actually conduct it.

Simple Gantt charts don't show the interrelationships among tasks. You need a network diagram for this or a project management program that produces complex Gantt charts that indicate summary activities and relationships between them. Also, a Gantt chart alone may not provide enough detail to communicate schedules to individual team members in a complex project. For this, you want a project list that includes work package assignments and schedule dates.

TIME IS MONEY

As project manager, you need to be able to create a personal timetable for each individual on the project team. Each individual working on the project also needs to be able to relate her personal timetable to the master schedule.

	❶	Task Name	Duration	Start	Finish	August	September	October	November	December	J
1		⊟ Project Alpha		8/23/10	Wed 6/15/11						
2		⊟ Gather customer requirements	Task Name (Name) Help on Name	8/23/10	Mon 9/27/10						
3		Conduct interviews	7 days	Mon 8/23/10	Tue 8/31/10		Bob Braveheart,Chris Tommasi,Donna Give				
4		Conduct research	8 days	Wed 8/25/10	Fri 9/3/10		Samatha Eggers[50%],Thomas Jones[50%]				
5		Examine documentation	2 days	Thu 9/2/10	Fri 9/3/10		Chris Tommasi				
6		Review options	9 days	Tue 9/7/10	Fri 9/17/10		Bob Braveheart				
7		Finalize requirements and sign-off	6 days	Mon 9/20/10	Mon 9/27/10		Bob Braveheart,Donna Givens,Tho				
8		⊟ Design and plan	20 days	Tue 9/28/10	Mon 10/25/10						
9		Determine infrastructure upgrage	10 days	Tue 9/28/10	Mon 10/11/10			Donna Givens[50%],Thomas J			
10		Cost/benefit analysis re customizations	10 days	Tue 10/12/10	Mon 10/25/10			Bob Braveheart			
11		Design data recover	10 days	Tue 9/28/10	Mon 10/11/10			Samatha Eggers			
12		⊟ Test	70 days	Tue 10/12/10	Mon 1/17/11						
13		Choose test pilot division	10 days	Tue 10/12/10	Mon 10/25/10				Bob Braveheart[50%],Tho		
14		Plan and schedule pilot	7 days	Tue 10/12/10	Wed 10/20/10			Bob Braveheart			
15		Conduct pilot	60 days	Tue 10/26/10	Mon 1/17/11						
16		⊟ Execute	100 days	Tue 10/12/10	Mon 2/28/11						
17		Migrate data	5 days	Tue 10/12/10	Mon 10/18/10			Samatha Eggers			
18		Manage switchover	30 days	Tue 1/18/11	Mon 2/28/11						
19		⊟ Organizational Readiness	180 days	Mon 8/23/10	Fri 4/29/11						
20		Communications	180 days	Mon 8/23/10	Fri 4/29/11						
21		Develop job aids	14 days	Wed 9/29/10	Mon 10/18/10			Amy Lynn			
22		Training development	26 days	Mon 9/20/10	Mon 10/25/10			Amy Lynn			
23		Conduct training	2 days	Tue 10/26/10	Wed 10/27/10			Amy Lynn			
24		Design help desk	38 days	Wed 9/29/10	Fri 11/19/10				Donna Givens		
25		⊟ Close-out	53 days	Mon 4/4/11	Wed 6/15/11						
26		Close contracts	5 days	Mon 4/4/11	Fri 4/8/11						
27		Provide lessons learned	1.43 days	Mon 4/4/11	Tue 4/5/11						
28		Conduct team review	3 days	Mon 6/13/11	Wed 6/15/11						

Gantt charts are useful for seeing the timeline for activities, including the connections between them along with the people who will do the work.

Other Schedule Considerations

As you work through building your schedule, there are some additional things you need to consider. Although some of them might seem obvious, you would be surprised at how often people overlook the obvious!

For more tools used to illustrate the schedule, refer to *PMBOK Guide* section 6.6.3.2.

Revisions

Assume that your schedule (and every other aspect of your plan) will require several revisions. Be sure you save each version with a unique identifier (such as the date) so you don't accidentally refer to an earlier version at some point in time. As feedback arrives from both team members and outside resources, you might redraft the task estimates and dates several times until you come up with a workable, approvable timeline (schedule) for the project.

Learning Takes Time

Even in the most routine jobs, some time is required for learning the procedures in the company and adapting to the new work environment. This is especially true of some consultants who must become familiar with your company's way of doing business before they can get down to work. When you schedule a project, allow for these various training and development requirements. You might even want to identify training activities as specific tasks in your WBS or network.

 RISK MANAGEMENT

If you must share your preliminary drafts of the plan with management, make sure "DRAFT" or "INCOMPLETE" appears on each page. That way, you won't be held to an unfinished plan by senior managers who assume that an early version of the project plan was the final one.

The Heat Is On

Every project is a rush. With that in mind, how do you, as project manager, avoid succumbing to unrealistic expectations and goals? Assuming the people commissioning the project are somewhat rational human beings, your best tool is the schedule. Management will constantly challenge costs, time, and resources. You must make them believe, through a well-documented schedule and plan, that your estimates are realistic and not unduly padded.

Team Member Estimate Errors

Chances are, you're counting on the core team members and experts to provide the best and most accurate scheduling estimates possible. But rather than carefully thinking through the process for which they are responsible, some members of the team might simply choose a number and feed that into your plan. If it's unrealistic, you're stuck with it.

To avoid this problem, insist that your project team use a method like PERT (that includes "optimistic," "pessimistic," and "most likely") or some other recognizable method to reach their estimate. And be sure you know which method they are using and challenge them to defend their methods. You must be comfortable that the estimate is reasonably accurate and defensible.

 NOTES FROM THE FIELD

The management scientists of the Special Projects Office of the U.S. Navy developed PERT, or the Program Evaluation and Review Technique, to help coordinate more than 3,000 people involved in the development of the Polaris missile.

Make sure the estimators consider elapsed time in the duration estimates. For example, one of the tasks in a project might be to buy new equipment. In order to complete the estimate successfully, they need to build in time to order it, install it, test it, and go through some conversations with the support staff. What may look like 4 days of effort (32 hours) could result in a 12-day duration when all the "dead" time between activities is accounted for. Have the team estimate both numbers—the effort and the duration. If they don't understand the difference, have a training session with them before they complete the estimates.

The Just-in-Time Strategy for Scheduling Resources

The just-in-time strategy for getting materials and supplies is credited to Toyota, but the technique is now common practice worldwide. Just-in-time delivery depends on accurate scheduling and project coordination. With an accurate schedule in place, you can order just what you need and get it delivered exactly when you need it. This means that supplies, equipment, and even people arrive only when the project is ready for them.

By having goods delivered (or people hired) exactly when they're needed, you save money for storage, reduce upfront costs for ordering materials, and are assured that you don't have extra materials or people on hand that are costing you extra money.

The key to making this approach work is, you guessed it, communication. For example, a temp agency hiring 20 people for your project will want enough time to hire the needed people, but you would need to notify them as soon as possible if you know the project might be delayed. The window for just-in-time delivery must be agreed upon in advance; otherwise, the whole schedule falls apart.

Having a contract with suppliers that lets you adjust dates is the essence of just-in-time delivery. That way, you don't have to warehouse items from the supplier. You need to make just-in-time delivery a mandatory contract clause: no delivery until a written request is made and guaranteed delivery within a set number of days or hours after you put the order in. This type of requirement is especially helpful when you are working with a project that uses a large amount of physical materials, such as construction projects.

NOTES FROM THE FIELD

In a series of projects I ran recently, I ran into scheduling conflicts with the operations calendar. Of course their calendar is pretty significant, because they are the part of the company that generates the revenue! They were building additional facilities at the same time my projects were scheduled for delivery. The facilities project fell behind and caused the operations people to adjust their calendar. That had a domino effect on my schedule since I lost access to the operations people, who were key to my project. And all of us were trying to meet year-end targets for completion. It created a significant amount of stress for all those involved. It reminded me that it is important to be aware of other projects that were affecting my stakeholders in addition to mine.

What Happens When They Want to Rush Me?

At some time, you'll be asked (or maybe told) to shorten the schedule, even though you know it's nearly impossible to get the work done any faster. Before you cave in, sit down with everyone pressuring you and go over the schedule, day by day, if necessary. Be friendly and cooperative and explain each task and the assumptions about your time estimates represented in the schedule.

Your goal for this process is to communicate why the project requires a certain amount of time. In a truly impossible situation, you might need someone senior to you (usually the project sponsor) to go to bat when others attempt to force an unworkable adjustment to the plan on your shoulders.

Now you're ready to learn about how to fine-tune a schedule to meet your stakeholders' objectives.

Review Questions

- Can I distinguish between estimates on level of effort and duration for tasks in the WBS?

- Which estimating approach do I consider the best for my project?

- Have I collected optimistic, pessimistic, and most likely estimates for the key work on my project?

- How can I use Gantt charts and milestone charts in my project?

The Least You Need to Know

- No schedule is ever perfect, but the goal is to make the best estimate possible. Use your own judgment and the experience of others to help you make your estimates.

- Scheduling involves estimating the task durations for the project and plotting the dates on a calendar. You need to account for holidays, special events, and unknown circumstances.

- Base time estimates on optimistic/pessimistic scenarios. Your degree of confidence in the accuracy of these estimates should dictate the ultimate schedule, which should be a compromise somewhere between the two extremes.

- A Gantt chart is an excellent tool for studying overall schedules, but it doesn't necessarily show all the interdependencies among tasks. Thus, using both a project plan along with a Gantt chart is a good idea.

Critical Path and the Schedule

One of the pioneering efforts to show the interrelationships among activities on a project was undertaken by the E. I. Du Pont Company. In later publications about the project, Du Pont referred to the method as the critical path method (CPM). Du Pont tested the CPM in the construction of a major chemical plant and in several maintenance projects. In Chapter 10, you learned the good news: scheduling is a simple matter of estimating durations for tasks and then plotting the dates on a calendar. Now here's the bad news: even using computer-based project management software, scheduling a complex project is, well, complex. Because an accurate schedule is essential to managing projects of all sizes, don't cut corners. You need to consider some of the complexities of scheduling before you finalize your project plan. That's what this chapter is all about—taking the initial schedule that you have built and dissecting the complexities to make sure you haven't missed something important.

You learn how to calculate the critical path and float in this chapter, but you should get a computer program to help on projects of more than 25 or 30 tasks. You can easily then change and revise the schedule as you work through the issues and changes in a project.

In This Chapter

- Determining the critical path
- Understanding dependencies between tasks using the network diagram
- Making important adjustments in complex project schedules
- Leveling the resource utilization
- How to adapt a project to meet a schedule

Determining a Project's Critical Path

When you have determined task durations and are confident in your estimates, it's time to assemble a schedule using real dates. On a large/complex project, however, one more step remains in the way of assembling a working schedule. For projects with multiple parallel tasks and subprojects, you must determine a *critical path* to identify the time required to complete the project. (Most small projects with few tasks can skip this step.)

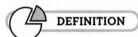 **DEFINITION**

The **critical path** is a sequence of tasks that forms the longest duration of the project. Think of the critical path as the activities within your project you have the least amount of flexibility to complete.

If a task is delayed on the critical path, the project is delayed. Tasks not lying on the critical path are more flexible. For example, you could delay printing of the training materials for the customer relationship management (CRM) software as long as they arrive before the training is scheduled to start.

Adding together the duration of tasks on the critical path determines the total time the project will take. Because each task on the critical path must follow its predecessor in order, all tasks following a late task will be late. Yes, the delay will hold up the entire project. That's why the critical path is, well, critical.

For more technical information on the critical path method, refer to *PMBOK Guide* **section 6.6.2.2.**

Not Just Floating Around

Tasks not on the critical path also must be completed. You can't build a house and ask someone to move in before the water and sewer are connected, but such tasks can occur later in the project's time frame without substantially delaying other tasks downstream. This gives them a flexible start and finish date, which in project management lingo is called *float*. The equation *Latest possible finish date – earliest possible start – duration = total float* calculates the latest date you can start, given the duration that an activity will take and still finish on time for the next activity to start. If the total float for a task equals zero, then that task is on the critical path. The amount of float is the amount of flexibility for starting a task.

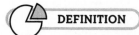

DEFINITION

The amount of time that an activity may be delayed from its earliest possible start date without delaying the project finish date is called **float.** Float is also known as *slack* or *slack time.*

The Different Views of Critical in Project Management

The term *critical chain* is used to describe a concept quite different from the schedule-based definition of tasks on the critical path. The concept of the critical chain is one of the ideas preferred by Dr. Eliyahu M. Goldratt's Theory of Constraints (TOC). The TOC states that any system has at least one constraint. Otherwise, it would be generating an infinite amount of output. Bearing this in mind, the TOC in project management is explained through use of the chain analogy: A chain is only as strong as its weakest link.

If you look at your project as a chain in which each department, activity, or resource is a link in the chain, what constrains your project from achieving its goals? Only through identifying and focusing on the weakest link, the critical link in the chain, can you make substantial improvements. In other words, if the weakest link dictates the pace of an organization's ability to achieve its goal, it makes sense that attending to this critical link will allow the organization to achieve a substantial rate of throughput faster.

To illustrate how you can apply the TOC without getting into too much theoretical detail, the critical chain concept illustrates that you can improve project control and scheduling through identifying the critical links in a project's chain and then focusing creatively on reducing these problems. The objective is to develop solutions of compromise based on fresh thinking that can help you continuously improve project performance through time. The performance is improved continuously because, as you fix one weakest link in the chain, a new weakest link emerges. Since project performance is never perfect, you will always have a weakest link to work on.

If you're interested in the application of the critical chain concept and the TOC on project management, visit the Avraham Y. Goldratt Institute on the web at goldratt.com. An adequate presentation of TOC is beyond the scope of this book, but for people interested in continuous quality improvement, there's a lot of substance in Goldratt's work.

For more information on the critical chain method, refer to *PMBOK Guide* **section 6.6.2.3.**

Establishing the Critical Path

The critical path is easy to determine in a project documented with a good network diagram. Simply add each parallel path's tasks together, and the path requiring the most time to complete is the critical path. Let's say for a project, the building of the interfaces takes 138 days. That makes it the critical path. Critical tasks—those on this path—not completed on time will delay the project unless you can make up the time further down the critical path or an on-the-path task finishes ahead of schedule.

To see more technical detail on the critical path, refer to *PMBOK Guide* **section 6.6.2.**

> **RISK MANAGEMENT**
>
> When its tasks go late, the critical path becomes the roadblock to project completion. That's why you should put extra effort into estimating these tasks. If you lack confidence in the task schedule or resource availability, delay the project until everything fits into place. When the project is already underway, put your best people on the tasks on the critical path and focus your energies on monitoring them.

Myth or Reality?

The concept behind critical path is simple: if you delay a task on the critical path, you delay the project. This seems to make perfect sense to most people new to project management. The path on the project has to go from beginning to end.

Unfortunately, as in all things involving people and plans, complexities occur. First, some tasks on the critical path may be less important than others. Some tasks may be there for other reasons (which you'll learn about in a bit), not managerial priorities. Because of this situation, many managers also create a priority task list, a list of the most important tasks on the project. You can use this managerial list of priority tasks, along with the list of tasks on the critical path, to focus attention on the important work of the project.

Always remember that regardless of the logic of it or the managerial importance, when you change task dependencies, duration estimates, and other network details, you need to reevaluate the critical path and reassess the schedule. There's no way around it. You can't change the sequences without impacting the schedule.

What's a Network Diagram?

The *network diagram* (also called the *project schedule network analysis diagram*) shows the path of the project. If properly sequenced, a network diagram will do the following:

- Show the sequences and relationships between activities necessary to complete a project

- Identify relationships among milestones in the project that can be used for monitoring progress and completion

- Show the interrelationships of activities in different parts of the work breakdown structure (WBS) hierarchy

- Establish a vehicle for scheduling activities

- Help reduce uncertainty in the project by breaking it into many small phases that have been analyzed and sequenced in advance of starting the work

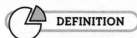 **DEFINITION**

A **network diagram** is the logical representation of scheduled project activities and defines the sequence of work in a project. It is always drawn from left to right and reflects the chronological order of the activities.

Network diagrams reveal the workflow, not just the work. Networks are always drawn from left to right, with lines drawn between activities to indicate the dependencies among activities. Arrowheads are placed on the lines to indicate the direction of the workflow through time.

Network diagrams simply sequence the work activities and identify their relationships in time. Networks are not as good as a WBS at demonstrating hierarchical relationships (milestones) in a project, but you can use them to demonstrate the sequence of activities and relationships among activities in different milestones in the WBS. Therefore, it's customary to complete your network diagrams after the WBS.

So everyone who uses network diagrams can figure out what's going on, a number of basic rules are used for reading the diagram:

- Boxes hold the description of each task. Lines connect the activities to one another.

- Groups of tasks that lead to a deliverable are identified by parallelograms.

- Tasks that can happen at the same time are shown in the same column, but in different rows.

- The dependency between tasks is shown by drawing lines from task to task indicating that the task on the left side must be completed before the task on the right can begin.

- Lines among tasks can cross rows to show how activities are related to each other.

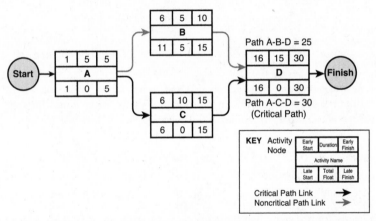

This is an example of a simple network diagram. As you can see, all the tasks have finish-to-start dependencies.

One ray of hope for you is that all the common project management software programs will create a network diagram for you if you enter the information correctly.

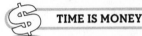

TIME IS MONEY

The network diagram can also help to determine whether "crashing" or "fast tracking" the project makes sense. *Crashing* is a term used when project managers want to compress the time to catch up on the project schedule by adding more people if the budget allows it. *Fast tracking* is when a project manager determines that activities can be done in parallel without compromising the project. In each of these instances, the activities may not have been planned that way, but the network diagram allows the project manager to see that crashing or fast tracking is an option.

Normalizing the Schedule

You must review the schedule to determine whether the resources you assigned are actually available within each task's schedule window. Obviously, you need to start with the activities on the critical path, those that have no float, and work the rest of the schedule from there. Move things around based on the float available to ensure that you don't overload someone and that others are fully utilized. After individual assignments are finalized and reviewed by the team, you must adjust the schedule to accommodate any other necessary changes. Senior management needs to review and approve it as well, as part of the project plan.

When you use the critical path in a project, you can schedule the tasks not on the path (called *noncritical*) in a number of ways to accommodate various needs of the organization. Three strategies are as follows:

- Schedule all noncritical tasks at the earliest date possible. This offers a way to free up resources earlier for other projects or the later critical tasks.

- Schedule all noncritical tasks as late as possible. This shows how much work you can delay without causing the critical tasks (and thus the project schedule) to slip.

- Schedule a subset of noncritical tasks. As you meet milestones, complete the rest of the schedule. This gives the manager scheduling flexibility and a way to assign resources to critical activities without causing political problems.

 TIME IS MONEY

If an activity defined in the WBS doesn't seem to fit in the network diagram, it usually means it's either too small or too large and needs to be broken down into smaller activities.

When assigning people, the rules are simple:

- Make sure you know the specific availability of all the people (as much as humanly possible).

- Assign the best-suited available people to each task, particularly those on the critical path.

- Use equipment and people efficiently to ensure the smallest gaps in working schedules.

- Redo the schedule until you get it balanced. (Get help from experts if it takes more than three tries.)

Loading Up and Leveling Out

Many ideal schedules forget to deal with conflicting availability of equipment, potential overuse of key people, and the needs of other projects and priorities. For example, the ideal employee to design the new employee interface may be unavailable the week you need him because of his "day job." If you can't reschedule the task to accommodate his schedule, you may have to choose someone else.

After working on your schedule, you likely will find that some team members have too much work—more than they can accomplish in a standard work week. Others may not have enough. The amount of work each team member or piece of equipment is assigned is called *resource loading*. As you would expect, it's easy to overwhelm your best people with an impossible workload while underutilizing others.

To compensate for overloaded workers, redistribute scheduled work from people with too much responsibility to those folks not fully booked, also known as *resource leveling*. As you level resources, you must consider skills and availability. For example, given the impact of the tasks that sit along the critical path to the overall success of my project, you can probably guess that I will assign my best people to those tasks. I am not going to risk my project by gambling by assigning these tasks to someone else. And if these "A" players are overallocated in their work, I will look at tasks where I have more float and identify people working them. I will often reassign them to work under the key player for a while. These "A" players usually have the skills and experience to supervise work, and it takes some of the load off them.

 TIME IS MONEY

Another key reason for understanding the float you have for activities is so you can recover if needed. In other words, if you have an activity that is getting behind, you can shift a person (or more) to help get the activity back on schedule before it is too late. You will only know who you have available if you know what float you have for each activity. And you must do it with enough time to make your corrective action effective.

The Reallocation Questions

Before you reallocate and level the resource commitments, you need to ask yourself these questions:

How many hours per day is each person or piece of equipment available? Can you expect employees to work eight hours a day? They probably do, but all that time is not necessarily applied to the project. After all, they do have to go to the bathroom, take phone calls (some personal, most legitimate business calls), get coffee, talk to other project team members informally (sometimes personal, but more often it's discussion about work on the project), and talk to other employees in the company (sometimes personal, but frequently it's important networking with other team members or peers). As a manager, you should completely support these activities. Comfortable employees who feel they have control over their work life are that much more productive. As a manager, however, you probably recognize that a work day usually consists of only about six and half hours of productive work time as a result.

Is an assigned piece of equipment allocated to multiple projects for multiple project managers? Depending on shared resources is not an optimum state for a project manager, but frequently you have limited control over the resources you get on a project and have to take other priorities into consideration. Too many times in the past, I have had teams composed of individuals who have a minimal time allocation to another project. ("No more than a couple of hours a week, I promise.") Then, during project execution, I don't see him for a couple of weeks due to legitimate problems on the other project. ("Sorry, Sam is the only one who understands payroll, and we lost the ability to create payroll checks; we need his to help us figure out the problem.") Have a contingency plan built in for these people.

Have you factored in time lost to anticipated interruptions? You can expect downtime due to weather, holidays, vacation and sick time, doctor's visits, and other personal requirements.

Have you factored in sufficient time for administrative overhead? This means allowing time for attending company meetings, allowing for company travel time, completing time reports, completing weekly status reports, and conducting project team meetings. This may also include reviewing team deliverables, as well as internal reviews of prototypes or documents.

Are you using people with specialized skill sets appropriately? Are team member assignments accurate in terms of matching skills and task requirements? Should you reallocate these people or reassign work? Have you considered the productivity of the people, as well as their relative skills?

Are you scheduling people without appropriate skill sets? Frequently, I send team members out to be trained on a new skill and expect them to come back fully proficient in that skill. Depending on the skill, you should assume reduced productivity for a certain period of time to allow that person to become fully proficient after applying the new skills in the project environment. The period of time should be directly related to the complexity of the new skills.

Have you planned for the time required to acquire additional people? Depending on the environment you work in, getting the authorization to bring in additional staff regardless of whether they are full-time employees or temporary contract staff will be more or less difficult. In some organizations, that may take as little as a week or as long as two months. My experience suggests you plan on an average of four to six weeks. After you have the authorization, time is required for getting applicants, interviewing them, checking references, making an offer, and waiting for the prospective employees to finish commitments at their current place of employment. Then, when they do come on board, they will require time to get up to speed on the project's purpose, its goals, and their job. If you're the project manager for a certain project and you only have nine months to finish the project, you can see why taking six weeks to bring on a new project team member is a problem. During all of this time, remember that your project is supposedly making progress.

Ready for Leveling Out

After making adjustments in response to all the preceding questions regarding people's schedules, you're ready to do the final leveling of resource commitments. One of the tools to help you do this is the resource histogram, a visual tool that allows you to chart resource task allocation for each period through the project. In the following figure, notice how the histograms chart the availability of the resource and the effort of that resource through the life of the project. Most computer programs will calculate this for you. By the way, most project management software programs will display a histogram for you as long as you have correctly entered all of the project information.

In weeks 1 and 6, the resource is overallocated, but it is underallocated in weeks 2 through 5. In this example, you would want to smooth out the peaks and valleys as best you can by moving work packages out of period 1 into period 2 or 3 as time is available. You can move the activity within the available float for that activity (remember critical path?). You can extend the duration of an activity because you have available float. You also could reassign some or all of the work to underallocated people if they have the right skills for the job. But you'll have to refer to your skills inventory to do that.

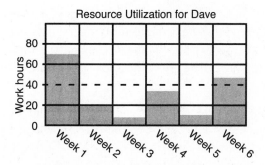

The resource bar graph can help you visualize resource utilization during phases of a project. Here you see that Dave is overallocated during weeks 1 and 6 and underallocated in weeks 3 and 5.

 RISK MANAGEMENT

The tendency will be to overallocate work to the "star" performers. Using the leveling process, you will discover that problem and look to reallocate the workload. The first place to look to reduce the load on the "star" is to ask yourself a question: Does that activity really require that high level of knowledge or experience? You will probably find places where you can shift the load to others who are less talented, but highly competent and able to handle that activity.

Options for Adjusting the Schedule

When you realize that no matter what you do, people will be overworked, here are your options for reworking the schedule:

- Reduce the scope of the project or keep the current scope and add people, keeping in mind that more people and equipment will impact the budget. Obviously, you have to do this with approval of the steering committee.

- Give a work package more time or split it into two or more work packages, modifying who is responsible for completing them to make the process work. You can also adjust the basic finish-to-start precedence relationships (but only when appropriate) by adding lead or lag time to tasks that enable some of the work to occur in parallel. Move a task to a time when more people or equipment are free. This will mean calculating the entire schedule again to make sure the moved activity doesn't impact the critical path.

- Outsource the work. Remember that outsourcing work, while reducing work done by the implementation team, also adds new tasks for vendor management. Outsourcing also assumes that the vendor people have the right expertise and are available and uncommitted.

- Negotiate for additional time in the schedule with a later completion date and a budget increase. You'll need stakeholder agreement to do this. Don't negotiate the time required to complete the activities (these should be good numbers if you've done your estimating correctly). Instead, negotiate the balance among the time, resources, and results (goals) of the project.

- Deliver components of the project in a phased approach, thereby extending the total project schedule but still giving the customer acceptable products or services at various intervals.

- Find more productive (better trained, more experienced) people. This choice may increase the budget, but you might get most of the added employee expense back in terms of increased productivity, if you choose wisely.

Charting the Final Schedule and Seeing Whether It Works

When the final schedule is in place and approved (along with the rest of the project plan), distribute it to all team members and post it in a common area so team members can measure progress. This helps you maintain a healthy competitive attitude as the various team members rush to meet or exceed their scheduled delivery dates. At that point, you cease to be a project planner and take on your role as project manager. Of course, you still need a budget before you have an approved plan. With the schedule in hand, the budget will be the next piece to tackle.

Review Questions

- Can I explain the idea of the critical path?

- Do I understand how to determine the float I have in my project?

- Am I clear on how a network diagram shows me the workflow during a project?

- Can I use the ideas presented in the chapter to assign resources to tasks on the critical path?

- Could I use the process to level the workload to make sure some people don't have too much work while others have too little?

The Least You Need to Know

- Understanding the concept of critical path is important in keeping a project schedule on track.
- When assembling a project schedule, you must be able to determine how much float you have to work with.
- Use a network diagram to give you and your team a visual picture of the project.
- Normalizing the schedule is important as you consider the people who will do the work.
- Put your best people on the tasks within the critical path because these are the tasks with the least available float.

Budgeting and Cost Control Options

"Hey, how long do you think it will take to design the new web-based portal for the CRM?"

"If you mean how long before we can have the portal into the test environment, I'd guess about six months."

"What do you mean, you guess? I need an estimate for the budget."

"Okay, I estimate it will take six months to put the portal into the test environment."

Unfortunately, this kind of dialogue goes on all the time as project managers work to build their budgets. Based on this type of estimate, it's no wonder so many projects run into trouble. However, there is a better way, and that's what this chapter is all about. All budgets start with estimates, so that is where you want to begin.

How to Avoid the Classic Budgeting Mistakes

It's important to understand that after you establish a budget, it becomes sacrosanct. You're stuck with it. Changing an entrenched project budget is like trying to modify the U.S. Constitution.

 **TIME IS MONEY**

The conceptual budget process is people + resources + time = budget.

The following classic mistakes are ones that you (or a project manager friend) have probably made. The idea is to not make them again:

Classic mistake 1: A senior manager stops you in the hallway and asks for the estimated budget for the project you have just been assigned. Maybe it's her authority or maybe she just caught you off-guard, but you feel compelled to answer. You blurt out some numbers and immediately realize that was probably a mistake. The reason? The manager is on her way to a meeting and will use that number to talk about the budget. The problem here is that by speaking off the top of your head, you may misinterpret the scope of the project or the scope of work. You can avoid this predicament by looking concerned and replying, "I wouldn't want to give you an inaccurate number, so I don't want to offer a guess right now. But I'm currently working on it. How soon do you need it?"

Classic mistake 2: Some project managers try to develop a budget without completing the work breakdown structure (WBS) to get the effort that will be required to complete the project. The problem here is that you have a poorly defined project and are likely to be overly optimistic in what you can accomplish. It's best to wait until you complete your WBS, sometimes even down to the work package level, before you begin the budget process. Without understanding the time it will take and the people who will need to complete the work, estimating a budget is just pulling numbers out of thin air.

Classic mistake 3: Sometimes project managers fail to account for the risks in completing the project. They failed to complete a thorough risk assessment that I covered in Chapter 8. As a result, they don't have enough flexibility in the budget (or the schedule) to handle the risks effectively.

Classic mistake 4: The project manager did not apply the proper experience and skill levels of the people available to the project work that needed to be done. By not properly matching the work to the skills and experience of the people, it took longer to complete the work than they expected. As a result, the quality of the project suffers, and it usually misses on both budget and schedule.

Three Levels of Accuracy for Estimating

You have three levels of accuracy to use in establishing your budget, which are applicable at different phases of the project:

- **Ballpark estimate.** During the project definition phase, the ballpark estimate is only useful if you are experienced enough to have a true "gut-level" feel for what the entire project might cost while you are still defining it.

- **Rough order of magnitude.** During the project definition phase, you might recognize aspects of the project that are similar to a project you worked on before. If so, you can often complete this type of estimate in a matter of days using your previous experience. You may hear some managers use the term *parametric estimate* for this type of estimate.

- **Detailed estimate.** The two earlier estimates can occur in the project definition phase, whereas this level of budgeting occurs in the project planning phase when the project team is developing all the plans for the work they will need to complete. The project manager then rolls up all the estimated costs and develops a budget. For that reason, project managers often call this technique a "bottom-up" estimate. This type of estimate may take months on a large project.

No matter which type of estimate you use, be sure to document the following:

- The basis of the estimate (how it was developed)

- All assumptions that were made

- Known constraints

- Confidence level

For more information on estimates, refer to *PMBOK Guide* **section 7.2.3.2.**

 NOTES FROM THE FIELD

During training classes on project management, I am often asked by new project managers about "padding" the estimate. I'll talk about contingency budgets later, but you must be careful with the concept of padding. Management often thinks that project managers pad the numbers on the estimate. That is why they often try to cut the estimate before the budget has even been built. Therefore, that is the reason for details in your explanation in how you arrived at the estimate. If your estimate has real detail behind it, they will be less likely to cut your funding arbitrarily.

Sources of Data for Building the Budget

Now you are in the position of doing some detailed analysis so you can turn the estimate into a real budget. Of course, the work the project team is doing comprises a significant amount of the money that will be spent on the project. However, you will need to estimate other costs, too:

Internal labor. Project managers often leave out or miscalculate these costs. For many projects, the project manager may be using company staff from accounting, IT, market research, marketing, and so on. All these people may need to be accounted for in the budget to really know what the project will cost. Even though many of these people will be on salary and therefore viewed as what is called a *sunk cost,* don't think of them as free. That would only be true if they had infinite hours to work, which of course they might object to. It is wise to find out if you must account for their labor as either daily or monthly rates.

Internal equipment. These costs may also be considered—items like computers, photocopiers, and printers are just a few examples. Depending on how the company wants the budget drawn up, you may also need to consider office space, even if you are not renting it separately. For example, if the project team is taking over space normally used by the accounting department, the project might be charged for the additional space required to house the accounting staff.

External labor and equipment. You should also include cost of these in the data you collect. For example, if the project team will be augmented by consultants who have broad experience in the implementation of similar projects, their costs will need to be folded into the estimates. Likewise, you must also factor into your estimates any independent contractors needed to supplement the team.

Materials. These costs are an important consideration. Office supplies are a perfect example, as people will need paper, pens, and a variety of other materials over the course of the project. Determine if you need to account for that expense in the project budget.

Travel. If project team members will need to travel to various sites for any number of reasons, don't forget to estimate the cost of those trips, including airlines, hotels, meals, and so on.

Direct and Indirect Costs

Before you put any numbers to paper, you must know the difference between direct and indirect costs on a project. Your budget must account for both of these types of costs, although how this is done will vary from organization to organization.

Direct costs are those costs specifically required by the project. Indirect costs are those costs not specific to the project because their value can be shared among many projects. You need to find out (usually from the finance officer for your project or from the accounting department) how your company allocates indirect costs for projects. You then need to establish the appropriate line items for indirect costs as part of the overall budget.

Direct costs include the following:

- **Labor.** The cost of the people working on the project. Benefits for the employees may be charged as direct costs or as a percentage of all overhead for housing the employee (which might include the cost of facilities, benefits, and so on).

- **Supplies and raw materials.** The cost of materials consumed by the project.

- **Equipment.** The cost of tools and machinery.

- **Travel.** The cost of travel associated with the project.

- **Legal fees.** Direct legal expenses charged specifically for work on your project.

- **Training.** Training for project team members and for the project end-users and customers during project installation or implementation.

- **Marketing/advertising.** The cost of project introductions, announcements, promotions, and public relations. These costs can be quite large on a project that introduces a new product.

Indirect costs include the following:

- **Facilities.** The physical location required for the project participants and shared resources, such as the company intranet or communication network. The exception is when facilities are purchased or leased specifically and exclusively for the use of the project.

- **Site-specific requirements.** State- or county-specific charges for business operations.

- **Management and administrative overhead.** The cost of paying for the managers and support staff (such as human resources people) used by your project but who don't directly report to you.

Indirect costs may be allocated on a percentage basis from some central accounting or management organization, such as a corporate office or the department responsible for the project. You will need to find out if you are required to include these costs because they could doom your project to budget overruns before it even starts.

You need to gather other possible sources of data to accurately put together your estimates. Talk with your project team, subject matter experts, and project sponsor to identify anything you may have forgotten.

> **RISK MANAGEMENT**
>
> "Money talks" is one of life's truisms. You'll find that this is especially true when you control a project budget of which outside providers want a share. Don't take money, gifts, or vacations of any kind on a vendor's tab. This keeps the bids on the level and the lawyers out of your life.

Building the Actual Budget

How do you establish a budget? You take it task-by-task, step-by-step. Doing the budget for a small project might take an afternoon. For large projects, such as implementing a new software package, a team might take a couple of months to bring expenses into line and to remember all the tasks.

The budget should help the project manager control the project; however, it's common for the project manager to find the budget controlling him. A realistic budget is central to keeping control of the project. It's okay to have one that's a little too conservative, but you can't turn lead into gold.

The budgeting process can be intimidating to project managers. How much will it really cost? What if the price of travel suddenly doubles during the course of the project? (That goes in your risk assessment.) How can I control an important staff member who demands a salary increase? What if I make a mistake? The process of building a budget should be an orderly one; otherwise, it's impossible to get reasonable numbers. You must thoroughly understand the components of each activity and then use the bottom-up method to cost out each one. Yes, you might make an error, underestimate, overestimate, or blow it completely, but all you can do is try, using your best estimating capabilities. Even so, business conditions might change, the project might get bumped into a new direction, or a task might fail. So what you are making in your astute budgeting is a set of assumptions that may change. Wish for luck while remembering the following:

- Costs are tied to project goals. Remember from Chapter 1 that all projects are tied to improved performance, so you must have enough money to complete the project to meet the goals.

- Costs are tied to time frames and schedules, and doing things faster usually costs more money. The estimates you developed for the tasks in your WBS, coupled with the schedule you developed to complete the project, are critical to this. If the steering committee wants the project done faster, this will undoubtedly cost more money. It's your job to estimate, to the best of your ability, how much more they are looking at if they ask to shrink the timeline.

Getting Expert Opinions

When establishing detailed estimates, the costs usually require expert input. With specific activities developed in the WBS and a schedule at the ready, ask the people who will be doing the work about their estimates for time and materials (see Chapter 13). It's important that each contributor understands exactly what you want. For example, if you want an estimate for doing systems testing, you might want to get written estimates and make sure they match your requirements. If you are using vendors, use the *answer-back process* to make sure you have a valid and complete estimate.

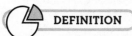 **DEFINITION**

If a project is highly technical, large, or complex in scale, ask for an answer back. In the **answer-back process,** the vendor takes your specs and builds a simple model that allows your experts to ensure that a clear understanding exists and that no significant parts or systems were neglected.

There are others who may help you in developing your estimates for the project:

Other project managers or experts. People in your organization who have handled similar projects in scope or size can provide excellent advice and study cost estimates for problems. They also might be able to provide exact estimates if a project they have worked on had elements common to yours. Or they might be much more experienced project managers and be willing to help out. Expert project managers estimate budgets accurately not because they have years of experience, but because they look at the budget and final costs of similar tasks on related projects. You can do it, too. If you completed a similar project in your company in the past, review the project close-out files and lessons learned to discover how that project was budgeted and how close it came to meeting that budget.

Your management team. Although sometimes unhappy about a project's cost, your management might be able to provide advice from their own years of experience with similar projects. Plus, by bringing them in early, they'll see that you're carefully covering your bases and are spending their money in an equitable manner. That observation will assist you in getting the final budget approved because management already will have a strong grasp on the realities of the project and its budget requirements, not to mention faith in you and your abilities. This concept is referred to as *preselling* the project budget.

Purchasing department staff. The purchasing department may or may not save you money because this department may help you in your quest for success or may stand in your way at every turn (I'll cover this in more detail in Chapter 14).

Standard pricing guides. Many government-regulated organizations and some private companies offer standard pricing in printed-guide format. Do you need to know how much Federal Express charges to move a box from point A to point B? Just look it up in the free user guide online.

After you have gleaned and carefully listed these cost estimates along with the names of the contributors, it's time to do a task budget roundup. In this process, you take all the estimates for Task A and combine them. Use a worksheet (probably in a spreadsheet), or enter the numbers in your project management software. After you wrap up costs for all the tasks separately, you can add the total of the entire plan to ascertain the project's total cost. With a computer, most unknown or unverified estimates can be indicated separately. Your manager and most stakeholders will want to see the budget in two formats—by cost center and by month—to assess cash flow and cost allocations. Some project managers will also want to present the budget by project milestones, WBS summary levels, or project phases.

For more on group decision-making techniques, refer to *PMBOK Guide* section 7.2.2.10.

 RISK MANAGEMENT

Are you assembling a budget using a spreadsheet program such as Excel? Don't accept the final numbers without calculating them separately using a calculator. Otherwise, an error in an underlying formula might be invisible.

Refining the Budget

When the budget numbers are in, although subject to correction, the next step is to fine-tune the numbers. You might have to go through this process several times as new estimates arrive and are revised or as tasks enter the project that were forgotten or ignored in the initial estimating pass.

You need to follow all these required steps as you refine your estimates:

1. **Doing a first cut.** This is a first pass on the budget, which you will probably do yourself. The first cut should never become the actual budget numbers because that will kill a project manager and project faster than anything. First cuts are often remembered as real budget quotations. Run like crazy if you're asked to stop budgeting at this step.

2. **Doing a second cut.** Ask others to carefully review the budget and focus on the resources required for each task estimate. These include the cost of labor, supplies and materials, equipment, overhead, and fix-priced bids from vendors (which account for all the vendor costs). This estimating process might demand the use of outside providers or might require more than one take as a complex subset of work is reliably broken down. You should also look at historical project costs to help guide your estimates. All estimating should involve the relevant stakeholders.

3. **Getting it right.** The third pass is the one in which you (and the team, of course) do the fine-tuning. For example, you need to make sure you know whether you need to budget the cost of company employees working on the project or whether that would be considered a sunk cost; the answer affects your budget numbers. Again, the relevant stakeholders need to be involved in these refined estimates.

4. **Wrapping it up.** If the budget appears to be workable—that is, affordable—it gets wrapped into the project plan while simultaneously heading for the steering committee for approval.

5. **Presenting it for approval.** At this point, the budget should not be a surprise to anyone on the approval cycle because you have presold the budget throughout the development process. Your complete draft for the budget is now ready for approval (see Chapter 15 for presenting the budget). Even though people have seen it before, they may still ask you to find ways to cut it, to modify the project, or to scrap the project as not worth the money (more common than you might think). If you're lucky, it gets approved right there. If not, continue to revise and present until you get consensus and signatures on the bottom line.

Adding a Little Insurance Money

Are you uncertain of the level of risk in a project? Want to provide a buffer of extra money? Most project managers add about 10 to 15 percent to the budget to ensure completion and treat it like an insurance policy. *Contingency reserve* is a standard procedure in managing any project. There's no way you can fully calculate or anticipate every risk, so when you present your draft budget, clearly identify the contingency reserve. It will prevent management from arbitrarily cutting money from your budget because they think you have padded the numbers.

> **DEFINITION**
>
> **Contingency reserve** means adding extra money to a budget in case overruns occur. This is a standard project management tactic (also known as a *contingency plan*) used to mitigate unexpected cost overruns.

Instead of overpadding the budget, negotiate for the money you really need, or, as suggested previously, adjust the project scope and objectives to be less expensive. Or use a technique like Program Evaluation and Review Technique (PERT), which includes some of that padding as part of the calculation. Remember, it takes three estimates for effort—optimistic, pessimistic, and most likely—and calculates the effort using a formula. Formulas work wonders in establishing credibility.

At the same time, remember it's often easier to get required money at the beginning of the project than to keep coming back for more because your estimates were bad.

Mastering Budget Control

Who holds the purse strings? You? Your management? A combination of both? Whatever the arrangement, you need access to the money as required. Work with your sponsor to get signature authority for the project. That way, you can pay bills and purchase supplies in a timely manner. In another arrangement that will cause you nothing but headaches, you theoretically own the budget but must get multiple signatures from senior management each time you need to spend a chunk of it. This slows projects to a crawl because some members of the executive suite might be out of town and unable to sign. Besides, executives often let authorizations requiring their signatures sit in their inboxes because they're too busy with their own projects.

The Time Value of Money

Everyone knows that what a dollar buys today will be less a year from now. For that reason, it is prudent to calculate the time value of money invested on a project. These four techniques, in order from fairly simple to very sophisticated, will help you validate the budget you have constructed:

- Cash flow analysis

- Payback

- Net present value (NPV)

- Internal rate of return (IRR)

For the purposes of illustrating each of these approaches, let's take a look at two projects and consider how they would be analyzed using each of these techniques. We're going to keep it simple, so let's imagine two projects where the initial investment is $100 and the cash received over three years flows as shown in the following chart.

	Year 0	Year 1	Year 2	Year 3
Project A	($100)	$25	$40	$60
Project B	($100)	$60	$40	$25

Cash Flow Analysis

If you look at the chart, at the end of year 3, both projects would show an equal amount of money ($125), and therefore, from a cash flow perspective, they are equal. This is fairly easy to compute.

Payback

If you look at the payback on the two projects, things change in the analysis. Because Project B receives money faster, you can see that it takes only 2 years to recover the initial investment. In Project A, it will take the business 2.6 years to receive the payback from the investment in this project. From this analysis, Project B begins to look better.

Net Present Value (NPV)

The net present value (NPV) method is a sophisticated capital budgeting technique that equates the discounted cash flows against the initial investment. Mathematically, it looks like the following figure:

$$NPV = \sum_{t=1}^{n} \left[\frac{FV_t}{(I+k)^t} \right] - II$$

Calculating net present value.

In the figure, *FV* is the future value of the cash inflows, *II* represents the initial investment, and *k* is the discount rate equal to the firm's cost of capital. If you assume that the cost of capital is 7 percent, then you can calculate the NPV for the two projects and come to the following answers:

- NPV for Project A = $7

- NPV for Project B = $11

Now you begin to see a fairly significant difference in the return on the investment the company would make in the two projects. It would tell the management of the company that there is more money to be made on Project B, particularly if capital is scarce.

Internal Rate of Return (IRR)

Using the following formula to calculate internal rate of return (IRR), you also see a significant difference between the two projects. When you calculate the IRR for Project A, you find a return of 10 percent. When you calculate the IRR for Project B, you find you have a return of 14 percent. Again, this can help management understand the money to be made in betting on the two projects.

$$IRR = \sum_{t=1}^{n} \left[\frac{FV_t}{(1 + IIR^t)} \right] - II = 0$$

Calculating internal rate of return.

Using the Cost of Money to Make a Decision

The reason for the better return for Project B is due to the fact that the money flows in earlier. Although that may seem obvious in a simple example like this one, it will be far less obvious in large, complicated projects.

Obviously, these methods, particularly the more sophisticated ones, rely on a set of assumptions that in reality will probably turn out to be wrong. Who can really predict the future? So a project manager might run two or three scenarios where she changes the assumptions to see what happens. As an example, suppose that the projects were dependent on the price of oil. The project manager might run scenarios with oil at $60 per barrel, $80 per barrel, and $100 per barrel to see what happens. (She would not generally calculate a scenario for a cost of $10 per barrel or $200 per barrel as they are highly unlikely.) As you can imagine, using these different scenarios would cause the results to change.

What you are doing in this type of analysis is helping management decide where to place the bet on projects, and you hope that your project will be the winner. It also feeds into your risk assessment where your scenarios would run from "optimistic," to "pessimistic," to "most likely."

For small projects, you probably can use the simpler methods. However, the project manager for one of these projects would probably want to run the more sophisticated NPV and IRR calculations in building a responsible budget. And remember to go back and review the risk assessment once the calculations are complete.

All in all, if you estimate carefully and document your assumptions thoroughly, you'll get a good budget approved, one that gives you enough money to get things done on time.

 NOTES FROM THE FIELD

In Chapter 1, I discussed the classic triple constraints in projects—schedule, budget, and scope. If you ask management which one is the most important, they will tell all of them! And that may be true. In my experience over the years, the truth is that one constraint is usually the most important. If the most important constraint is the budget, recognize you won't get more money to complete the project even if you may need it. If you are managing the budget correctly and you realize you don't have enough money in the budget, begin the process of changing the scope. You will need to adjust the scope to something you can deliver given the budget you have.

Review Questions

- Can I identify the levels of accuracy for estimating my project budget?

- Can I identify others who might be able to help me refine the budget?

- Do I have a clear understanding of indirect costs for my project and whether I should account for them?

- Is the contingency reserve for my project a separate line item, or have I built the reserve into various tasks within the plan?

- Do I understand how to calculate the time value of money?

The Least You Need to Know

- Establishing a reliable budget is likely the most difficult task a project manager faces. Don't get caught in one of the classic estimating traps.

- Be sure to factor in direct costs (such as labor and equipment) and indirect costs (such as facilities and site-specific requirements).

- For the best accuracy, always complete the budget after you complete the WBS and the schedule.

- For larger projects, take the time to calculate the net present value and internal rate of return for your project before you complete the budgeting process.

CHAPTER 13

Building a Winning Project Team

As you build the project team, you need to carefully consider the knowledge and skills of each individual and what he can contribute. You also need to think about which phase or phases of the project life cycle they will be involved in. You require the largest number of people during the execution phase, and smaller numbers in the definition and planning phases. However, the people you choose for the planning phase should usually be the key thinkers and innovators. They must help you plan the project, and their technical knowledge will be very valuable.

This chapter explains how to scope out required skills, assess current talent, and develop a list of people required to complete each phase on your project. I also offer guidelines for filling the gap in people skills when adequately trained resources are not readily available.

In This Chapter

- The importance of a well-chosen core project team
- Determining who you need on your core team
- Matching required skills to available talent
- Places to find people for your project
- Assigning people to the team
- When you can't choose your team members

The First Step

The first step in building your organization and human resource plan is to determine what kinds of people you need. As you consider the kind of background your team needs, ask yourself these questions to help you think through your requirements:

- What kinds of experience do they have or need?
- What is their availability?
- What knowledge and skills will they need?
- Do they have a personal interest in the outcome of the project?
- Will they work well in a team environment?

You will probably think of other questions, but this list should help you begin to sort through the possible candidates and select the appropriate ones.

One of the key considerations in building the project team should be that except for some of the very technical people, each key team member needs to have an understanding of the business. You can have great technical people, but you cannot give them the in-depth knowledge or experience of the business. Having business analysts who can stand toe-to-toe with organizational people and talk about the business, ask the right questions, and question the answers they receive is the only way to build real credibility with the organization. Staff your project with strong business analysts who can challenge the ever-present parochial view that "we're different here."

You'll actually be doing most of your hiring after the plan is approved and you move into the project execution phase (that starts with Chapter 16), but you need to verify personnel costs and resource availability before you put the plan into effect.

Building the Core Project Team

Choosing the core team could be the single most important decision you make as a project manager. Strong team leaders effectively combined with knowledgeable experts (where necessary) build the momentum required for successful project planning. And good planning is paramount to a successful implementation of the project.

The core project team usually consists of the most important players—those who will be associated with the project from start to finish. The core team will be involved in the project design phase and the planning phase, and then will bring others on board for the execution phase. While the core team doesn't usually have signature authority for spending money on the project, they are directly responsible for the overall success of the project's planning and execution phases.

Rank is not always a consideration in forming the core project team; for a larger project, skill or experience might be more important factors. On small projects, the core project team might be only you and another one or two key people with whom you will be working on the project.

NOTES FROM THE FIELD

One good project manager I worked for years ago did a great job of selecting his project team. He analyzed what he needed and found the best people who matched the work in the WBS. He found people who had the technical skills, but also were very knowledgeable about the business. He went even further than most project managers I had seen by planning how the team could collaborate by thinking through the seating assignments for his team members. He wanted certain people who would be working together frequently to sit close to each other so they could develop a relationship and collaborate easily as the project progressed.

The membership of the core team may change slightly as you move out of one phase of the project and begin the next phase. For example, one person may be the team leader for the testing plan during the planning phase, but another may take the lead for testing during the execution phase of the project. Throughout the project, however, your core project team should consist of your most trusted employees and central advisors.

For complex projects, to have a tool to help you determine your personnel needs and match those needs with qualified individuals is useful. One such tool is the responsibility assignment matrix (RAM), as shown in the following table. In addition to helping you match individuals to a group of tasks they might lead, you can use it to help figure out who you need to consult on particular decisions or issues and who will actually be responsible for carrying out certain duties. It may also provide some backup if someone is absent for a stretch of time. Signature authority is usually reserved for managers who control critical aspects of the organization the project will depend on. They are key stakeholders, and you will not be able to use their facilities or people without their approval. Bob is a case in point in the following matrix.

Responsibility Assignment Matrix (RAM)

Phase	Ali	Bob	Callie	Diane	Ed	Frieda
Requirements	B		P		I	R
Design		S		P		B
Development	B	I	P	B	I	
Testing	B	S	B	B	P	B
Training	P	I				B

P = Primary   B = Backup(Assist)   R = Review Required   I = Input Required   S = Signature Required

In the matrix, I have given the primary responsibility for certain tasks to those who have the knowledge or experience the team needs. Often, project managers will give them a title, such as team leader. For example, Callie is an experienced developer who has worked on projects similar to the development needs that you anticipate will be important for the system implementation. Therefore, Callie becomes the team leader for development. Ali, on the other hand, is less experienced and will need someone like Callie to help direct her work, or assign work for her at times. And Bob is the manager for IT infrastructure at the company, so he will need to be consulted or be asked to sign off on certain aspects of the project.

You may also decide to use the RAM as a tool to help you bring new people onto the team or as a way to determine who to recruit if you happen to lose people along the way, which almost always happens!

 TIME IS MONEY

As you build your core team, look for people who can work within an ordered system of checks and balances. Avoid people who might impose their own agenda on the project or the classic "prima donna" types. If you have a choice in the matter, choose individuals who will accept your role as project manager without resentment or hostility.

Only when you have the tasks and the work breakdown structure (WBS) in hand can you identify all the resources required to complete the project. The project sponsor and the core project team may help you do this; however, it isn't until after the project plan is approved and the execution phase begins that you'll actually start working as a fully functioning project organization. (I cover how to organize the project team during the execution phases in Chapter 18.)

For more information on planning for the people you need, refer to *PMBOK Guide* **section 9.1.**

The Complete Execution Team: Where the Work Is Done

The project implementation team includes the core team and other people who will actually do the work to develop the project deliverables. On almost any project, this team is made up of people with differing personalities, skills, ability, knowledge, and temperament. Your mission is to evaluate the project prior to choosing implementation personnel and to build an execution team that takes advantage of each team member's skills without taxing his weaknesses.

Unfortunately, this isn't as easy as it sounds. Building the team and keeping it together are two of the most difficult tasks for any project manager. Whether through neglect or confusion, it's easy to let the team spirit slip away, and a spiritless project comes in with a bang and leaves with a whimper. Don't let this happen to you and your project! Even though I have spent a lot of time talking about activities, budgets, and schedules, your most important job will be managing the project team. Read this chapter, and learn how to find the right people for your project to reap implementation success.

 WORDS FROM THE WISE

> Some of us will do our jobs well, and some will not, but we will all be judged by only one thing—the result.
>
> —Vince Lombardi, Hall of Fame football coach

Matching Skills to Tasks on the WBS

For most projects, assigning people to the tasks involves two steps: deciding what skills and experience you need, and matching people to the tasks. You can answer with confidence the questions about the people skills you need for your project by using a structured approach that starts with the project's WBS. For each task in the project, answer questions similar to the following:

- Is there a specific technical skill or combination of skills required to complete this task?

- How much experience should the person or people have to complete this activity? Does a person need to have specific experience doing this activity, or can general experience be applied? If so, what general experience is required?

- Does this person have the knowledge or education required to fulfill the role that you need filled?

- In addition to technical skills, are any specific interpersonal skills required to complete this task effectively, such as good written or verbal communication skills, diplomacy or negotiating skills, or management ability?

- How many of these skilled people will you need for each task, and how will you organize them by job title and job function?

List the skills and experience next to each WBS level, or use a worksheet like the following example. With a form like this, often called a *skills requirement worksheet* or *skills matrix*, you can list the actual skills you'll need to complete your project on a task-by-task or milestone basis. Use this type of worksheet to determine the skills, and then decide whether you can find these people internally or whether you will be forced to find them elsewhere.

Skills Requirement Worksheet Project:
Produced by: H. Lieberum   Date: 05/03/14

WBS	Tasks	Skills Required	Experience
2.0	Storage	Data management	Oracle DB
		Data modeling	
6.0	Billing system	Accounting	Financial systems
		System development	
13.0	Interfaces	Development and testing	Retail environment
		User interface with drop-down menus	

 TIME IS MONEY

If you have a college or university within a reasonable distance of your company or facility, check to see whether they have classes in project management at the graduate (usually) level. You can often get students who are smart and motivated to work as interns on your project. Professors are often anxious to give their students practical experience on a real project (and students are often just as anxious). You will need to consider the risks of untried resources and work with the professor on how the students will be evaluated, but their participation might be well worth it!

In addition to completing the skills requirement worksheet, to decide on the team members you need, consider questions like these:

- If you could choose anyone you wanted for your team, who would you choose and why? (*Hint:* Your answers should involve both skills and personality for each person you choose.)

- Given the team that you actually get to work with, what levels of supervision will be required? You must be brutally honest here, especially if you're evaluating the skills of people who also happen to be friends or colleagues. Regardless of the talent involved, there's no sense in pretending your team members will be self-sufficient if they won't be. Some people simply need more direction than others, and these people will need some of your time.

- Where will the people come from? Do you have the talent in your own department (assuming these people have the time to be assigned to your project), or must you raid another department or hire outsiders such as consultants or contractors for talent? (I tell you where to obtain people in the following section.) The source of the people affects their cost and availability and maybe even the quality of their output. All these things affect the schedule and budget you have yet to create and get approved.

Answering these questions allows you to compare the talent required for the project to the people actually available. Are the people you need ready, willing, and able? If so, are they affordable? Will your project demand already overburdened co-workers take on yet another responsibility? How much will outside resources—such as consultants, experts, and temporary labor—really cost?

Wow! This whole thing is sure interrelated. That's why you need to put on your thinking cap while you're planning and involve your trusted advisors. The better you understand your choices, the better chance you'll have to make good ones. It's also a good reason to involve others like your team leaders in the discussion.

Where Will the People Come From?

Staffing a project can be difficult because co-workers are already buried in their own work and hiring outsiders is expensive. Typically, your options are limited by people's availability and their cost. But an organization that wants or needs to complete a project must make staff available, even if it means pulling people off other projects or bringing in outside help. Staffing options include the following:

- Using your own staff and other people from your department

- Using staff from other departments

- Contracting with consultants, outside vendors, or temporary agencies

- Hiring and training new staff

As with most business options, each of these choices has an upside and a downside involved. Just working with unfamiliar faces can mean a few surprises. You might have to adjust the project to accommodate each personality and productivity level while keeping a wary eye on the project dollars and timing.

WORDS FROM THE WISE

Motivation is a fire from within. If someone else tries to light that fire under you, chances are it will burn very briefly.

—From *The 7 Habits of Highly Effective People* by Stephen R. Covey

Your Own Staff and Other People from Your Department

If staff members with appropriate skills exist in your department and aren't already (fully) committed to other projects, using them is the easiest alternative. You have easy access to these people; you have a working knowledge of their strengths and weaknesses and, depending on your rank, you may have control over them.

However, don't kid yourself. If you use internal people, you will need to change their performance contracts to include the project goals. Think about it: if they have to choose between two competing tasks, they will choose the one they are getting paid for, their day job! If you want them to commit to the project in addition to their regular jobs, the project must show up on the performance evaluation and have a positive (or negative) impact on their year-end bonus. Otherwise, you will always lose this battle.

You may also want to set up two organization charts: one that shows them in their regular job, and one that shows them in the project organization. Visually, this sends a strong message. By that, I mean that in the functional organization, for example Information Technology, you would see a worker, Bob, as a manager of infrastructure with seven people reporting to him. In the second organization chart for the project, you see Bob as the team leader for infrastructure development that includes five people, ranging from developers to database administrators. The people in IT know they need to listen to Bob because he is their boss. On the project team, the org chart shows Bob as the boss of the infrastructure development team.

If your project requires outside expertise (either from inside or outside your organization), this will require time and money. Projects with high visibility can be problematic politically, too. If other departments see you utilizing vast amounts of resources on a single project, you may have to justify your resource use as other projects slip. Further, you may be considered hard to work with because you use only people from your own group when more experienced talent is known to exist elsewhere in the company or organization.

Staff from Other Departments

Working with others in your organization makes for good communication and camaraderie among those involved. In a large organization, this might get you the technical or specialized staff you need, or it might allow you to bring in competent people whom you watch with awe as they keep the team moving efficiently and effectively. For example, you might need a financial wizard from the finance department to track your budget and streamline purchase orders.

If you need to put a team together with resources from other departments, consider these questions before you go any further:

- Who do you have to deal with in other parts of the organization to get approval for a prospective team member's participation? Is this politically workable?

- How much do outside services cost? Would it be easier to use outside resources than to get approval to use the inside people?

- How much training does each team member require? Is it worth it?

- Will team members come willingly, or are you imposing your agenda on workers who would prefer to have no part in the project?

- Is another manager offering you a team member because he wants to get rid of the person? (This is called *exporting the problem!*)

 NOTES FROM THE FIELD

Recognize that when you borrow people from other departments within the company, you will inevitably face the situation where their manager sets the priorities for their work. Realize that unless they were assigned to the project full time, their "day job" will interfere with their ability to do project work—and their day job will always be the highest priority. If they were supposed to be working two days per week on the project, be aware of the fact that they have essentially been given a second job. Identify those people, and the work they will do, and develop a risk mitigation strategy within your risk plan.

Negotiate carefully with line managers in advance to set the expectations as much as possible. Don't assume anything here. Don't forget to consider other aspects of the day job. For example, to get time with the accounting people will be hard when they are closing the books on a month or a quarter. Factor that into your plan and your schedule!

Contracting with Consultants and Temporary Agencies

Outsiders are always available—for a price. With careful selection, you can fully staff a project with exactly the right mix of people. Hire them when you need them and let them go when they're done. This is a flexible arrangement in that you have no responsibility (other than paying the bill) to keep them on or even to provide office space because all but some temp agency employees will already have space of their own. The biggest risk here is that you will lose them if they find a permanent job. You will need to work out how that situation will be handled in advance with the agency, but don't forget to identify mitigation strategies in the risk register.

Also, consultants can be expensive. The key to using outside consultants is to schedule their work carefully. The cost for a highly trained consultant priced at $1,500 per day by his firm is mitigated if, with careful scheduling, he comes in, works using his own well-developed methodology, and leaves. But should the work fall behind, he may spend several days cooling his heels while the clock is running. In this situation, he will become an expensive liability, regardless of his admirable skills and experience.

RISK MANAGEMENT

Be careful of using the term *head count* when you talk about additions to your project team. Head count is the term used to describe the fixed number of internal employees approved to work in an organization or on a project. Hiring a new person "increases head count." On many projects, using an outside consultant or other temporary worker only increases costs. Sometimes it's easier to increase costs than to raise head count because head count enlargement shifts the permanent overhead costs for the company. Thus, if you need a person for a project and you don't have a job for that person after the project is done, it's usually easier—and in the long run less expensive—to propose an outside team member than to propose additional head count.

Good consultants are masters at selling themselves; otherwise, they would be out of business. Remember, just because someone proclaims himself an expert doesn't necessarily mean he has a track record to back up the claim. Make sure the vendors you choose have been around the block a couple of times. Also, watch out for the "bait and switch." That is when a consulting group shows you résumés for experienced professionals for your project, but when the day comes to actually start, a group of newly minted MBAs shows up. You will spend time training them and constantly worry if they can keep up.

Even hiring low-level labor must be handled carefully. The temporary agency's polished salesperson may overwhelm you with smooth promises and glossy brochures, but eventually, you'll just need hard-working developers to write that code. Remember the gloss and polish you pay extra for probably won't make any difference if you just need good code developers.

You'll want to work with the procurement professionals in your company. They are experienced in writing contracts with incentives for good work and penalties for poor performance.

Hiring and Training New Staff

If the project is a long-term commitment or is ongoing with a finish date far enough out, you might find adding to the head count is the most expedient method for bringing in the manpower and expertise required. For example, after implementing a new system, you know you will need people to support the new system after the project is finished. It might make sense to hire them so they are familiar with the deliverables and the history of the project. Of course, you noted the word *training* in the title of this section. You must be fully prepared with time and money to train your new people in everything from their task requirements to the culture of your organization. But adding new workers often brings a fresh point of view, takes some pressure off other staff members, and is an easy way to add a much needed skill set not available elsewhere in the company.

For more information on developing the project team, refer to *PMBOK Guide* section 9.3.

 TIME IS MONEY

If your skills analysis reveals you need to employ more people, the company will likely have detailed hiring guidelines that include job description formats, pay scales, interviewing procedures, and reference requirements. Learn about these now before you have to start recruiting people. And don't forget to establish a good relationship with your human resources manager. This person can be a lifesaver when you need to get people on board quickly.

Keep in mind that not everyone you hire will like being a part of the team or will make a good team player. Individual contributors with specialized creative skills, such as engineers, designers, and writers, may sometimes appear to you and other team members as difficult to work with. That's okay if their expertise is a must-have for the project. Although you should avoid mercurial personalities with no people skills whatsoever, a genius with a compelling vision might make the difference between a mediocre project and a great one. Just keep him out of supervisory roles wherever possible. Another approach is to assign him to tasks with little dependence on others. That way he won't need to interact too often. Or you may want to use him as a subject matter expert that you only bring in at certain times to take advantage of his genius, but you don't have to supervise him.

You must structure the project team to work like the gears in the car's automatic transmission. Appropriate matches of worker to co-worker, manager to worker, and manager to manager are crucial.

In a long project, this team assembly becomes more important. Someone who gets along with a colleague for a five-week project may grate on the person's nerves during a project spanning a longer period of time. Conflicts are inevitable, but do your best to assemble team members that favor cooperation rather than discord.

Assessing and Assigning People

Now that you have looked at the first step—deciding what skills and experience you need—let's take a look at actually identifying and assigning people to tasks on the project.

Skills and Knowledge of the Project Team

Before actually assigning people, I usually try to consider two key aspects of the question:

- What level of skill and knowledge is required?
- How must the skill and knowledge be applied?

In the level of skill or knowledge, it usually breaks out into three distinct levels, which I grade as follows:

- **A:** Must be proficient enough with the skill or knowledge that they can teach others
- **B:** Can effectively utilize the skills and knowledge to complete the tasks they will be assigned
- **C:** Must at least know something about the area they are working on

In addition to that, I want to assess how well they can apply the skills or knowledge during the course of the project. In this aspect, I would also grade them in this fashion:

- **1:** Can manage others who must utilize the skill or knowledge
- **2:** Can work independently with little or no supervision from the team leader or me as project manager
- **3:** Must work under the supervision of someone, either me or the team leader

You can then create a matrix with team members and the work they will complete within the WBS. You probably know the answers to these aspects for people within your own firm, but clearly need to think through this grading system when going outside for resources.

If, after matching people to jobs, it still looks like you have the right talent available for the project, it's time to study other ramifications of your choice of project team members. Also, you need to think about the location of the various people. Sometimes, all the people are in the same location, so it's easy. However, at times, you may have people scattered all over the country or the world (see Chapter 19 on managing a virtual team)! Consider the political aspects of whom to choose because you need people from all the stakeholder groups to buy in. They are more likely to accept the project solutions if they have some of their people working on the project. Also, your boss may ask you to include someone on the project as a developmental opportunity, as he might need experience to grow into his next job. You might think of this as an imposition. However, what you may really have is a bargaining chip to gain further concessions on other aspects of the project.

RISK MANAGEMENT

Skills inventories and contact lists also are useful after the project starts. Your goal should be to take an accurate inventory of the skills you need for the project, to prioritize the skills according to amount of experience required, and then to assess the proficiency of your project team members against that inventory. Why? What happens if a key staff member assigned to your project quits or gets sick? Pull out your skills inventory to identify potential replacements. If you don't have a network diagram and skills inventory ready, you will waste valuable time trying to find someone who can take over for the lost resource, and the project may suffer delays or other problems as a result. Always make this situation a part of your project risk plan.

The Best of the Best: Making Your Selections

After you've considered your options and the talent available to you, create a list of possible people and vendors for each task on your list. This list should include the alternatives available. For large, complex projects, rank the alternatives in priority order, and include the strengths and weaknesses of each choice. A worksheet like the responsibility assignment matrix (RAM) shown previously in the chapter can be useful in identifying people and their strengths and experience for a project team. (Guard your list closely and rarely share it with others!)

If you use a skills inventory, you will discover almost no perfect matches of people and project requirements on your list. Because no one can perfectly fit your needs, the selection process usually involves trade-offs. For planning purposes, identify people with the closest match of required skills and ask yourself whether the skills deficiencies are workable. Can you use two people who complement each other's skills on the project? Can you make up for the lack of skills in other ways? The more critical the tasks, the more important the match of skill requirements to people becomes.

Sometimes You Have to Compromise

Obviously, you want the best people possible for your project, but even after making compromises and trade-offs, it's not always appropriate to use your first choice for every task, especially if another person's skills are adequate.

For example, if you were the project manager for a project for installing a new billing system, you might have two people who could do the job of designing the new billing system. One of them has extensive experience in billing systems but is relatively new to the company, and you have not worked with him before. Another person does not have the experience of the first one, but you have worked with him before and know what to expect if he joins the team. So you will have to decide which trade-off you are willing to make—experience or familiarity. Which will it be? Every choice involves risks and trade-offs.

The other key reason for compromising might be budget constraints. With the example of the billing system design, the more experienced person might be your choice, but the person is too expensive. You don't have the budget to spend on the work that needs to be done, and the compromise might be to let the less skilled person do the work at a lower cost and just bring the more expensive person in on an as-needed basis.

The Problem of Imposed Team Members

You don't always have the advantage of being able to choose and organize every member of the team for your project. Other managers within your own organization may impose the team and its structure on you. Frequently, people are selected because they are available and not because their skills or talent match what you really need. Imposed team members are common in every business for a variety of practical and not-so-practical reasons. Be sure to include the risks of imposed team members into your risk analysis and to determine the best strategy for mitigating that risk.

In dealing with imposed team members, you can consider a number of alternatives to make things work:

 **TIME IS MONEY**

Don't forget to change your performance reward and recognition system to incorporate the success of the project into each and every person's evaluation criteria. Provide an actual performance report to your team members at regular intervals, so they will know how they are performing.

Review Questions

- Is my WBS well developed so I can understand the knowledge and skills I need in my team?

- Have I identified the core team who will not only help me plan the project, but also lead the implementation?

- Am I clear on where I will get the people to staff the project, both inside and outside the company?

- Did I assess the people with A, B, C and 1, 2, 3 before I assigned them?

- Did I identify all the trade-offs required by assigning people to the project tasks?

The Least You Need to Know

- Planning for the right kinds of people on your team is important to the success of the project.

- The core project team usually consists of the most important players involved in the project from start to finish.

- A comparison of project needs and people skills can help you match the right people to the right jobs on your project.

- Look for the right combination of skills and experience in team members, whether it's within or outside of your company.

- Part of your risk plan needs to include a strategy for replacing people you may lose over the course of the project.

- When you have team members imposed on you, analyze the risk that may entail and look for other ways to deal with the situation effectively.

Getting Supplies, Equipment, and More

After you have defined the tasks, established a basic network diagram, and selected the team members, you must create a list of additional resources you'll need for your project. You have also determined your project schedule and budget, so you are ready to begin the process of procuring those additional items, which is the focus of this chapter.

The Additional Resources You Need

As you figure out what you need to complete the project, you have to consider additional fundamental resources required to implement almost any project (besides people and money, which have already been discussed):

- Equipment
- Facilities
- Materials and supplies

You and the core project team need to identify these other resources for the entire project. Ask yourself what resources are already available. Professional project managers often use a resource inventory to list everything available for the project (including equipment, facilities, and supplies).

As you begin to plan for procurement, consider a variety of inputs to help you. You need to review these items:

- Scope statement in your project charter

- Deliverables you are responsible for

- Procurement policies within your company

- Market conditions for the equipment, supplies, and so on

- Constraints identified earlier in your planning process

- Assumptions you have made

After you (and the core planning team) identify additional resources, you still need to know one more thing before you can complete your plan for project resources: the estimated quality and output of people and equipment resources. This is important because it enables you to make a trade-off analysis between similar resources. If time is most important, choose the fastest resource. However, if a slower resource really saves money in the long run and if you have the time to spare in the project schedule, then a slower but cheaper resource might be a better selection. If you don't make these estimates in advance, you won't be able to put the best budget and schedule together for your project.

 TIME IS MONEY

If you need help building your estimates, check out one of the several estimating software programs available.

Planning for Outside Vendors, Contractors, and Suppliers

During the planning phase (where you are now), establish a list of probable vendors, suppliers, and contractors for your project, and get estimates of cost and availability. Before you talk to vendors, you need to be crystal clear about the materials, equipment, and work you want from them. This will come into play during negotiations, and a well-defined statement of work (SOW) or scope statement is essential.

For more detailed information on this type of planning, refer to *PMBOK Guide* **section 12.2.2.**

When you evaluate the need for vendors, consider doing a make-or-buy analysis. This technique determines whether you can effectively produce the items you need internally within the company or whether your best alternative is to purchase what you need. A good way to begin that analysis is to develop the specifications you need for your project based on your earlier requirements, which include the following:

- *Design requirements* detail what is to be done in terms of the physical characteristics of the product, and the risk is on the buyer.

- *Performance requirements* describe measurable capabilities the end product must achieve, and the risk is on the vendor.

- *Functional requirements* express the way the item will be used as a way to stimulate competition and lower the cost since most products don't exactly match the functions to the usage. This is often linked to a performance specification, and the risk is on the vendor.

Don't forget to include indirect costs when you begin this analysis. Often an internal source looks good until you factor the indirect costs into the equation. Also, keep in mind the overall perspective for the company and not just the project. For example, it might look like the resources for supporting the new customer relationship management (CRM) system can reside in-house after it is installed. However, considering the implementation of patches, help desk, and other technical support, it might make more sense to hire a company that specializes in supporting this type of system for your company since your internal IT department would just not have the skills or staffing levels. Factoring that into your vendor analysis is important because you may want to include these types of vendors on your project team during the execute phase.

For more detailed information on factoring indirect costs, refer to *PMBOK Guide* **sections 12.2.2 and 12.3.4.**

You might also need people with special training or experience to provide input into the procurement process.

NOTES FROM THE FIELD

When you are looking for expertise, don't necessarily focus on your particular industry. For example, when I did a project regarding improving the scheduling of pipeline maintenance for a major energy company, one area of expertise I looked for was people who could give me expert advice on turbine engines. What better place to look than in the airline industry, an industry that has hundreds if not thousands of turbine engines operating every day! I decided the project team would talk with maintenance experts at the national airline on how they did the work on their turbine engines and see what we could learn and apply to our project. It worked wonderfully, and the pipeline people really respected the airline people and vice versa.

Determining What Kind of Contract to Use

Different types of contracts entail different levels of risk for you and the vendor. The more risk the vendor takes, the more profit she expects on your project. You need to choose the right contract for you and the risk tolerance within your company for these types of purchases. The three primary contract types used most often are as follows:

- *Fixed-price or lump-sum contracts* let you know exactly how much you will pay for goods or services. They place much more risk on the seller's part, and therefore most vendors will not enter into this type of agreement unless you provide them with a very clear and concise scope statement.

  Vendors who are hoping to work with you on a long-term basis on future jobs might bid the first job at a loss to blow away the competition and get the work. This is called *buying the job*.

- With *cost-plus-fixed-fee contracts,* you pay the vendors for their costs—both direct and indirect—plus a fee over and above costs, which is the vendor's profit. This puts more risk on you as the buyer and less on the seller, but it enables you to offer incentives to the vendor if she meets or exceeds certain targets for the project.

- *Time-and-materials (T&M) contracts* are a combination of the fixed-price and cost-reimbursable contracts and are often used for consultants or other professional services resources. T&M contracts resemble the cost-reimbursable contracts in that they are typically open-ended since the full value will not be realized until the project is finished. However, they resemble a fixed-price contract because you negotiate fixed rates that you will pay for the services of different people (a senior programmer, for example).

For more technical information on various contracts, refer to *PMBOK Guide* section 12.1.1.9.

Getting an Estimate

No matter which type of contract you choose, you should ask for an estimated cost. You want to know that the estimates are good ones and that the eventual commitments will be met. You may hand this type of work over to the procurement people (which I'll talk about later in the chapter). However, if you don't have a procurement group, or you just want to do it yourself, here are some guidelines for getting the best estimates for your project:

- Whenever possible, get written estimates from suppliers with whom you or your company has had extensive and positive experience.

- Make sure that all providers (people, materials, and equipment suppliers) bid competitively. Get a minimum of three bids or more if you can. When you have trimmed the list down, ask the final two providers to present you with any revised estimates. When two companies know they are down to the wire with only one other competitor, they will often factor in other savings and give you an even more attractive estimate to capture your business.

- Be aware that some companies are now beginning to hold what is called an *e-auction* for bidding that is similar to the auctions on eBay. This approach might be particularly appealing if you want to speed up the process due to a short time frame.

 WORDS FROM THE WISE

Business people see me as a master negotiator because I usually wind up with what I am aiming to get. In other words, I negotiate to win and then I win.

—Donald Trump, chairman of Trump Enterprises

Now you can get to the bottom line of working with outside suppliers. Never view an estimate as final. Negotiation is a fine art. When you are ready to begin negotiations, you should plan for and include the following ideas in your thinking:

- Based on your work breakdown structure (WBS), determine the maximum amount of money you expect to pay as well as the minimum amount.

- Determine how you will evaluate the competing bids. Will you just decide on the lowest price, or will quality, reputation, or other factors (such as financial stability) be just as important as price?

- Decide whether you want a single source or multiple vendors for your project. On a large project, you may want to deal with just one vendor who can provide all the resources you require. On the other hand, hiring a collective group of smaller vendors that are considered "best of breed" in their area of expertise might be the right model. Your answer often depends on the risk assessment you have done.

- Review past performance on similar projects. You want to make sure that the vendor is capable of delivering on your project based on the experience of others.

You need good estimates for your plans and good working relationships with your vendors to get these estimates. Work with suppliers, study the goods or services they sell, and check up on their reputations. Never let a powerfully persuasive salesperson push you into a commitment before you've approved the plan. It may be harder to resist than you think.

If you follow these simple steps, you'll get more accurate estimates from suppliers of all sorts of goods and services:

Step 1: Get written estimates for your service, supply, material, and equipment needs. On large projects, you may want to put together a formal request for proposal (RFP) to attract the maximum number of potential suppliers. Advertise the RFP if that's what it takes to get good estimates and quality vendors. Offer detailed specifications of your project and its needs by return mail, fax, or email. Vendors will assume bidding is competitive, although the words "Competitive Bid" stamped on the RFP will help make it clear from the start.

 TIME IS MONEY

Keep in mind that, as you develop the rest of the plan, your resource choices will affect the quality, schedule, and budget for your project. If you aren't able to get the resources you planned to use, you have to adapt the scope, schedule, and budget accordingly. It's a good idea to verify the availability of as many resources as possible before the project plan is approved.

Step 2: Fully explain, demonstrate, and document your requirements for equipment, materials, and supplies for the estimate or in the RFP. Be as precise as this sample bid request for professional services: "The Company expects the consultant to research and recommend billing technology that will satisfy the requirements listed in the statement of work and that will operate within the technical environment at the company." In your RFP, here are some questions you might ask them to address:

- What is your understanding of our need(s)?

- What will be the overall or life-cycle cost? The definition of life-cycle cost is the purchase price plus cost to operate over a specific period of time.

- What are your technical capabilities to complete the work? Please give examples that illustrate these capabilities.

- What is your management approach, and how will you use it to ensure the success of the project?

- What is your financial capacity to fulfill the terms of the agreement during the life of the contract?

Step 3: Before you read a single proposal, sit down with your project team and develop the selection criteria. Determine whether certain elements of your evaluation are worth more than others and develop a weighting system that takes those priorities into account. Also, consider developing certain minimum standards that any final vendor must meet to win the contract. You may be able to eliminate some vendors right away and not waste time on someone who wouldn't win against the competition anyway.

Step 4: Make sure the vendors know acceptance and performance clauses will be inserted in the final order for goods or services. This means goods or services that don't meet specified standards will be returned and replaced at no cost to you or will be deducted from the invoice. Also, make sure the vendor will be responsible for picking up the shipping tab for return freight if materials or supplies are inappropriate or substandard upon delivery. Include delivery requirements in the description of your needs. (Ordinary but unavailable materials have sunk more than one project.) These specifications must indicate when the goods must be delivered and to what location; otherwise, the contract is void. If the company turns out to be a no-show, you're still in trouble project-wise, but at least you won't owe a bill for a shipment that arrives three weeks too late.

Also, make sure you find out how changes will be dealt with and include those details in the contract. All projects change over time, and you will need a clear process in place when you change the scope of work you have asked a vendor to supply. It will also help when one or more of the stakeholders request a change because you will be able to explain to them how the price will change (increase) and what impact it will have on the schedule (delay).

Step 5: When getting estimates from consultants or other service providers, ask for a formal proposal for their services. A formal proposal will tell you a great deal about a firm. Do they use "boilerplate" wording in response to your request? If so, it may mean they are not really familiar with your requirements but are hoping to impress you with their credentials. Be more interested in how they will work for you, not what they have done for others.

Step 6: When hiring consultants or service providers, also ask for a description of their current workload. Many will boast about current projects without realizing that what you're looking for is a person with the time to take on your tasks. The biggest concern most customers have is the classic "bait and switch," as mentioned in Chapter 13.

Step 7: Check references, compare estimates, and use the estimate from the most likely choice of vendors for the rest of your planning purposes.

Step 8: Hold a bidder conference to allow you to meet with several vendors at one time. A bidder conference is an invitation to all potential bidders to meet with you and some of your key team members. This will allow them to ask more detailed questions prior to submitting their proposals. Often, project managers will revise their RFP based on the questions they received during the bidder conference and then send it out to any vendors still interested in proposing on the contract.

Step 9: Provide each vendor who submitted a bid the courtesy of a reply. And, if it is practical, give them the time to discuss why they lost the bid either in person or over the telephone.

 TIME IS MONEY

One way to get reliable bids and estimates is to have vendors develop their own WBS for their portions of the project, complete with the acceptance criteria and the list of resources they will use. They can then assign individual costs to each task and resource in the WBS, just like you need to do for the rest of the project. This document can help you determine the quality of the estimate and their understanding of the work you want done.

Working with the Procurement Department

Sometimes you won't be given the opportunity to get estimates or to order resources without going through the procurement department. This can be a relief because it takes the work out of your hands. But the procurement department can be the bane of projects (and project managers) if they are simply an organization that believes their job is to provide as much bureaucracy as possible.

If you're lucky, you'll find a professionally run organization with experienced purchasing agents who take the time to understand your needs and to handle your bid requests with aplomb. Be aware, however, that you may be faced with the uphill task of (literally) fighting with your organization's procurement personnel to place an order.

The only way to know what you'll be up against during a project is to test the waters. Begin by ordering something simple, such as a desk for a team member. The resulting cooperation of the procurement department—or lack thereof—will let you know whether you need to add tasks to your project that read, "Work with procurement to explain need, secure bid, and gain approvals to order desks."

 TIME IS MONEY

Look into using a database program to maintain the equipment inventory for your project. You can assign codes to equipment categories for easy sorting. Some of the more sophisticated project management programs allow you to include equipment inventories as part of the project data.

The best way to solve problems with a bureaucratic procurement organization is to learn its procedures, follow its processes, and make friends in the department. If the department causes more problems than it solves, try to work around it when you can and learn to work within the process when you must. The test of the project manager's mettle is to make it all work—easy and hard.

For example, while running a project for the procurement department of a global oilfield services company, I developed a good working relationship with the director. She had built a strong, professional group that worked hard to save the company and the project managers money with vendors. One of her greatest frustrations centered on project managers who did not give her and her team enough time to find and negotiate the best deal. Far too often, she would receive a request to find a vendor who could provide a piece of equipment and have it delivered to the work site in two weeks. As you might imagine, those project managers paid premium prices for that equipment! I suspect those projects went over budget on a regular basis.

The Final Steps in Procurement

For planning purposes, getting the bids for people, supplies, materials, and equipment may be enough to finish the budget for your project. But don't forget to build in some contingency funds for your equipment and supplies just in case circumstances change after the project starts.

After the plan is approved and you have the go-ahead to proceed with the project, however, you'll have to get an attorney or the corporate legal counsel to draft the actual work agreements with any suppliers or outsider vendors. Require vendor signatures on all agreements before work commences or money is exchanged. All these procedures are part of the procurement process, and procurement is a major portion of your job as the project manager.

For more information on procurement, refer to *PMBOK Guide* **section 12.3.**

Review Questions

- Are my requirements detailed enough to let vendors know exactly what I need from them?

- Which type of contract is best for the type of project I'm running?

- Should I send out an RFP to a broad audience or just rely on vendors we have already used in the past?

- Have I established a process for comparing bids so that I am evaluating vendors on the right criteria?

- Have I identified who will help me with the vendor selection and the final contract?

The Least You Need to Know

- After you have identified all the tasks for a project, identify the specific resource requirements for each task or milestone, including people skills, material requirements, information needs, and other resources.

- Before you get your project plan approved, verify the cost estimates and availability for all the resources in your project. Otherwise, you can't put together a reasonable schedule or budget.

- Getting accurate estimates from suppliers of materials and equipment requires a clear description of your needs and a careful review of the vendors' capabilities.

- Establish a good relationship with the procurement department, and learn its procedures before you need to procure anything.

- Always check out the vendors before you sign a contract.

Getting the Plan Approved

Okay, you've assembled a charter, a work breakdown structure (WBS), a network diagram, a schedule, a description of the team you require, and a budget. You understand the activities for the plan and the resources needed. And you have determined how you want to integrate the project's deliverables into operations after it is completed. After all this effort, you may feel that what you want to do is start working on the project, but you're not finished yet. That's right: you need to get your plan approved before you can start working.

This chapter reminds you of all the good reasons for planning in the first place and provides advice for getting your project plan approved so you can start working. Don't fret. You are almost ready. With an approved plan in hand, you'll finally be ready to start working on the project.

In This Chapter

- The importance of planning
- A last-minute reality check
- Putting the whole plan together
- Selling the plan to management and getting it approved
- After approval

Reasons to Plan in the First Place

Sometimes people complain that plans take too much time. They would rather start to work on the project than think about the plan. Some people think that plans are created only because other people want to see them. Your boss asks for a plan, so you write one. The customers want a plan, so you draft something to make them happy. Plans prepared carelessly rather than thoughtfully are a waste of time for the reader as well as the writer. Plans written only for the benefit of someone else rarely meet their goals of guiding the project to a successful conclusion. However, one of the biggest problems in business today—not just in projects but everywhere—is an attitude of ready, fire, aim. Don't get caught in that mentality.

 WORDS FROM THE WISE

One of life's most painful moments comes when we must admit that we didn't do our homework, that we were not prepared.

—Merlin Olsen, member of the Pro Football Hall of Fame

Finally, if you're not going to take planning seriously, don't bother. Just remember that without a good plan, you're like a surgeon who decides to remove an appendix with a can opener. You'll likely get the offending organ out, but you'll also make a mess of things in the process.

A good plan can help you avoid most problems, but not all. Even so, you should know that no amount of planning will make your project go exactly as you planned. Your plan will go off course because of things you didn't know in advance, and every project will encounter some things that cause you to deviate from the plan. Of course, you won't be able to think of everything. Remember, every project is unique, so you will be learning as you go. However, the better plan, the more likely you'll get where you want to go. And the better you keep the plan up to date, the more likely you'll be able to make the best adjustments to keep the project on course.

The Reality Check Before Approval

Before submitting the plan for final approval, you need to perform one last *cross-check* of your planning efforts within the project team. This involves a line-by-line matching up of the WBS, schedule, budget, and network diagram, assuming you created these pieces. Computer-based planning software can help by finding conflicting dates and durations on the critical path, missing links (only if they're entered correctly), and missing activity data. Even when you use a software program, however, always check the logistics and flow of your project personally and carefully—don't assume everything is accurate.

For more detailed information on cross-checking, refer to *PMBOK Guide* **section 4.2.**

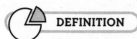 **DEFINITION**

> One of the best tests of completion, whether for the doors on an airplane or the workability of a project plan, is **cross-checking.** To cross-check a plan, one person lists a procedure and another verifies it. With two people carefully verifying the plan, chances for errors greatly diminish.

You can get your project team to help you with this effort. Run all steps of the plan past your core team members before asking approval. The final fine-tuning of the project plan is no exception. After all, if you missed something, others might be able to fill in the gaps. If you've asked the impossible of a team member, you'll have an opportunity to hear about it before the work starts.

Follow these steps for cross-checking a project plan:

1. Match the activities, durations, and dates to the schedule.

2. Match the resources to the schedule.

3. Match the activity to those shown in the WBS.

4. Verify the numbers on the budget, and check to make sure they match your existing estimate.

5. Study the activities on the critical path. Do any activities require more time? Have you separated the labor required from the duration on each activity?

6. Verify that the milestones (if you chose to include them) make sense as a means of highlighting the key points in a project.

7. Confirm that the start and finish dates are still reasonable. Also verify that you have accounted for all holidays and vacations in the schedule.

If you utilized a project management software program, it is much easier to cross-check a project. If you are not convinced you need to cross-check, you might consider rereading earlier chapters on why these components are important. If you're unwilling to prepare this level of detail in plans, whether formal or informal, be prepared for some surprises. A plan is an absolute requirement of success in project management.

What to Do If Discrepancies Appear

Inevitably, discrepancies will appear in the cross-checking process. As you might expect, larger projects tend to have more mistakes than smaller, simple ones. After finding the errors, you must modify the plan to correct them. If your plan requires significant modifications due to omissions or changes, perform the cross-check from scratch one more time after the changes are made. It's always possible to "fix" errors by introducing new ones. For that reason, review your notes from the previous process, and do it again.

One way to encourage review is to have a dedicated wall or cubicle where you can display the latest project data. Team members can check it and flag changes or problems. Team meetings take up a lot of time, so you should limit them. In today's networked world, you might consider an internet collaboration site and tools to share project information, but don't let a site and tools replace your involvement as project manager.

 TIME IS MONEY

> An efficient way to present a plan is with a summary presentation backed up by hard copies of a Gantt chart, WBS, worksheets, and network diagram. Presenting a management overview hopefully will avoid a line-item review of each activity, its schedule, and its budget. If it comes to that, however, the backup data you've provided will do the trick.

Other Last-Minute Issues to Consider

Upon integrating the various components of the project plan, you might find issues that you have not addressed in your other planning efforts. Not all of these are worthy of an activity in the plan, but if you ignore them or don't address them somewhere in the schedule, the project will suffer. Typical things that get left out of the plan but shouldn't include the following:

- **Space and facilities.** Do you have basic office, manufacturing, or other accommodations arranged that are suitable for your team? Do these costs appear in the budget?

- **Transportation.** Does your team need transportation above and beyond normal commuting, such as air travel and accommodations to other locations, and have you budgeted for this?

- **Permissions.** Do you require written or at least verbal permission to use specialized equipment, to trespass on private property, to cross international borders, or to do something similar? Remember that these activities will take time to complete.

- **Licenses, permits, and clearances.** Do you need official permission to use hazardous chemicals, to block access to a structure or roadway, to enter restricted government facilities, to move confidential equipment or materials, or to do something similar?

- **Insurance.** Are your team and other resources underwritten for accidents and infringements that might occur? If insurance is required, what existing policies protect you, and how can you fill the gaps with additional coverage?

- **Weather.** How will the weather impact your plan? Can you hold the dates together if rain or snow delay construction, hinder delivery of materials and equipment, or impact team member performance? If severe weather would create a danger to your team, do you have an evacuation plan in place to move them to a secure location?

- **Project management activities.** It is remarkable, but not surprising, that sometimes project managers forget to identify and schedule the various tasks and activities required to manage a project. Be sure to include them in your plan.

For more information on activities to manage and control the project, refer to *PMBOK Guide* sections 4.3, 4.4, and 4.5.

These are just some of the more common risk factors that might impact your project's timely completion. Before reviewing your plan for approval, make sure you have accounted for the time to manage these situations in your plan.

Putting It All Together

Project planning documents are interrelated. If you make a change to one, you need to adapt the rest. For example, if you make a change to the scope of the project, it will affect the work that needs to be done, the schedule, the budget, and perhaps the project team members you will need to complete the new scope of work. If you don't keep the plan up to date, it doesn't matter how good the initial plan was. An out-of-date plan is a statement of what didn't happen—not a guide for the future. Typically, the plan will also include narrative and organizing information to help readers (and team members) understand how the entire project fits together. The complete project plan for a large project might include a table of contents like the following example:

1. Executive Summary of the Project (or Project Overview)

2. Project Objectives

3. Project Assumptions and Risks

4. Project Milestones

5. Risk Analysis

6. Project Organization

7. Project Budget

8. Quality Assurance Standards

9. Contact Points and Information Sources (if relevant)

10. Project Approvals

There is no magic formula for the right level of detail in the plan. If your project involves a large number of people and millions of dollars, you want to develop a detailed plan that allows you to coordinate the myriad resources properly.

The project planning stage dominates almost one third of this book, but the actual time required to complete the plan (including the work plan, resource assignments, schedule, and budget) is usually about 20 to 25 percent of the total time devoted to the project. But the quality and thought that goes into a plan, not the time, determines its value in the project management process. This is why it's so important to understand the issues in creating each component of the plan as I've covered them in previous chapters.

Use the following project checklist to see whether you have all the plans ready for the review and approval process.

Project Planning Phase

❏ A. Develop project plan

   ❏ 1. Finalize scope definition

      ❏ a. Project objectives

      ❏ b. Project requirements and specifications

   ❏ 2. Develop work breakdown structure (WBS)

      ❏ a. Identify work activities and milestones

   ❏ 3. Develop organization breakdown structure

      ❏ a. Match project work activities and performing personnel

   ❏ 4. Work out project scheduling and cost estimating

      ❏ a. Identify activity dependencies

      ❏ b. Sequence activities

      ❏ c. Develop project schedule

      ❏ d. Estimate costs

      ❏ e. Develop budget/funding profile

      ❏ f. Determine scheduled start dates

      ❏ g. Set project milestones

      ❏ h. Establish measurement baselines for schedule and cost performance (project metrics)

   ❏ 5. Originate subsidiary management plans

      ❏ a. Risk plan

      ❏ b. Issues resolution plan

      ❏ c. Organization and human resources plan

      ❏ d. Procurement plan

      ❏ e. Quality assurance plan

      ❏ f. Project change control plan

   ❏ 6. Develop organization transition plan

      ❏ a. Project communication plan

      ❏ b. Change management plan

   ❏ 7. Deliver project plan memorandum to decision authority

Conducting a Peer Review

Gather a group of qualified people who can review your project plan and give you feedback on various facets. They will each have a different perspective on the plan and may point out risks or activities that you and your team may have overlooked. See Chapter 23 for more on conducting a peer review.

For more detailed information on peer reviews, refer to *PMBOK Guide* section 13.2.2.1.

NOTES FROM THE FIELD

In a peer review, you are asking the reviewers to look at the project from a technical point of view. Keep the focus of the peer review technical in nature. Technically, you want people to identify any risks that you haven't thought of. Or you may want their advice on how your mitigation strategy will help if a risk does occur. You would also like them to identify any tasks or activities that they believe are missing from the project plan. Often, when you work on a plan for a while, you mentally "fill in the blanks" without realizing it. People with a fresh view will not suffer from that symptom and can bring a great perspective to the review process.

Reviewing the Plan with the Key Stakeholders

By using the strategy I have outlined in this chapter, you are not only getting a project plan approved, you are beginning the process of engaging with key stakeholders. During the individual reviews, you should be attempting to presell the project and the plan you have put together. Any concerns that a stakeholder might have should be addressed by your plan and highlighted, if appropriate, during the formal presentation. It is important that these key people recognize that you are listening to them and acting on the advice they are providing. This approach will begin building goodwill with these key stakeholders, and that goodwill will undoubtedly become important later on as the project progresses.

Getting the key stakeholders involved in reviewing the project plan may require one or more structured meetings and probably advance preparation by each of the team members. As you prepare to present the information to the sponsor, steering committee, or whatever governance board will ultimately approve the project plan, put yourself in their place. What will they want to know? How can you best address their needs and concerns as you prepare to move into project execution? Who among your team members will they want to hear from and question about the project plan? Answer these questions before you prepare your materials for the meeting.

RISK MANAGEMENT

While you work on a plan, your project might change in relevance, and you might be plugging away at something currently as important as yesterday's newspaper. Avoid this problem by continually feeding progress reports to your project sponsor and other key stakeholders during planning. And learn to take the company's pulse on a regular basis to see how the business climate might be changing to ensure that the business case for the project is still valid.

As you prepare to review the plan with key stakeholders, first consider how formal the project plan needs to be for this preliminary review. Also, think about how the key decision maker(s) in the group like to see information. For example, many people respond very well to charts, graphs, and models. Others need pages of written text with only the occasional diagram thrown in. Again, tailor the information to the person that will be reviewing the plan ahead of the formal presentation.

This presentation can also be a test of how the larger steering committee will want to be briefed on the project as you progress, so pay attention to what they like about the way you present your project plan, what they don't like, and the types of questions they ask. Their reactions will give you clues on how to present the information in the formal presentation for approval.

You should also know how much detail you will need to provide. Sometimes in a preliminary review like this, the stakeholder will not want a lot of detail. If that's the case, leave the details out of the plan, but bring along any supporting information you have prepared. That way, if they ask you a question, you can respond quickly without having to say "I'll have to get back to you with that."

As you review, take good notes and review them with the key stakeholder before you finish. You want to make sure that you can address any concerns they might have about your project in the formal approval meeting.

Finally, proceed through the key stakeholders by moving from least important (if there is such a thing) to most important. That way, you will have added or changed some things that may be critical for the most important stakeholders to assess.

Presenting the Project Plan

Before you present your project for final approval, study the presentation from the point of view of the preliminary reviews with key stakeholders. Is the presentation clear and organized? Is the level of presentation appropriate for the scope of the project? Did the project sponsor review the presentation and suggest any changes?

When you present the plan to the steering committee, be prepared to justify your choices, dates, and budgets. You may need a compelling reason why each activity is required and the associated budget justified. (Even if the reviewers don't ask, you should be prepared.) Also, be prepared to talk about risks and contingencies if things go wrong. Most of these should have come up during the preliminary reviews with key stakeholders.

Use judgment in what you present from the plan. Always start with an overview of the plan, and then move on to details. Remember, the people who approve the plan will have a copy of the complete document to review anyway; you don't need to go over every detail in the presentation. The goals of the presentation are to present the overall structure and objectives of the project, to answer questions, and to establish your credibility as the project manager (and project planner).

Too much detail in the presentation can be as damaging as too little. If you present too many details in your presentation, you'll be bombarded with questions and arguments from management about the details. Ask your sponsor to give you direction on the level of detail. Consider using milestone summaries of activities so that management sees the big picture during your presentation. Keep the meeting short (one hour, if possible) and focused. Senior managers usually dislike meeting for longer than an hour. Keep it crisp, but make time for their searching questions and time to get their approval. While you would like them to hold their questions until you finish, don't be surprised if they begin asking questions in the middle of the presentation.

The result of your presentation will be either the approval (by signature) of the project or a request to make revisions. If you've done a good job in the review meetings, revisions may not be necessary. If you've done a good job of planning, you'll have to communicate this fact to the people who approve and sign off on the plans.

At the conclusion of the review process with the steering committee or governance board, get the project plan formally signed by the project sponsor and any other appropriate stakeholders on the steering committee. You should view the project plan as a contract between you and the project steering committee and just like any contract, all the appropriate people need to sign it to make it binding.

 NOTES FROM THE FIELD

In the real world, the plan for a large project (or even a small one) will go through multiple versions on its way to approval. Sometimes the steering committee will tell the project team to go back and make changes. Don't think of that as a failure! These plans may be debated, discussed, enhanced, expanded, and revised several times until the project plan is complete and approved.

Plan Approval

The final step before the ship sails, so to speak, is getting the project and its cross-checked plan approved by the people paying the bills. The people who approve the plan will vary by company, project, and assignment. As mentioned in Chapter 6 when I discussed the stakeholders on the project, make sure you know who will approve the work and the budget for the project. Sometimes multiple departments will be involved. Sometimes you'll get to sign the approval sheet on your own. In any case, the most important aspect of the approval is getting the money freed up (the budget) so you can start work on the project.

Finally, you get great news: your plan is approved. They've signed on the dotted line. The accounting department has assigned a budget number and account codes for the project. You're ready to go!

The plan you created and got approved isn't the only plan you'll use during your project. You'll typically have three or more versions of the plan during the course of a project. First, there is the original approved plan, which is usually called the baseline plan. Second is the actual plan, which reflects the actual work accomplished to date. Third is the future schedule based on work to be completed during the project. You could also have a number of contingency plans developed for a complex project over time.

Just remember to keep the plans numbered or dated and up to date. A good computer program should be able to manage multiple versions of the project plan at a time so you can compare various stages of the project as you proceed.

From Plan to Action, Finally

After getting a plan approved, it might seem like you've done an awful lot of work and still not gotten anything done. The central role of the plan in the project management process often leads people to the mistaken conclusion that the creation of the plan is project management. But it's not. Most of the time spent in project management involves management. As you've already surmised, project management involves much more than just a plan.

Still, don't be surprised if people identify your project management skills with your ability to create an impressive-looking project plan. Worse things could happen, and as long as they pay you for it, well, you don't have to tell them that it wasn't really that hard.

 WORDS FROM THE WISE

The longer a project's duration, the less likely that changes in organizational priorities and happenstance will allow it to reach completion as originally planned.

—A project manager's standard axiom

You'll soon get to work and put your approved plan into action. Most project managers will tell you that planning a project is the easy part; executing the plan is the real work! Now the execution or implementation phase is about to begin. In the next phase, I'll show you how to take the baseline and create both plans that reflect work done and schedules for remaining work. But that's to come. For now, just enjoy your completion of a demanding phase of project management.

Review Questions

- Have I done a cross-check on the project plan to discover any discrepancies?

- Do I have the framework for putting the plan together for review?

- Did I review and presell the project plan to key stakeholders?

- Have I drafted a presentation and reviewed it with my sponsor with enough time to make changes before the steering committee review and approval?

- Do I have the right level of backup information available in case of questions?

- Is my project team ready to go when the plan is approved?

The Least You Need to Know

- You need to cover all your bases in planning. Don't forget to include the team's transportation, food, and lodging expenses.

- Always analyze risky activities. If a less-risky approach is possible, modify the plan to accommodate it.

- Scrutinize all planning documents from the WBS to the network diagram to ensure that they match and work together.

- You'll probably have to present your plan to management and customers before it gets approved, and it probably won't get approved the first time around.

- You must sell your plan to the stakeholders and get their commitment to the plan, its schedule, and perhaps its budget before starting work on the project.

The Execution Phase

Well, you've done it! You've defined a project and gotten the plan approved. You're ready to begin, and the beginning is a very crucial time in any project. If you begin the execution phase (also commonly called the *implementation phase*) of the project the right way, it enhances your likelihood for success.

The execution phase of a project is where all the work actually happens. To start toward the finish line, you must first get your team aligned to deliver the work that you have planned so carefully. To do that, this part of the book tells you how to establish your leadership, organize the team with clear roles and responsibilities for top performance, institute operating guidelines, and provide good communications that keep all your stakeholders informed and supportive as the project unfolds.

Getting Started on the Right Track

At this point, you now have an approved project plan in hand. You have identified most of the key team members, sought permission to use them, and established a budget and a source of funds to pay them. You're ready to get started. Here is the way to do so.

For most projects, everyone who will participate in the project will have questions. These questions are answered at the project kickoff event and the first project meetings with the team and individuals. These activities are the first steps in the execution phase of any project. The kickoff meeting serves to get everyone in sync with each other and to build a feeling of team spirit. The project kickoff is like the locker-room pep talk before a big game. It gets the juices flowing, reinforces the goals for the project, and gets the team lined up to win the prize.

In this chapter, I tell you how to hold a project kickoff meeting that motivates the team and gets everyone moving in the same direction—toward the project finish. You also see how to make the first project meetings part of the key strategy in your project game plan.

In This Chapter

- Kicking off the project
- Making sure the first project meeting goes smoothly
- Getting project members coordinated and enthused
- Managing global projects

Always Get Your Own Act Together First!

Before you have the kickoff meeting, consider both your leadership style and your management tactics; the two are intertwined and are central to the implementation of projects. Your leadership skills and the appropriateness of the management tactics you adopt for each of the various people on your project team are of paramount importance in achieving project goals. The first time you get to try out these strategies and tactics may be at the kickoff event.

 TIME IS MONEY

Remember, you will never have everything completely in place, and changes will be coming no matter how carefully you have planned things (I'll talk more about changes in Chapter 22).

In Chapter 17, you'll learn a lot more about becoming a leader on your project. I mention it now only because, to get a project kicked off, you must be both a manager and a leader. Use the project kickoff to gain the trust and respect of the project team so people feel comfortable taking your direction. You can also use the kickoff to explain the reports and administrative procedures you'll use to help people get work done on time and within budget.

For more information on managing project teams, refer to *PMBOK Guide* **section 9.4.2.4.**

Doing It Now and Doing It Right

After you've decided you're really ready, you need to decide how to kick off your project. Whether handled formally or informally, the kickoff events of the project need to accomplish the following objectives:

- Communicate the goals of the project to all team members to ensure that everyone is crystal clear on her contribution to the project.

- Attain the commitment you need for the project and get people enthusiastic about making things happen.

- Establish the leadership style for the project and get the team ready to follow you.

- Identify critical deadlines and milestones within the project.

- Review the overall schedule and work plan with the appropriate team members.

- Explain basic operating procedures, including required reports, meetings, and other ongoing communications necessary between you and other team members (I'll talk about that in more detail in Chapter 18).

- Explicitly give the people responsible for the initial tasks the approval to begin work on the project.

If you add all these objectives together, you'll see that the overall goal of the execution phase is to establish a set of conditions so work can be accomplished. These conditions start with clear communications about the plan and other procedures associated with your project. The project kickoff is the first step in opening up the channels.

The Formal Kickoff

Although some projects don't require more than a small meeting and a memo to get started, when a formal project kickoff event is appropriate, make it both celebratory and informative.

The type of event will depend on the size, importance, organization, and budget for the project. Use your judgment. Look at the kinds of events given in your company for similar projects and ask about the events that worked and the ones that didn't.

To help set the tone, develop an agenda for the meeting and distribute it to all who will attend a couple of days before the meeting.

RISK MANAGEMENT

If a customer is paying the bill, keep the event as simple and economical as possible and still accomplish your mission. One more reminder: if you hold the kickoff in a public place, make sure the competition is out of earshot.

It's a Go

Regardless of the sophistication or format of the kickoff event, the event should put team members on notice that the project is a "go." It should emphasize that each individual's contribution is vital to the success of the project. The kickoff event can also help individuals relate their goals and work responsibilities within the overall project to the efforts of other team members. This is a first step in establishing a "team" spirit.

In more formal kickoff meetings, always schedule the event so your project sponsor and all other stakeholders, customers (if appropriate), managers, and key team members can participate.

Give the sponsor a spotlight (most of them love it) to endorse the project and "wave the flag." Remember the support of senior management is a critical success factor for projects. Seeing and hearing from one of the executives from the organization gives the whole project team a sense that the company really means business regarding this project.

The kickoff event should also establish the priorities, tone, and energy for the project. Avoid too many individual details; leave those for the first project meetings and one-on-one sessions with key project players. These meetings should take place during the first week after the project kickoff event.

For more information on organizing the team, refer to *PMBOK Guide* **section 9.1.2.1.**

NOTES FROM THE FIELD

In my role as a coach for project managers, I am sometimes invited to attend meetings as the project begins the execution phase. One of the gaps that I often see with less-experienced project managers is clarity around responsibilities for tasks that cut across organizational lines. In one example, the operations team members understand that the project team members are responsible for developing reports. However, the project team needs the operations team members to explain how they will use the reports so they can be formatted correctly. However, neither side understands that this task takes both of them to complete it. Instead, they work in isolation and complain about the lack of responsiveness of the other side's team members.

Between Kickoff and Team Meeting: Using the Time Wisely

The time between the project kickoff and the first formal project meeting (I would recommend three days to a week between events) gives team members time to reflect on their roles. Feedback after the kickoff event is invaluable to plugging up holes in the project plan. During the period before the first project meeting, team members may approach you with questions or problems.

Based on any feedback, you can fine-tune your project plan and look into problems team members throw at you. You can also run issues and problems by senior management to level out small issues before they turn into major problems. Gathering feedback allows you to come to the first project meeting prepared with answers to objections and explanations of issues that were inadequately addressed in the plan.

During that time, set up what project managers usually call a "war room." Often this is a conference room that is reserved for the exclusive use of the project team for the duration of the project. It should be outfitted with phones, internet or intranet connections, and plenty of wall space to post information. Project members should be able to come here at any time and work, and other members of the company can stop by and see what's going on. Although it is not top secret, you should also have cabinets with locks on them to store sensitive material.

The First Project Meeting

After the kickoff event, you're finally underway! Schedule the first team meeting to take place approximately one week after the kickoff. This first meeting will be the first true test of your leadership skills as the project manager.

Invite all working members of the project implementation team. (Do not invite customers and the executive management team.) Since this first team project review meeting is a meeting to get work started, it should accomplish the following.

1. Establish a model for future meetings by doing the following:

    -   Start on time.

    -   Before the meeting, develop and distribute an agenda of topics and ask people to review them before they come.

    -   Conduct one agenda item at a time, and conclude it before moving on to the next item. (Avoid getting hung up on the order of topics.) Establish a "parking lot" for items that come up that are not on the topic. Write the list on a white board or piece of chart paper and label it "Parking Lot." Before adjourning the meeting, decide when you will handle these items (for example, a future meeting, assignment to one or more people, and so on).

    -   Encourage open communication; meetings give individuals a chance to express ideas.

    -   Take notes. Really the only notes that are probably relevant are action items assigned to people with due dates and any decisions made by the team.

    -   Establish time and place for the next project team meeting. I recommend you try to establish a regular meeting time, such as every Tuesday afternoon at 3:00. It's much easier for people to manage their schedules if they know that for the duration of the project, they need to devote their Tuesday afternoons to the project meetings.

    -   Agree on and reiterate any follow-up activities or required action items. Assign people to these tasks and get their commitment to complete them, including a time frame for completion.

    -   End the meeting on time. If you need to stretch the meeting a little longer, ask the group for permission and decide *how much longer* you will meet. When that time is up, close the meeting down.

- Distribute (brief) minutes to all attendees within two days of the meeting that covers any decisions reached.

- Make sure the minutes indicate action items and responsibilities so people don't conveniently forget what they agreed to do in the meeting.

2. Introduce the members of the team and their project roles.

3. Review the first priorities for the project and repeat or reiterate briefly the other objectives and overall schedule.

4. Review individual plans for getting work started.

5. Discuss methods and tools you will use to manage, control, and operate the project.

6. Deal with objections to the current project plan, and work them out if possible.

7. If the group needs to make decisions, follow these steps:

   - Discuss the problems and seek opinions from all.

   - Don't allow one person to dominate the discussion.

   - Test for readiness to make a decision.

   - Make the decision.

   - Assign roles and responsibilities.

Here is an example of how minutes might look after a project team meeting:

Project Team Meeting Minutes

Meeting: Project Team

Date: 02/07/2014

Time: 2:30–3:30 P.M.

Chair: Bob Braveheart

Attendees: Kim Winford
  Jo College
  Ben Adminovich
  Joe Goniski
  Mary Scarlotti
  John Andreotti (by phone)

Decisions:

Agreed to the case for change and the business case for the project.

Items	Person Responsible	Date	Status
Action Items:			
Research vendors to build	Kim Winford	2/07/2014	Completed the server rooms
Investigate the credit policy	Ben Adminovich	2/07/2014	Completed as reported by the project team
Review requirements for new billing system with Accounting	Joe Goniski	2/07/2014	In progress
Submit RFP for laptops	John Andreotti	2/07/2014	In progress
Analyze reporting needs for management team	Bob Braveheart	1/31/2014	In progress
Parking Lot:			
Question of data entry	Project manager Project sponsor	4/15/2014	Parked
GUI interface for customers	Project manager	4/15/2014	
Data storage and data mining	Parked until late May	3/30/2014	Parked

In beginning a project, it is important that your team realize that it is a team. In teams, specific things happen through your leadership and management. Team members need to understand and do the following:

- Realize they'll be working on tasks that involve more than one person, meaning they must communicate with each other.

- Identify and solve problems together and then live with the results. That includes supporting the solutions publicly and not complaining if it wasn't their answer.

- Accept the fact that if one person makes a mistake while working on the project, the entire team may suffer. That means they need to support each other to prevent mistakes if possible.

- Recognize that changes will occur to the project over time, and the team must be flexible enough to adjust.

One-on-Ones: The Individual Starting Events

In addition to the kickoff and the first project meeting, you'll also need to meet with key individuals at the beginning of the project to make sure they have all the information they need to get started. These initial meetings with new players may continue throughout the project as different aspects of the project get underway.

Use formal meetings with project team members, known as *one-on-ones*, to clarify priorities and to discuss schedules and plans. Many of these people will have worked with you on the project plan already, so you won't need to go over all the details with them. However, you will need to turn their focus away from planning and start delegating work to them so things start happening. This is a great place to review the network diagram and show each team member how her work fits into the broad project plan for the project. For larger projects, you may have your team leaders conduct these types of meetings with the people they will supervise. If at all possible, attend these meetings, but only as a resource if there are questions that only you could answer. Let the team leaders do their job with their team.

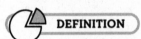

> **DEFINITION**
>
> **One-on-ones** are meetings (often scheduled and formal) between two people involved in a project. These meetings are used to discuss priorities, to resolve issues, and to communicate overall responsibilities to the project.

Make sure you also schedule these one-on-ones with key players on a regular basis throughout the project. For a short project, the one-on-ones with key personnel might happen daily or weekly. For a longer project with more players, the formal one-on-ones might be monthly or even less frequent depending on your other level of interactions.

In the first one-on-one meetings, clarify and review the following with each individual:

- Reasons she was selected

- Performance expectations

- Individual priorities, tasks, and milestones

- Administrative procedures and project management methods and tools in use, such as reporting of progress on work packages and time covering both frequency and level of detail you want in those reports

- Challenges and issues

- Processes for solving problems

- A schedule for future one-on-one meetings

- Action items for future meetings

Always take notes in these meetings, and suggest the other participant does the same.

Setting the Right Expectations

Your ability to organize and control the first team meetings will be a major step in establishing your leadership of the project team. If you do this well, the meetings will serve as a model for subsequent project meetings and will set a tone of open communication and professionalism that will make managing your project a lot easier. If you waste time in the meetings, you'll also lose credibility as the project manager. The number-one criticism of most meetings is that they don't produce anything of value. Don't let that happen to your meetings. Preparation, organization, and focus are critical to making the first team meetings a success.

Start from the end result you want to achieve during any project meeting and work backward. Express this as a written goal for the meeting and get everyone to agree to it before you start. Examples of what you are trying to achieve might be the following:

- Are you defining issues or making a decision?

- If the team is making a decision, are the decision makers present and properly prepared to make a decision?

- If the team is discussing issues to be worked on, are the proper people present to make work assignments?

- Do the meeting participants have the necessary content knowledge experts present?

For more on establishing team expectations, refer to *PMBOK Guide* **section 9.3.3.1.**

Information Everyone Needs to Get Started

The purpose of the kickoff and the initial team and one-on-one meetings is to inform people and get them in sync with the project plan. From the beginning, people who work on the project need access to relevant information in the plan so they can do their jobs. Tasks and schedules should never be a secret (although budget and other financial information may be held confidential when people aren't responsible for the costs). The project plan should generally be an open book to help guide people to the promised deliverable.

During the initial stages of the project, provide every member of the team with access to the plan and make it available on an internal team website. You can do this before the kickoff event, in a team meeting, or during a one-on-one at the very start of the project. For team members who will remain with the project from the beginning, I recommend identifying the location of these documents prior to the kickoff event and then discussing them in the first project meeting and one-on-one sessions. As new team members join the project during later stages, make sure they get the information as well.

Every team member needs the following pieces of information from the project plan in order to contribute appropriately to the project:

- **A summary of the overall project goals.** The project summary outlines and explains the purpose of the project, its goals, and the overall schedule.

- **The team member's role and task assignments.** Lay out in writing the specific tasks and milestones for each team member. At the beginning, keep the milestones and task overview general and have specific tasks introduced by you or other supervisors and managers at a later date. Also, tell team members that you require regular status reports. Explain why the reports are essential to tracking the project and keeping it on time and within budget. Set the report intervals for weekly, biweekly, or monthly intervals, depending on the nature of the project.

- **A list of who's who on the project.** The directory or list of key project team members should include a description of each team member, her role (and title) in the project, and contact information (telephone numbers, office location, and email addresses).

NOTES FROM THE FIELD

Projects increasingly are becoming virtually staffed by transient, dispersed teams. Achieving the potential of the project under these conditions requires distributed project leadership using "virtual walking around" techniques via computer networks, video conferencing, and the internet. These techniques help people communicate, collaborate, and manage shared activities in an integrated way.

For more on virtual teams, refer to *PMBOK Guide* **section 9.2.2.4.**

In addition to information about the project plan, you need to inform every team member of the administrative procedures that will affect her life: reports, forms, legal documents, and so on. Don't drown team members in reports. If your reports to them are crisp and timely, their reports will be on time and accurate. For a large project, you may want to provide a "Project Administration Handbook" on the project website that assembles examples of all the forms, reports, and other documents required from project personnel, along with other relevant documentation of the project plan. For small projects, a simple list and an example report will probably do the job.

If confidentiality or other legal agreements are required for your project, now is the time to get them signed. If your organization contracts with the military or other government agencies, rules may be more strict. Look into the proper forms of agreement and reporting that are required and ensure that the appropriate team members understand the requirements at the beginning of the project.

Managing Global Projects

Having a project manager who must manage a global project is not as unique as it used to be. I am defining a "global project" as one that crosses boundaries between countries and is staffed by people from those countries. They often have different languages (although fortunately for many of us, the common language of business is English), and they certainly have different cultures.

Global projects, by their very nature, require a high level of sensitivity and awareness by the project manager. What may seem totally acceptable in one culture will not be acceptable elsewhere. You need to consider these areas when you face the management of a global project. If members of your team are in multiple locations, be sure to also build in travel to these other locations. The best way to establish relationships is for team members to meet you in person— particularly at the beginning of the project.

Schedule

The schedule that you must develop for team meetings, for example, needs to take into consideration national holidays in the various locations where your project team is located, which will vary greatly. In some cases, the work week itself may be different. For example, the work week in many countries in the Middle East is Saturday through Thursday, and the work week in France is only 35 hours compared to the 40-hour week we generally take for granted in the United States.

Also, with time zones that can be several hours apart, including when daylight savings time begins, planning how people who need to communicate and work together can be a challenge. In one project I managed, some of the people were in Indonesia, which was exactly 12 hours difference from our location in Houston, Texas. It meant that someone would be up late at night (and early in the morning) anytime we had a full team meeting.

Budget

With a global team, there will obviously be additional travel expenses. You will want to visit the project sites regularly, and you will want at least some of the team leaders to come to you to meet together occasionally. You will need to factor that into your budget and track it carefully. You can eliminate some of the travel costs using video conferencing, but again, find out what charges you will incur when you use those facilities.

Technology

Using technology to link the team members can be a tremendous help. However, plan carefully and arrange for a collaboration project site so team members can save their work and provide access to others who may need to see it or build on it. In providing a collaboration site, consider security and access rights so the information you want to keep confidential (the pay rates of contractors, for example) stays confidential. Also, you may want to limit the access to some people to "read only," while others may have the right to edit materials. Finally, a common convention for naming and managing version control while the project is progressing will be critical to preventing problems later on.

Quality

Since you will not be on location to supervise much of the work being produced as part of the project, you will need to have a robust quality plan (covered in Chapter 23). Make sure your team members know how you will measure the quality of their performance. Also, a global project will require your team to have strong processes for the way work is produced and tracked, including problem resolution. They will not be able to walk over a few desks and confer with their teammates when a problem arises like they would if they were co-located. All these issues need to be clearly communicated from the very beginning of the project.

Human Resources

In other countries, you may need to comply with other national or regional laws as you manage your team members. For example, bringing members of your team to various locations may require visas for work-related activities. It's a good idea to find someone within your company's human resources department who can advise you on these kinds of issues, or hire a consultant with the background and experience to advise you on the correct course of action. You will need to know the rules from the first team meetings.

> **RISK MANAGEMENT**
>
> Do your homework to make sure you're familiar with certain customs. We know one project manager who had a kickoff meeting with his team at a local steakhouse that was known for great food. Unfortunately, part of the team consisted of people from India who would not even enter a steakhouse let alone eat there, and, as a result, refused to attend the opening team dinner.

Procurement

Many countries will require you to purchase a certain amount of materials from the local or national economy, which you will need to factor into your budget. However, if those types of rules are also combined with a poor location infrastructure, you should consider that in your risk analysis. The best example is a project manager I met from Egypt who was managing a project in Sudan. His supplies were regularly disrupted due to the continuous eruption of civil war there. Because of local laws, the project manager had to cope with local vendors who could not deliver at certain times. Again, getting expert advice from within your company or from a knowledgeable consultant is your best course of action in developing your procurement plan and negotiating the contracts.

Review Questions

- Am I ready to begin to execute the project plan?

- Do I understand how formal my project kickoff needs to be? Do I have the agenda for that meeting to help make it successful?

- Who else should attend the kickoff besides the project team?

- Have I set the right expectations within the project team on what I expect from them?

- Do I have the right collaboration tools in place for the team?

- Are the team members located in different places? Have I considered how I will manage the work and the people?

The Least You Need to Know

- Getting a project started right involves communication.
- All projects need starting events that clarify project goals, responsibilities, and operating procedures. These events can be simple or elaborate but should always be commensurate with the size and importance of the project.
- Prior to the first project team meeting, have team members review the project and point out any holes in your plan that need patching.
- Focused, productive, and informative team and individual meetings are the best way to get things started on the right track.
- Managing a global project team will require extra thought and effort on your part.

Leadership: Providing Direction

Since it's up to your project team to complete the work specified in the plan, you, as the project manager, must employ appropriate methods to motivate, coordinate, facilitate, and administer your team. If you don't, the work may never get done. As a project manager, you must also identify and implement the appropriate leadership style to keep the team motivated, which is what you learn about in this chapter.

The Importance of Establishing Your Leadership

Whether managing the remodeling of a major hotel in downtown New York City or the installation of a new software package for the company, you must take command if you are going to lead your project to success. You can use every technique in this book, but without assuming a leadership role for the project, you'll get nowhere. Being a leader and the manager of the project are two distinctly different roles.

In This Chapter

- Establishing your role as leader and manager
- Leading the way for change
- Recognizing the four sources of power
- Competing with other projects for attention
- Leading a technical project when you lack technical expertise
- The ever-changing roles of a project manager

As a leader, you must command respect and take responsibility for guiding the project. One key way to command that respect is to be a trusted and reliable source of information on the project. As a leader, your team will expect you to be honest, competent, and in charge.

RISK MANAGEMENT

Project managers who are technically knowledgeable are sometimes prone to interfere with the work of their team members to the point that they actually become a hindrance. Remember, as a project manager, your job is to lead and manage the project, not approve all the details of the work.

As a manager, you will monitor and control the project through to completion using specific techniques and procedures that establish the framework and structure of the project. You'll review the plan, complete reports, balance the budget, update the plan, fix the schedule, update the plan again, report on the updates to the plan, and yes, update it again. You'll also do a lot of other administrative stuff that will drive you crazy. You'll continue to "manage upward" in keeping the key project stakeholders informed and involved about project decisions.

Some people get so caught up in the management of a project that they forget about leadership. It's possible to complete the management part of the project and not attain the status and influence of a leader. That's why I've written this chapter—to make sure all those project management traits get transformed into leadership skills as well.

For more information on the responsibilities of a project manager, refer to *PMBOK Guide* **section 1.7.1.**

Filling the Big Shoes

You must be a leader who provides strong guidance but at the same time offers a receptive ear to people with problems. Your team members may not always fill the big shoes you've offered them. The well-known Murphy's Law often ensures that anything that can go wrong on projects will, from the tiniest issues to the most colossal.

As a leader, you must also know the plan inside and out and be able to talk to the team about priorities without sounding frustrated or rushed. If a team member has a problem that requires discussion, as a leader, you should always be seen as a resource to seek out rather than as an obstacle to avoid.

Managers go to meetings and complete paperwork. Leaders must gain the trust and respect of the project team. People must feel comfortable taking your directions; otherwise, they'll make up their own course of action. Yes, as a manager, you must develop protocol and administrative procedures for ensuring that work is getting done on time and within budget (coming up in Chapter 18). But establishing yourself as a leader is more important than any report or process.

Your leadership style and management tactics are intertwined and are central to the successful implementation of the project. Your skills and the appropriateness of the management tactics you adopt for each of the various people on your project team are of paramount importance in achieving project goals. Lots of hard-nosed books tell you how to become a leader, but I favor a simple, soft approach involving only eight tips:

- Listen to your people and ask lots of questions.

- Be a reliable source of information when your project team needs it.

- Observe what is going on and take notes.

- Know enough to know that you don't know everything.

- Be available when people need you. If you need to leave for any length of time (such as vacation or extended travel), make sure your team knows how to reach you.

- Make decisions when called upon to make decisions, but also know when to refer decisions to other stakeholders with more authority.

- Delegate the work that needs to be delegated.

- Don't micromanage. You manage the project; your team members must manage their work.

A Style That Gets the Job Done

Business writers have described a wide range of effective leadership styles that can be adapted to meet the needs of different people, organizations, and projects. You need to choose from three basic styles to lead your project—and you might find yourself using all of them during the course of the project:

- *Task-oriented leadership* emphasizes getting the job done and concentrating on methods for assigning and organizing work, making decisions, and evaluating performance.

- *Employee-oriented* or *people-oriented leadership* concentrates on open communication, the development of rapport with team members, and an ongoing direct concern for the needs of subordinates.

- *Reward-based leadership* ties positive feedback and other rewards directly to the work accomplished. The reward-based style assumes that a high level of performance will be maintained if work results in meaningful rewards that correlate directly with the quality of the person's efforts. Rewards include pay and promotion but also encompass support, encouragement, security, and respect from the project manager.

The approach of matching your management style to the specific needs of a situation is often called *situational management* or *contingency theory*. Project managers must effectively apply the best style for the job—whether task-oriented, employee-oriented, or reward-oriented leadership—to meet the needs of individual team members.

As you try to implement a style, don't assume that because you like something done a certain way, your team members will have the same preferences. Individuals differ from one another in experience and personality. Each person has a different concept of how to do the job, who should get credit for the effort, and how each individual should be rewarded for his work. For these reasons, different leadership styles and management methods must be used to monitor and coordinate different projects.

For more on the interpersonal skills required of a project manager, refer to *PMBOK Guide* section 1.7.2.

 NOTES FROM THE FIELD

If you go to Amazon.com and look for books on leadership, you will find more than 90,000 book titles. A lot of people are interested in understanding how leadership works, particularly in business. One of the key roles of a project manager is that of leader. However, you won't find many books on that topic—you have to take the concepts in the book and figure out how to apply them on a project yourself. However, the basis of all leadership is really power and how you get it and how you use it. So pay attention and assess which is the best way for you to access power for your project.

Four Sources of Power for Project Managers

There are four key sources of power for a leader:

1. Expertise: This is a strong source of power—perhaps even the most important of them all. With this power, people will respect you as a leader because you have the following:

- A track record of success that others recognize

- A special knowledge that few have

- Insights and intelligence that others recognize

- Personal integrity and honesty

The power of respect for your expertise takes a long time to establish, but once you have it, it is very powerful indeed.

2. Relationship: This power is based on the relationships you have with others who wield power. These leaders know who you are, and that traditional source of power is transferred to you. The important point for a project manager to remember with this source of power is to continually cultivate each relationship and never take it for granted, since if the relationship disappears, your source of power also disappears.

3. Rhetorical: This source of this power is a strong set of communication skills that allows you to influence the way others think. It includes your ability to explain complex issues in a way that others can understand. As a power source, it allows you the ability to sell ideas to others and negotiate to arrive at the outcome you want to achieve.

4. Reason: This source of power comes from the ability to explain *why* some actions or ideas are key to the success of the project. The ability to logically lay out with a plan or issues provides legitimacy and authority to accomplish your objectives.

Obviously, as a project manager, you would like to have all four sources of power, but if you are honest with yourself, there is one source that is more important. Recognizing the source of your power with key stakeholders is critical in leading a successful project.

How to Lead Change

It may seem odd to talk about leading change as part of a project management book, but if you think about it, all projects are changing the way operations work. Whether the project is the construction of a new facility or the introduction of a new technical system, it is always a change. As project manager, you must lead that change! (If you need to, go back to Chapter 7 and look at the case for change.)

Projects always create changes in a variety of ways, not the least of which are the following:

- Work processes

- Procedures

- Performance expectations

As many experienced project managers will tell you, the operations group that ultimately receives your project will make some crazy assumptions that will only get you into trouble (because they will never admit that they might be the problem!). Here are some things to consider:

First, operations sincerely believes that they do not own the project. Remember the premise from Chapter 1 that stated all projects are implemented to meet business needs. The operations people are the ones who actually have the business need that justified the project in the first place. If they don't own the project, you will always have difficulty defining and achieving success.

Also, most operations people will underestimate the amount of effort it takes to actually get operations ready for the project deliverables. You will often hear the operations managers say statements like "Just give it to me and my people; we're all pretty smart people, and I'm sure we can figure it out." That is a sure recipe for disaster. If it fails, no operations manager will admit that it was his fault that his people weren't ready. It is always the fault of the project and the project manager. (You will learn more about this in Chapter 21.)

Finally, most operations managers will not appreciate the time and money that it takes to evaluate and adjust the business processes to the new reality created by the project deliverables. It will be up to you as project manager to lead that effort and enlist the operations people in the effort. (More about this in Chapter 18, when the discussion returns to the working committee and how to utilize it.)

WORDS FROM THE WISE

A manager's personal style—how good he or she is at exchanging information—contributes more to ... efficiency than the results of any structures or organizational brilliance.

—Mark H. McCormack, founder of the International Management Group, the world's largest sports talent and marketing agency

Hopefully, you can see the power of providing operations with the answers to the questions like you read about in Chapter 7 for the case for change. Immediately, instead of approaching the deliverables of the project reluctantly, you are building an expectation and an excitement around the possibilities and potential of the project. If you deliver (and hopefully you will), by the time you are ready to roll out the final product, the people who would normally be your biggest problem group will be actually begging you to deliver! They will start driving you to deliver it faster, and you might need to slow them down. Wouldn't that be a change?

Building a good case for change answers the basic question "Why are we doing this?" and addresses the reasons for them to not only accept but also support the deliverables of the project. What a change!

Competing with Other Projects for Attention

Conflicts are part of any project, and project managers must be aware of other initiatives that may impact the success of their project. Let's look at some of the concerns that a project manager must attend to.

Lines of Communication

A project manager must set up a method of communicating with the other project managers who have responsibility for these competing initiatives, which may use the same resources as your project. This particularly important when another project's deliverables are key to your ability to deliver your project. The communication can be like the following:

- Holding regular meetings to discuss projects

- Exchanging status reports

- Having lunch with another project manager regularly to catch up on the latest developments

There are other ways, too, but the important consideration is to have some formal process in place. If the communication is too casual or informal, it is likely to get knocked off the agenda rather quickly when time gets precious.

I cover the importance of the communication plan in Chapter 19, but you might consider these other project managers as stakeholders for your project and ask them to consider you a stakeholder in theirs for communication purposes.

Where Do Projects Fit Together?

Rarely does any organization of any size have only one thing going on. Usually there are several, and all compete for time, attention, and resources (including money). Often, you concentrate so hard on making a project successful that you forget it is usually linked to others. For example, if the project will require training for the marketing personnel within the organization, the project manager must know of any other initiatives marketing has going because those initiatives may also have training requirements. Most companies will not be receptive to taking their marketing personnel off the job for extended periods for training regardless of the importance and requirements.

As another example, if the company is doing an upgrade of the financial software package at the same time your project is implementing the customer relationship management (CRM) software, as the project manager you could easily overlook the fact that your data will need to flow over to the financial application for billing and accounting purposes. If you forget to check on their progress, you may find they have made some technical decisions that have an adverse impact on the way the project can send or retrieve data.

Also, you will need to analyze and handle any dependencies or overlaps in timelines so if one project comes off schedule, it will not throw others off, too!

Finally, within most companies, there are the people that they go to regularly to help with important initiatives like projects. These people are great, smart, and respected for their abilities. However, that is the problem—project managers go to the A-list people all the time! Often they will be advising other projects and not just yours.

For more information on what to do about these overlaps, refer to *PMBOK Guide* **section 13.2.1.3.**

You will need to communicate with your project sponsor about such situations. Identify these people and be aware of when they have a heavy workload. If you do not keep these considerations in mind, you may well push them too hard and not get the results you need. So communicating with the sponsor about creative ways to lighten their regular work to give them the proper time to focus on your project may be communication time well spent.

Critical Path Conflict

By its nature, the critical path is very important to your project and to the other projects going on around you. You will need to develop a plan for keeping in touch with those project managers to make sure critical path conflicts don't develop.

In the early stages of planning the projects, no conflict may be apparent, and everyone goes their way to implementation. But experienced project managers know that things rarely stay the same as projects begin to unfold. This is why communication is so important. A change in schedule on one project may suddenly put its critical path in conflict with another project when no conflict existed before!

Keeping Your Project Front and Center

As I discussed for the concept of constraints earlier in the book, one of the risks to your project is lack of the limited resources required for success. There can always be a danger that your funding could be cut to fund another project or that resources could be pulled away to operations to meet their requirements for running the business.

Keeping your project front and center with key stakeholders can be critical. This will include working with your sponsor to fight for your project so you don't lose momentum or visibility, but also keeping your sponsor properly informed so he can handle these issues effectively and efficiently. Remember the tips I gave you in Chapter 7 on managing your sponsor. Those will help in this situation, too!

 WORDS FROM THE WISE

If a project is to succeed, it must have both a motivated project manager and a motivated project team. A project team takes its attitude from the project leader, so one of the greatest motivational tools the project manager possesses is enthusiasm, positive attitude, and confidence.

—From *Human Resource Skills for the Project Manager* by Vijay K. Verma (Project Management Institute, 1996)

Leading a Technical Project When You Don't Have Expertise

You don't have to have technical knowledge to provide leadership on a technical project or to supervise engineers working in a discipline you know little or nothing about. Instead, you need to be an efficient project manager capable of listening intelligently and understanding and handling the human and business issues at hand. Yes, it's possible that technical people may try to "snow" you with jargon, but you can work around these efforts to stall the project. Your greatest asset in this regard will be team leaders whom you can trust and who can help you understand the issues.

Sometimes a project manager who is the most skilled technical person on the team actually creates a problem. I was once asked to help a project team that was having considerable difficulty in maintaining its schedule. The problem was a very talented and technically superb project manager. He was so good that no one felt confident enough to make a decision without running it by him first. Needless to say, that created a bottleneck to progress. Once the project manager began to manage the project instead of trying to do all the work, the project began to move faster, and the project team gained confidence in its ability.

Always talk regularly to each member of the technical team, insist on periodic updates, and ask (with genuine enthusiasm) to see results, no matter how small. At the same time, never allow a single team member to be the only repository of key project data. Instead, insist that more than one member of the technical team understand, or at least be involved in, key technical areas. Keep copies of work descriptions on backup tapes/disks, and archive them regularly (offsite, if possible!) as additional backup and protection from acts of God and disgruntled workers.

Being All Things to All People

As project manager, you change roles from day to day. One day, you may feel like a hands-on manager in charge of a group of productive, motivated employees. The next day, you may be relegated to a position that's really little more than that of petty bureaucrat, shuffling papers and scheduling dull appointments all day.

The role of project manager also changes as the project proceeds. At the beginning, during the initiation and planning phases, your role focuses on creating a vision for the project and working with stakeholders (managers, customers, and other project beneficiaries) to reach consensus on the goals and objectives of the project. During this planning phase, the project team may occasionally complain that all they seem to do is crank out plans and status updates. However, gently remind them that all that planning will pay off when they move to the execution phase. Then, as the project proceeds into the execution phase, your role involves supporting, coaching, and otherwise guiding people to the promised land of project completion. You'll also have to spend time communicating the project status to the stakeholders so they remain happy with the results you are achieving as the project proceeds.

In all these roles, you will be expected to excel. Obviously, you can't be all things to all people. But as a project manager who is also a leader, you better be, at the very least, a lot of the right things to most of the project team.

 NOTES FROM THE FIELD

One of my customers is a global company that has a strong focus on project management. For the project managers, that's good news, because what they do is considered very important to the bottom line. However, the company has a policy of moving managers every 18 to 24 months to new positions so they don't get stale and learn even more about the business. For a project manager, that often means that their projects are "orphaned" because they lose their sponsor. The real issue behind this problem is that too many project managers rely on the relationship power of the sponsor to get things done. When that source was gone, they had nothing to fall back on. On the other hand, good project managers in the company have worked to develop another source of power for supporting their project. As a result, these project managers are in a much better position to carry on when the sponsor leaves.

Review Questions

- Am I clear about the importance of leadership while managing a project?

- Do I understand the four sources of power and which ones are most useful, or appropriate, for me?

- Can I see how my project drives changes in the company and why I need to pay attention to those changes?

- Do I know which other initiatives might have an impact on my project and what that impact might be?

The Least You Need to Know

- Project managers must not only lead the project team, but also lead change.
- Understand the source of power you have in leading your project.
- No project is an island. Keep your project front and center to maintain support and momentum and keep track of the situation surrounding your project.

Establishing Operating Guidelines

When you initiated the project with the stakeholders, you already established some basic rules for the project in the charter (see Chapter 7), including authorities and reporting requirements. In this chapter, it's time to extend those rules and expand the operating procedures for the entire project team.

Before I talk to you about procedures, though, I want to tell you about processes.

In This Chapter

- Recognizing the project process groups within every phase of the project
- Understanding the Plan-Do-Check-Act cycle
- Getting the work done
- Setting up a work authorization system (WAS)
- Creating administrative procedures
- Keeping a project diary

Project Process Groups in Each Phase

In each phase of the project, basic management process groups will aid you in organizing the project. You can
further divide these project processes into the following categories:

- The *initiating process group* begins each phase of the project and authorizes the work in that phase.

- The *planning process group* defines and refines the goals for each project phase and includes selecting the best course of action from all the alternatives.

- The *controlling process group* ensures that the goals of each phase are met by monitoring and measuring progress regularly to check for any deviation from the project plan so corrective action can be taken when necessary.

- The *executing process group* consists of coordinating people and other resources needed to carry out the activities in a phase.

- The *closing process group* brings an acceptable and orderly end to a phase.

The general project processes may vary in intensity depending on the project phase. For example, the initiating processes are much more in evidence during the beginning of any of the four project life-cycle phases. Focusing on the initiating processes during the beginning of each phase helps to ensure that the project stays focused on the business need it is supposed to deal with. Controlling processes are important processes during the execution phase of the project, but they should be recognized and used from the beginning to control costs and schedule. Finally, the processes overlap, so that the closing of one phase provides input for the next.

For more detailed information on project management process groups, refer to *PMBOK Guide* **sections 3.2 and 3.9.**

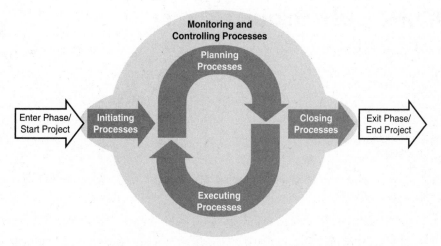

*Because project management involves so much integration, the monitoring and controlling processes
are constantly interacting with all the other processes to achieve success.*

Project Processes vs. Project Procedures

Unlike the project processes, the operating procedures for your project should help you guide
people to work on the right tasks at the right time. Operating procedures also help you stay
abreast of the status of every activity and cost associated with your project. You need to delegate
the work and gather information without undermining the motivation of the team with too much
administration, paperwork, and redundant communications. In other words, your operating procedures should help you manage the project but not keep you from getting the project done.

Operating procedures should also enable you to gather the information necessary to make
changes in a timely fashion, thereby maintaining control of the schedule, the resources, and the
costs and ultimately guiding your project to completion on time and within budget.

Sometimes the establishing of these operating procedures and reports can appear to be bureaucratic. However, you will really understand the value when you manage people who only work on
your project part-time because they have a day job within operations. When people don't report
to you, managing their work can be very difficult—and sometimes politically risky. However,
good operating procedures and reports can really help you mitigate the risks. Establishing
responsibilities through the RASIC (see "Using a RASIC Chart" later in this chapter) can set the
right expectations for the part-time team member and her boss. Good reporting procedures will
allow you to recognize when people are starting to miss work on the schedule and give you time
to do a course correction before things get badly out of hand. The point is to look at these operating guidelines in the right frame of reference to help everyone to produce a successful project!

The Plan-Do-Check-Act Cycle

An underlying principle within the project processes comes from the work done by W. Edwards Deming, a professor and author, and others in the Total Quality, continuous improvement, Six Sigma, and Lean Six Sigma movements. The planning processes correspond to the Plan, the executing processes to the Do, and the controlling processes to the Check and Act components. And since a project, by definition, has a definite beginning and ending, the initiating and closing processes are designed to address that finite nature of projects.

The Plan-Do-Check-Act Cycle

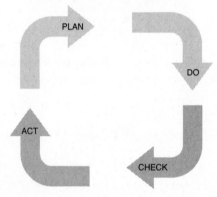

The Plan-Do-Check-Act cycle was the basis for upgrading manufacturing. This model was adopted by the Project Management Institute (PMI) and incorporated into the Organizational Project Management Maturity Model (OPM3). It has contributed to improved design, service, product quality, testing, and sales.

To read more about these techniques, refer to *PMBOK Guide* section 8.1.2.

The Things That Need to Get Done

Getting work done on the project should always be the first priority. To get the actual work started, you'll need to delegate all work that isn't your own responsibility. Do this in meetings, in written communications, and through reviewing the project plan with team members and the working committee. As you start the project, however, you'll also need to develop a process or work schedule for the many activities that won't necessarily be found on the work plan or task list for the project.

RISK MANAGEMENT

Not paying attention to the business process changes that your project creates will get you in deep trouble quickly, particularly on a large project that touches a large number of people.

Handling Business Process Changes

After your project has developed the project plan, the next important series of tasks to get both the project team and the business users working on is the business process changes that will occur.

The business process changes occur naturally as part of any project deliverables, but it is critically important that both sides work together to analyze the various changes that will occur and then let the business decide how to address these changes. Let's take a look at a decision-making process and some ways you and your team can decide how to move forward.

Start with the Project Team

Issues that create the need for process changes may come from a variety of sources, such as the business analysts on the project team, the new technology vendor, or the business itself. For example, the business may decide that the project is an ideal time to make a change in a business policy or procedure that is not created by the project, but provides the natural opportunity to address it.

Process for Business Process Changes

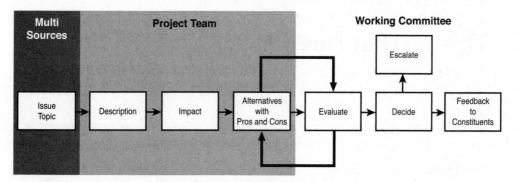

Issues or decisions may come from a variety of sources and then move from left to right through the project team, to the working committee, and finally to either the senior management or the constituents (the organization affected by the issue or decision).

Regardless of where the issue of a process change originates, the process illustrated in the figure is a good model to follow. Here's how you can break it down:

- Develop a complete description of the proposed process change.

- Evaluate the impact on the business as they see it.

- Develop a list of alternative actions that may address that process change with the accompanying pros and cons.

- Conduct a cost-benefit analysis on each of the potential options.

Starting with the project team is an important step and one you should not shortcut. Very few people are capable of making these kinds of decisions when working from a "blank sheet of paper." The decision-making process is always much faster and more effective if those who must make the decision have something to react to and work from.

Now It's Time for the Working Committee

At that point, the working committee (see Chapter 6) takes over and conducts a detailed evaluation of the alternatives provided by the project team or even develops other alternatives if they identify possibilities the project team did not anticipate. Use the following table as a template to evaluate the business process changes in a measured and methodical way.

Process area _____

Process change _____

Background information _____

Issue
(What decision do we need
to make?) _____
_____

Constraints _____

Alternatives _____

Plan
(How should we move forward?) _____

Test
(How should the project
team test to make sure this works?) _____
_____

Communications
(What do people need to
know? When? Who should
provide the information?)

_____

_____

_____

Training
(What must people be able
to do after training is
completed?)

_____

_____

_____

Leadership
(What support does the
management team need to
provide for success?)

_____

_____

_____

Benefits

_____

Transition
(How do we handle this
issue until the project is
fully implemented?)

_____

_____

_____

_____

After the working committee has completed its evaluation, it will need to make a decision as to which alternative to use. This is important for several reasons, but the most obvious is that the business will make the decision based on the best way to meet the business requirements versus the best "technical" way according to the project team.

Making the Decision

Part of the decision-making process should include having the various working committee members network the alternatives, including pros and cons, with other members of the constituencies they represent. This is important for two reasons. First, it gets input from others who will later be asked to support and adhere to the decision. If they have had input along the way, they are much more likely to support those decisions. Second, this wider audience helps to ensure that the working committee members have not missed something. This can happen! Often, these people may be managers who are not familiar with all the intricate details of a process and so may overlook, or be completely unaware of, an important detail they should consider before a decision is made.

I am *not* advocating some sort of democratic vote around these decisions, but only suggesting that more people need to be consulted. It will not only ensure that you reach a good decision, but more people brought into the process will provide a better guarantee that it is supported when you roll out the final deliverables. The ultimate decision should rest with the working committee since it will be held accountable for all the decisions it makes.

Using a RASIC Chart

A RASIC chart is a special type of responsibility assignment matrix (see Chapter 13) that can be particularly useful in decision making during a project. RASIC stands for the following:

- **R**esponsible for the task to be completed

- **A**pproves who performs the task and the final result

- **S**upports by providing resources or playing a role in implementation

- **I**nformed, as in must be notified of results but not necessarily consulted before the decision or actions

- **C**onsulted, as in has information or capability that might be necessary to complete the work

Creating a chart in a spreadsheet that identifies either individuals (for example, John) or a role (VP Product Development) can be used for clarifying how different stakeholders are involved in key decisions or work deliverables.

Automation Services		Superintendent/ Manager	Local Team	Automation Coordinator (operations)	Regional Automation Foreman	Automation Foreman (local)	Manager, Automation Support	Regional Automation Manager	Automation Communications Coordinator	Enterprise Automation Coordinator	Manager, Automation Services
Break/Fix Unplanned Event											
Low	Hardware		S	R	I	I	I			I	
	Software		S	R	I	S	I			I	
High	Hardware	I	S	R	I	S	S	S	I	S	
	Software	I	S	R	I	S	S	S	I	S	
Planned Event											
Enhancement											
Low impact		A	S	R	I	C		A		C	
High impact		A	S	R	I	C		A		S	
Project											
Medium to Large Scope		A	R	S	I	I		I	I	S	C
Training		A	R	S	I	C		I		S	I

Responsible	Owns the problem/project
Approves	Must sign off (approve) on work before it is effective
Supports	Provides resources or can play a supporting role in implementation
Informed	Must be notified of results, but need not be consulted
Consulted	Has information and/or capability necessary to complete the work/project

Here is an example of how a RASIC chart might be look for an automation project.

Escalating the Decision

You need to have an *escalation procedure* in place prior to the first "deadlock." If you have no escalation procedure in place, the situation could develop into a power play for some individuals and seriously delay the project team. A general rule of thumb that I have used in the past suggests that the working committee has three attempts to make a decision, and if it is unsuccessful after those three attempts, the decision is passed on to the sponsor or the steering committee for resolution. Of course, as project manager, you must alert the sponsor or steering committee at the first sign of trouble. Don't let them be surprised by a problem coming to them! If they know the situation in advance, they may even be able to work behind the scenes to get a resolution. Also, an escalation procedure has the added benefit that most people will work to resolve an issue and make a decision if they know a time limit is imposed. If there seems to be an open-ended process, then people can get into playing games or striking poses for other purposes completely unrelated to the project.

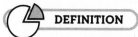

DEFINITION

An **escalation procedure** is a defined process or procedure used to elevate a decision to the steering committee of a project.

Finally, after the decision has been made, the working committee needs to communicate the decision to the organization.

Setting Up a Work Authorization System

When your project team begins to work, the question always arises: When should I start the work I've been assigned? The answer to that question is that you must put a *work authorization system (WAS)* in place from the beginning.

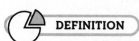

DEFINITION

A **work authorization system (WAS)** is a written method that sanctions the right work is done in the right order. It also provides direction that enables a team member to begin work on a specific activity or work package.

A telling story involved a project manager who did not have a WAS in place. During the course of the project, customers would approach project team members and ask them for minor modifications in the work they were doing. In their attempts to be accommodating to the customers and keep them happy, the project team members would say "okay" and begin to work on the modification. The project manager had no idea this was happening until a few days later when he asked for the work package that was scheduled to be delivered. Because this work was not ready, he discovered the reason. If the WAS had been in place, the team members would not have been able to accept the modifications. They would have had no authorization to do that work.

A WAS would provide the team members with a politically correct way to say "no." They could have referred the customer to the project manager by saying, "I would love to do that for you, but I need the authorization from my project manager. Please see her, and I'll get started as soon as the work is approved."

In large projects, make the authorization to begin work formal and in writing so that it can be tracked in a project audit if it is required. In smaller projects, it can be more informal, such as an email "okay." However, under no circumstances should it be just verbal as you pass in the halls. If a conversation does occur and you approve work passing in the halls, always follow it up with written authorization!

For more information on controlling the work, refer to *PMBOK Guide* **sections 5.6.1, 5.6.2, and 5.6.3.**

Administrative Procedures That Won't Hurt

Eventually, in spite of your good attitude and informal chats with people, you'll have to ask them to do administrative tasks, such as writing reports and reconciling expenses. Most people won't like it, but if you have a positive work environment, they'll usually comply with your guidelines (though you must make the requirements clear in advance).

As you develop administrative procedures, try to collect only the information you'll use. At the beginning, you may collect more information in the form of reports and updates than you really need. When you realize you're gathering too much data, give the team a break and tell them to simplify or shorten their reports. For the data you really need, store the information for ready access and make it easy to retrieve when you need to analyze it.

If your project is one of many similar projects in your organization, established operating and administrative procedures probably are already in place to help you complete your ongoing responsibilities to the project. These include report formats, time frames for project review, and other tracking procedures.

If review procedures and administrative reports are not already well established in your organization, you need to develop basic administrative procedures before you begin work on your project.

WORDS FROM THE WISE

When people fill out time reports weekly, without writing down what they did daily, they are making up fiction. Such made-up data are almost worse than no data at all.

—From *Fundamentals of Project Management* by James P. Lewis

The Reports You May Need

Your stakeholders, managers, and customers deserve informed communication about the project on a timely basis. A regular status report, targeted toward appropriate project stakeholders, contains information on current progress, schedule changes, and budgets. Other reports may also be required to both inform and motivate team members. On large projects, a weekly scoreboard and update report targeted toward the project team, including vendors who are part of the team, may be a good idea. An update report emphasizes important priorities, issues, or deadlines. The purpose of the update report is to convey information that might otherwise fall through the cracks. (If a major snag crops up, the update provides information to keep the team focused on their own work while you deal with the problem.) Cost-variance reports, load-leveling reports, supply inventories, and other formal documentation should also track specific aspects of the project.

Simple Forms to Create Useful Reports

Reports enable your team to follow the project "road map" and stay on track, but the reports need to be easy to produce. I suggest using a good project management software program or simple forms for gathering regular report information. These forms, which I often use on projects, may be useful for yours:

Schedule update forms. You need to update the schedule as the project progresses and evolves. Notify team members each time the timeline changes, for whatever reason, so they can review the master chart and adjust their duties to match.

Supply and equipment request forms. Team members will require supplies and possibly equipment you haven't considered. Give them a simple worksheet to complete so they can tell you what they need before they need it. This is a good place to involve the procurement team so the information they might require is included on the form.

Status reporting forms. Consider investing in a collaboration site on a computer network that reminds people about status reports and other administrative requirements. Have the status report provide the following information:

- Tasks completed since the last status report with dates completed

- Tasks in progress with forecasted completion dates

- Tasks planned with expected completion dates

- Budget expenditures (if appropriate)

- Issues that need attention

- Recommendations for project improvements or changes

- Questions, decisions, or other items that require other people's approval or input

When everyone uses the same format, it's easier to summarize, synthesize, and analyze the status information for the formal status report you'll write as the project manager.

Every Report Needs a Purpose

For each report (or form) you choose to use on your project, document the following:

- How often is the report produced? Some reports are produced weekly; others are submitted monthly or quarterly.

- What is contained in the report?

- Who is responsible for producing the report?

- What is the objective of the report?

- Who will follow up on action items identified in the report?

- Who is the intended audience for the report? For example, there are three potential audiences for status reports: team members on the project, company management, and customers or key stakeholders (if involved).

 TIME IS MONEY

> The report to management and customers is typically more formal but less detailed than the report made to the team members. The reports team members send to you (as project manager) probably have the most information; some of this information is for your eyes only, however, so always filter what you summarize for other staff and managers.

Writing status reports for various audiences enables you to synthesize the formal and informal monitoring you've been doing. It enables you to relate your progress to the original project plan and to understand any risks to meeting your planned goals.

Ask Two Final Questions Before You Start

Before any report or procedure becomes part of the bureaucratic process associated with your project, ask yourself the following questions:

- Is this report the best way to communicate this information?

- Would some other form of communication or action be more expedient and just as useful?

Chapter 19, which discusses how to make the most of your communications, will also help you answer these questions.

Why You Should Keep a Project Diary

In addition to taking notes at meetings, gathering information from project participants, and making general reports, a prudent project manager makes a personal project diary part of standard operating procedure.

The daily diary should include notes on progress, problems, and any issues that impact the project in a positive or negative light. Unlike "Dear Diary" entries, this notebook resembles a captain's log from a ship. Entries are to the point, dated (by page), and contain as much or as little information as required to document project progress and issues. The diary also tracks discussion points, decisions that were made, and any action items that you committed to at any given time. It should contain information about the outcome of key meetings, accomplishments, conflicts, and extraordinary events affecting the project's health and well-being. The project diary will become a key artifact when you begin to complete your lessons learned at project close-out. It will remind you of events that may have completely escaped your memory over the course of the project.

You can use a standard journal and write the information, or use a tablet such as an iPad. Many tablets have applications for capturing notes the same as pen and paper, but have the additional benefits of automatically recording dates and various folders that allow easier sorting and access.

The purpose of the project diary is threefold. First, it tracks your progress and can be reviewed later. The diary may pinpoint project issues that are hard to identify by reading a pile of status reports. Long-term problems, such as a failing team member, become easily visible as you flip through the book. Unloading the team member is easier when you can document her nonperformance through the written record.

Second, if management complains about a problem, such as budget overages or tardy delivery, your meticulously kept diary serves as the perfect memory of what really happened so you can explain the situation.

Third, your diary is an excellent tool for doing a better job next time. Review it occasionally to see what worked and what failed last time. Employ the positive and reject the negative. A good diary is fuel for laughs years down the road.

The Bottom Line

In implementing all the operating aspects and creating the administrative guidelines for your project, remember the management and leadership of the project make the difference in your success, not the forms or the computer programs. You must act as a manager and a leader, not just as an administrator. With this in mind, you're ready to attack some of the best ways to keep all the "adminis-trivia" under control and to make communications more effective.

Review Questions

- Do I understand the project management processes and how they are defined?
- Can I appreciate the need for operating procedures to manage my project?
- Do I understand the value of a WAS for focusing the work during a project?
- Do I recognize how a RASIC chart would clarify responsibilities for project work?
- Am I confident that I can use streamlined reports to assess progress in the project?
- Am I convinced of the value of keeping a project diary?

The Least You Need to Know

- Every project needs the project processes to track progress, report status, and move successfully from one phase to another, but no project needs long-winded reports with irrelevant details or meetings without objectives.
- Use the project team and the working committee to handle business process changes.
- Establish a work authorization system (WAS) to manage the work of your project team.
- Make sure that your reports have a meaningful purpose and are not a bureaucratic exercise.
- Be sure to establish the administrative procedures you want at the beginning of the project.
- Use a project diary to capture your notes and ideas as you move forward.

Making Your Communications Count

When you think about ensuring the success of your projects, your head may go immediately to defining the scope correctly, having a complete work breakdown structure, or managing risks. The Project Management Institute (PMI) recently published the *Pulse of the Profession* report on successful projects. The *Pulse* study—based on research from Forbes, PricewaterhouseCoopers, and Town Watson—revealed that the most crucial success factor in project management was actually effective communications to all stakeholders. The study also concluded that a stunning 56 percent of the dollars at risk were due to ineffective communications.

So what can you do as a project manager to avoid these problems? That's the purpose of this chapter—to help you develop your project communications.

In This Chapter

- Knowing your audience
- Building and executing a communication plan
- How communication and strong leadership go hand in hand
- Using communications to mitigate risks
- Communicating scope change
- Being a good listener

The Basics of Communications: It's All About Perception

Much of people's understanding comes from their perceptions. Every time you communicate with people, your project team, stakeholders, or anyone else, you must keep their perspective in mind. Before you communicate anything to anyone, analyze your audience. Ask yourself the following questions:

- What information do people need?

- Does the message I'm sending communicate a particular feeling or attitude? (You may need to alter the tone depending on how you answer the question.)

- What is the best media (for example, one-on-one meeting, town hall, email) for delivering the information?

- Who is the best person to deliver the information?

- How should I deliver the message?

- When should people receive the information?

- How will I receive feedback on how people react to the information?

 NOTES FROM THE FIELD

I had the privilege of traveling all over the globe to meet with project managers. My client had asked me to apply my experience to an initiative they had to mature the project management methodology within the company. An interesting trend surfaced in my interviews. I asked them to tell me the best predictor for a successful project. I had thought it would be scope definition or good planning. It turned out that more than three fourths of the project managers cited good communications, between the project team and the customer and within the project team. If there were strong communications, they could almost always predict a successful project. If communications were weak, it enviably led to problems within the project.

The following figure illustrates how perspectives influence people's understanding.

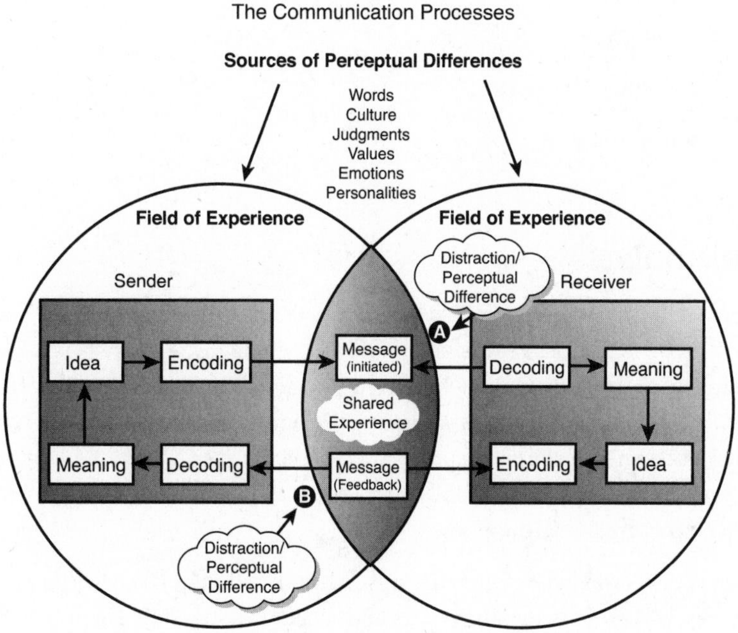

A basic communication model demonstrates that perception comes from people's experiences, culture, word choice, values, and judgments. We use all these elements to encode and decode messages, and communication only occurs when the circles overlap. Otherwise, misunderstandings are inevitable.

(From *Human Resource Skills for the Project Manager* by Vijay Verma)

What Does a Communication Plan Look Like?

Building a communication plan is critical to the success of any project. It is the most common way of letting the end-users of the project know what will happen to them and when. Let's look at several components of the communication plan in greater detail:

- Stakeholder analysis

- Sensitivity analysis

- Information needs

- Media requirements

- Delivery personnel and power bases

- Timing requirements

- Common definitions

- Feedback loops

- Macro and micro barriers

- Jargon and acronyms

Stakeholder Analysis

Some stakeholders will have more interest in a project than others. In the case of a project to develop a new customer information database for the company, the front office of sales and marketing personnel are probably much more interested in this project than others in the manufacturing facility, but all of them have an interest! The purpose of doing a stakeholder analysis is to see whether you can determine what they will be concerned about and how to communicate that information to them. These examples from the stakeholder analysis for a customer information database project illustrate the point:

- **Sales** is concerned about how the information will help them sell more products and services to their existing customers and whether it can help them land the business of some prospects that are not currently customers.

- **Marketing** is concerned with getting information that will help them identify buying trends that may result in new marketing literature. They will also hope to see trends that will indicate the types of new products customers are likely to buy in the future.

- **Research and Development** takes the information that Marketing provides and works to develop products that will meet the new demands and can be manufactured at a price that will produce a profit.

- **Manufacturing** is interested in correct order entry by sales so they can plan their production schedules in a way that will ensure enough products are on hand for delivery, but not too much that will require storage in a warehouse.

- **Purchasing** wants the system to feed information into their financial systems so they can track customer purchases to make sure they are not exceeding their credit limits and provide information to track their payment records.

- **Management** wants visibility into the buying patterns of their customers so they can make rational decisions about where to invest limited capital and human resources that will allow the company to continue growing.

For more information on stakeholder analysis, refer to *PMBOK Guide* **section 13.1.2.**

TIME IS MONEY

Remember, all communication starts with the stakeholder you are communicating with. Various stakeholders will have different information needs and will require a unique level of detail. A general email to everyone is not likely to satisfy anyone. While it takes time, think of that time as an investment.

Sensitivity Analysis

All these groups will have some sensitivities the project manager will need to consider when developing a communication plan. For example, sales professionals will be sensitive to any system that seems to add a layer of bureaucracy to the tough business of selling goods and services. They will rightly complain and follow with a statement like, "What would you rather I do, sit around all day entering information into a computer or be out on the street selling products?" The answer to that question is obvious, but if the project manager does not take that into account, the team will run into some serious resistance later on as they try to implement the new customer relationship management (CRM) system.

The management team and all others will have different concerns, but the way the project manager addresses them will be just as important during the course of the project.

Information Needs

Different groups within the company will require different types of information. In an example of a project to implement a new customer information database, salespeople will be much more concerned about how information is entered into the system since they will be the ones most likely asked to do that. Accounting and marketing people will be much more interested in the reporting capabilities and the accuracy of the information for invoicing and payments. They will want to know how much and what type of information they can extract from the system using queries and searches. They will be bored by the level of detail the salespeople will need on order entry.

Likewise, each group will have its own unique information needs. You will need to build each type of information required by each stakeholder group into your communication plan. And don't forget that there may be a single individual, such as your sponsor, to consider outside the information required by the management team in general.

Media Requirements

Think about how, exactly, you are going to deliver information to each of the stakeholder groups. When defining media, I mean the vehicle you will use to deliver that information. You will want to deliver the information in such a way that it has the best chance of success—that people will actually pay attention to the information! Let me reiterate a basic point that has hurt hundreds of projects over the years: sending out email messages is not communicating!

Recently, I had a customer who was in a tough situation that all project managers find themselves in at one time or another. The project was coming into the final months. Things had gone very well up to that point, but the final few months threatened to undo all the goodwill that had been built up over the previous 18 months. While many of the issues that surrounded the project were more complex than is necessary to detail here, there was a basic flaw in the communications strategy. The project manager had fallen into the habit of communicating with the business users through email only. As most of us know, between the tremendous amount of email (much of it unnecessary) everyone receives, coupled with spam, many people will ignore email after a while. And that is what happened to this project. The project manager had to go back and build a new and more robust communication plan to help the project finish with the amount of goodwill they deserved based on the terrific job they had done.

Although e-mail can be one component of the overall communication plan, you really need to make it a minor media at best. Consider, instead, a variety of other delivery mechanisms, such as the following:

- Town hall meetings
- Presentations
- Staff meetings
- Written memos
- Wall charts
- Web portals

The following table illustrates the various types of communications commonly used, and the checkmarks indicate the situations where it is generally most effective.

Types of Communication and Their Characteristics

Type of Communication	Group	Individual	Written	Spoken	Formal	Informal
Conference calls	✓			✓	✓	
Emails		✓	✓			✓
Instant messaging		✓	✓		✓	
Letters		✓	✓		✓	
Reports		✓	✓		✓	
Meetings	✓			✓		✓
Presentations	✓		✓	✓		
Telephone calls		✓		✓		✓

For more information on technology, refer to *PMBOK Guide* sections 10.1.2.2 and 10.1.2.4.

Delivery Personnel and Power Bases

Consider who would be the right person to deliver the message. That will depend on thinking through the power base that is required to complete that message successfully. As you can see in the following table, different sources of power will give you different results. For example, you'll notice that the most persuasive power base is expertise. As a project manager, that tells me that if I have a message where the desired outcome is to persuade people, I need to have that message delivered by someone who is considered an expert (whether internal or external) by the people being targeted for the message (hence the "+++"). If I ask an executive to order people to comply, I am likely to get a poor outcome (the "–"), which means I might actually be worse off than if I hadn't communicated at all!

The rule of thumb, then, is to pick the source that matches the result you want.

Power Base	Action	Results
Expertise	Persuasion	+++
Admiration	Ask	++
Reward	Promise	+
Position of authority	Order	–
Coercion	Threat	––

As you can see from this chart, what you need to accomplish determines the power base you come from. If you will need to persuade the stakeholder group, then a power base of expertise is the best direction. How would your project team apply that to the customer database implementation?

Say that you need to make a shift in the way sales reps keep track of their information on existing customers. If you were thinking about who should deliver the message, you might think that having a leader such as the vice president of sales make a declaration on the way it must be done would be a reasonable idea. However, you can tell from the chart that it may not achieve the results you had hoped for. However, you might provide one of the real "stars" of the sales department (someone recognized by the entire sales staff as successful) a demonstration or prototype of the new tool and get his suggestions on how it could enhance his ability to generate sales. After incorporating some of his ideas, you can then ask that sales rep to speak to his colleagues on the benefits he sees. What difference do you think that would make? The difference would be dramatic! The salespeople will really listen to one of their peers because he is respected as an expert, not by position (like the vice president of sales) but by performance—the test that really counts for salespeople.

Timing Requirements

The right timing for the message is important. If you provide information too early, people may ask questions you can't fully answer just yet! They may want more details than you can give them—particularly early in the project. If you wait too long to relay information, then the project is moving forward at a pace that will not allow people that are impacted to keep up, and they may feel like you are making decisions without them. Although you don't really need their consent, timing your information correctly will make them feel like you are seeking, and receiving, their approval. It will really provide excellent buy-in from the ultimate customers! So as you develop a communication plan, consider adding a timeline that provides guidance on when these communication activities will occur.

Common Definitions

Often certain industries, or even companies within an industry, will have a unique set language. It will be important that the project manager know the unique definitions within this language. This is particularly important if you are coming in from the outside. Again, your internal subject matter experts (such as the working committee) can be helpful here.

RISK MANAGEMENT

Make sure that all the key people on your project team are familiar with the common definitions associated with your project.

As a simple example, in projects I have traditionally managed, I have always used the classic names of Define, Plan, Execute, and Close-out; therefore, my team could understand the way I defined the phases. However, for one project, our customer defined the phases of their project as Design, Build, Commission, and Operate. We had to build a definitions file for team members where they could cross-reference the activities they were used to seeing and where those fell using the customer definitions for the phases. That seemed to most practical way, as using multiple definitions seemed risky.

Feedback Loops

In any communication plan, you will need to build in a feedback loop to assess how the information has been received. Occasionally there can be unanticipated interpretations or consequences based on the communications. If you consider for a moment, it makes sense. Making sure that everyone involved understands common definitions is one way to prevent those misunderstandings from occurring. However, different interpretations of the information can lead people to different conclusions than you had anticipated. Therefore, the only way you will know that has happened is if you have a feedback loop.

One way to build a feedback loop is to develop a relationship (or have your team members do it) with key people in various stakeholder groups and contact them after a key communication has gone out. Ask them what the reaction was—what people said around the water cooler. That will help you realize whether your communication was successful or whether you'll need to refine or modify the message next time.

Another benefit of a feedback loop is that it lets you know what rumors are circulating about your project. Address those rumors as quickly and fully as possible. Nothing will build the credibility of your project more than having a message delivered about a rumor that only started a few hours or days ago. The stakeholders will believe you are listening to them, and this will reduce their anxiety about your project considerably.

Macro and Micro Barriers

As you build your communication plan, think about macro and micro barriers. Some of these barriers are obvious; others are not so obvious; but all are important to consider and plan for to be effective.

Macro barriers are those large barriers that prevent effective communication. One such barrier would be simple geography. If the potential customers are scattered over multiple locations, obviously the ability to communicate is more difficult. You will need to consider how to handle the situation and overcome the barrier. Another macro barrier would be different languages; different languages, including culture, will be a major consideration as you plan your communications. Getting a project team member from that language or cultural group to assist in the communications will be critical to success.

Micro barriers are much more subtle. One obvious example would be attitudes that people, as a group, have about the deliverables of a project. Maybe a similar project was attempted a couple of years ago and was a complete flop! Now everyone thinks the business concept is flawed and will never succeed. Other similar micro barriers may surround the project and will need to be considered as you figure out how you will communicate to people.

Jargon and Acronyms

When you communicate, use only jargon and acronyms that are used by the stakeholders of your communication plan. For various functional groups, it is easy to slip into using jargon and acronyms that are common or popular with that function but are not familiar to others. A simple example of an acronym might be the use of AMA. If you were talking to a group of marketing people, they would probably assume you were referring to the American Marketing Association. However, if you were speaking to doctors, they would assume you were referring to the American Medical Association. The best strategy is to actually define the acronym when you first use it—or avoid them altogether!

 NOTES FROM THE FIELD

Every company I have every worked in has its own unique language. Many times, it is the hardest thing for a new person to understand. Also, various departments have their own unique language to communicate. During a project, unless you have individuals seconded from those departments or that company, always seek clarification when you hear jargon or acronyms—and encourage your team members to do the same.

Don't Forget the Project Team

In building a communication plan, don't forget that you need to communicate to the project team as well. When a project team is large or in different locations, you need to think about parallel communication plans—one for the stakeholders and one for the project team.

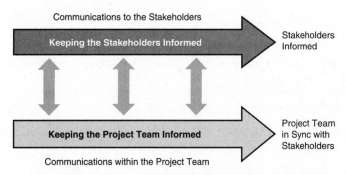

A parallel communication model that demonstrates communications to the stakeholders and the project team.

For more technical information on communication planning, refer to *PMBOK Guide* section 10.1.

Executing the Communication Plan

A plan is only as good as your ability to execute it. After spending the time to develop a communication plan, don't leave it on the shelf. Put the tasks into your project plan and execute them like you would any other task (or give some of them to your team members) during the project. Don't forget to assign some of those tasks to members of the working committee, too! You may need to coach or assist them by drafting the communication, but don't do it for them. Remember that all projects are really undertaken for business results, and you shouldn't let them off the hook for messages that really need to come from the business leadership. Also, just like any other part of the project plan, review and update tasks as circumstances change.

Communication and Leadership

Good communication and strong leadership go hand in hand. The project managers who consistently succeed in bringing their projects in on time and within budget are those who effectively manage the interactions and communications between people and organizations. The people working on your project and other members of the project team need to be comfortable with bringing issues to your attention. This goes for people who report directly to you, their managers, and your managers as well.

Three types of communications must occur for a project to be managed effectively:

1. **Vertical communications.** These are the up-and-down organizational communications based on the hierarchical relationships established on an organization chart.

2. **Horizontal communications.** Horizontal or lateral communications involve communicating and coordinating activities with peers.

3. **Diagonal communications.** The diagonal relationships are rarely shown on organization charts, but they are almost always important to the success of a project. Diagonal communications involve upward relationships with managers and officers from other departments. They also include downward diagonal communications with third parties, such as contractors, suppliers, or consultants.

If you have established the required communications in all three dimensions before conflicts occur, when the inevitable conflicts do arise between organizations, styles, procedures, or priorities, the channels you have established will be available for resolving issues.

For more information on managing communications, refer to *PMBOK Guide* **section 10.2.**

Purpose of Communications

Always think through the purpose of your communication. Do you want the recipient to do something? Do you want the recipient to think or feel a certain way? To determine what kind of response you want, complete this sentence: *The purpose of my message is* …. If you can't complete the sentence, how will those with whom you are communicating understand your purpose?

RISK MANAGEMENT

You can use groupware (software that lets people talk together through a computer network) for keeping status reports and general project information up to date. You can create a project website for a really large project to keep people informed of objectives, accomplishments, and project plans. You may also create tweets or project blogs to keep stakeholders informed—but remember your stakeholder analysis and don't use these tools for the wrong audience! Regardless of which medium you choose, you need to employ common sense. Never ignore the unexpected impact of your messages. Select the medium wisely. Even a casual disparaging remark to a team member can come back to haunt you later in the project.

Developing Effective Messages

Communicating on a project is an art. The better you get at it, the smoother your project will flow from beginning to end. You must provide enough information to keep stakeholders informed without boring them. Every word counts, so use the minimum required to convey the message. What you send, to whom you send it, and when you send it are always issues. If in doubt about a message, always wait. When you decide you need to say something, however, these guidelines should help you decide exactly what you want to say (regardless of the medium you choose):

- Always draft the message and then carefully edit it before you send it. This will help you be more concise in the message and ensure you have covered all the points required.

- Think about the audience's expectations, any actions required as a result of the message, and your expectations after the message is delivered.

- Justify your choice of delivery medium for the message and the timing of it.

- Start the message with an introduction that identifies the issue, context, or opportunity of interest.

- Make any required actions clear and specific in the message—and right at the beginning.

- Be as concise as possible without seeming insensitive or rude.

- Never surprise someone with information. For example, if you will be discussing something important in a meeting, make sure the right people know what you will say before you get there.

Listening as Part of Communicating

The ability to listen is one of the most important communication skills a project manager can possess. Only through listening can you determine whether your messages are understood. Focused listening helps keep you abreast of project progress better than any status report. Observant listening can also help you foresee political issues before they start bogging down the project.

Here are some tips for becoming a better listener:

• Stop talking and let others tell you what they want to say.

• Let people finish what they are saying. Try not to interrupt because you'll never hear the person's complete intent if you do. If there is a brief pause in the discussion, don't jump in prematurely. Allow the other person to finish before you take your turn.

• Eliminate distractions, such as telephone calls or people coming in and out of the office. Give the person your full attention.

• Listen with purpose and intent. Try to hear between the words for the underlying meaning of the message. Notice body language and facial expressions as people talk. These are often the clues to dissatisfaction or issues that are not being addressed. If you see something wrong in the person's face, ask some probing questions to get at the real concerns.

• Restate what you hear people say to make sure that you have the message right. You must receive and understand the message for good communication to occur.

Communications to Manage Risks

Risks will always occur as part of the project (see Chapter 8). Many of those situations will never occur, and the planning for mitigating those risks will remain just that—planning. However, a smart project manager will use communications as part of a strategy for managing risks when they do occur. Make sure communications are part of your risk mitigation strategy. People will often help in creating a solution, but they have to know a problem exists. There are three key points to remember when using communication to manage risks:

1. Never surprise key stakeholders about a risk. Keep them informed as the events begin to unfold.

2. Be sure to *frame* the issue correctly so you can influence the way the stakeholder responds.

3. Stay positive if at all possible.

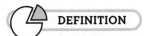

DEFINITION

Framing is a concept borrowed from psychology and applied to communications. It is defined as describing a situation by encouraging a certain perception and discouraging others. The simple way to think of it is with the common description "the glass is half empty" or "the glass is half full."

Communicating a Scope Change

It is inevitable that there will be changes in scope over the course of a project. Those changes might be large or small, but you will need to communicate to key stakeholders about those changes. As I discussed in Chapter 7, having a clearly defined process for managing scope change will actually provide the added benefit of helping you in communicating a change if it is approved.

As I pointed out earlier in this chapter about who should deliver the message, this is one area where the person delivering the message needs to come from the business and not the project team. Having a business person deliver the message will go a long way in creating acceptance of the change in scope. Also, the business person can explain the impact of the change and the options considered before a decision was made in a language that key stakeholders will consider important.

Finally, regardless of whether the change was approved or not, the person or group who requested the change needs to hear the rationale. Again, I would recommend it come from a business person, not the project team.

Integrating the Communication Plan

So much is made in project management books about the WBS and breaking down project tasks—and that is very important. However, as my clients illustrated earlier, communications are critical to a successful project. After completing the steps described in this chapter, you should go back to your project plan and begin adding in all the work associated with the communication plan. Just like estimating effort and scheduling the work, you need to apply the same rigor to your communication plan. Put the tasks in your project plan and determine when you will complete them. If they are recurring tasks, like status reports, show them as such in your plan. Just like all the work, there will be dependencies. For example, you won't be able to communicate about user acceptance testing until after the acceptance testing is completed and you have an analysis of what needs to be fixed and what is good to go.

Please don't treat your communication plan as an afterthought—make it an integral part of your project plan.

Review Questions

- Have a utilized my stakeholder analysis to build a proper communication plan?

- Do I understand the sensitivities and information requirements for each of those stakeholders?

- Is my project team using a common set of definitions that everyone will understand equally?

- Have I analyzed macro and micro barriers and planned how to overcome them?

- Have I built all the communication tasks into my overall project plan?

The Least You Need to Know

- Plan communications as thoroughly as you do the work for the project deliverables.

- Remember all the elements that you must examine as part of the communication plan.

- Be sure to get the leadership involved in communications.

- When developing important communications, create them carefully and ask others for their feedback before you send them.

- Use communications to handle risks and scope change.

- Being a good listener is an important part of being a good communicator.

- Be sure to keep your project communication plan evergreen and execute it!

The Monitoring and Controlling Processes

Like any good project manager, you need to monitor and control the work. Like the driver of a race car, you need to adjust your speed on the curves and compensate for the condition of the road. Control of a project starts with a detailed plan, good communication, and clear operating procedures that you've developed for the project.

To actually maintain that control over time, however, you need to monitor and deal with changes, problems, and unexpected circumstances. This part shows you how to compare the time, cost, and quality of your project at various points and then make adjustments to the activities, resources, and plan to keep things moving toward the ultimate goal. Sometimes you may need to slow things down to avoid an accident. Other times, you need to step on the accelerator to keep pace with the changes.

Finally, this part teaches you how to prepare the operations group for the final deliverables from your project.

Monitoring and Controlling the Plan

After a project is underway and you establish the operating procedures and start working on perfecting your leadership style, your key responsibility is to keep things going on time and within budget. After meticulously planning your project, you might assume that team members will simply stick to your plan and get things done as you have specified. Unfortunately, this almost never happens. On occasion, you'll need to intervene.

In this chapter, I provide you some basic monitoring and control techniques that can help you keep track of what is going on.

In This Chapter

- What project monitoring should accomplish
- Understanding earned value analysis (EVA) and Gantt charts
- The project review meeting
- Controlling with a project audit
- Monitoring the budget

Taking Charge and Getting Control

When a project is underway, it takes on a life of its own. But your job is getting the project done on time and within budget. Your job and your reputation are on the line. But how will you know if people are doing what they have promised to do? How can you meet your objectives and still get everything else done? It can seem overwhelming.

The purpose of controlling a project is to ensure that the project is staying on schedule, that the work is being completed within the budget constraints, and that the project is meeting the quality criteria. If any of these go awry, the business case for the project may be lost, not to mention the value to the company based on improved performance. Controls within a project ensure that all the key stakeholders—from the project team to the steering committee—can monitor the progress toward completion, compare achievement against milestones, and help correct problems if they appear.

Getting a handle on your project isn't really that hard. You have a plan, and now is the time to use it. Your plan is your main tool for maintaining control of the project through its lifetime. To move forward and keep everything in gear and well lubricated requires careful management of both the plan and its resources, especially the people. Otherwise, you won't meet the goals established at the project's outset. The schedule, budget, and procedures you've put together to this point provide you with the structure you need to evaluate where you are at any time.

 RISK MANAGEMENT

Control can imply bureaucracy, headstrong authority, or excessive power. Because of these negative connotations, people new to project management may be reluctant to implement project control. The controlling phase is not about domination, however; it's about gathering information so you can measure, monitor, and make course corrections as you progress toward your project goals. That's a good thing, because otherwise you'll never know if your project is on the right course.

Success Criteria for Project Control

I want to discuss why monitoring and controlling is important and then look at what to monitor and control. How you use your status reports and operating procedures (discussed in Chapter 18) to control your project will directly affect the end results your project will achieve. Let me walk you through the guidelines for using reports and operating procedures to help you achieve positive control of your project.

First, use the project plan as the primary guide for coordinating your project. I have devoted a major portion of this book to preparation of the plan because of its centrality in the project management discipline. If you diligently follow the steps laid out in previous chapters, your plan is most likely a good one and something worth following.

You should also consistently monitor and update the plan and the other control documents, including the statement of work, the requirement specification, the blueprints, and the functional specifications (if you are using these documents for your project). A plan or supporting specification that is never referenced again after the initial plan is built will not help you control your project to a successful conclusion. Instead, for your plan to be useful, you must update it regularly. It must always reflect the current status of the project and any changes that become necessary because of new issues, budget constraints, or schedule or product modifications.

As I've emphasized throughout this book, you should monitor the progress of the project against the plan on a regular basis. This should be done in an integrated manner at regular intervals, not in a haphazard, arbitrary way. You must be aware of and report any significant variances from the budget and the schedule immediately because these anomalies affect the business case and success of the entire project.

And don't forget to get involved. You won't have time to sit at your computer waiting for results and accolades from the big boss. Instead, roll up your sleeves and get down in the trenches with the team. That way, you not only have a finger on the project's pulse, but you also actually contribute to a workload that may otherwise weigh heavily on team members' shoulders.

Make sure you also adapt the project schedule, budget, and work plan as necessary to keep the project on track. As the project progresses, changes in the original plan may be required for several reasons. (I cover the more common causes for changes in Chapter 22.) The project manager's responsibility is to make sure these changes are appropriate, valid, and approved.

Finally, document project progress and changes, and communicate them to team members. Keep the quality and level of detail of your reports and communications consistent, reliable, and appropriate for each level of the project team.

What Should You Monitor?

To keep things running smoothly, monitor the following elements for every project, regardless of size or complexity:

- The completion of work packages as compared to the plan to confirm you are on schedule. The work breakdown structure (WBS) is also the best way to maintain cost control.

- The scope of work being performed, to make sure you don't have scope creep (see Chapter 2).

- The quality of work being performed (see Chapter 23) against the requirements for the project.

- The costs and expenditures as compared to the plan to make sure you stay on budget.

- The attitudes of people working on the project or involved with the project, including key stakeholders and management.

- The cohesiveness and cooperation of team members.

 TIME IS MONEY

Remember, when managing a project, you need to control time, cost, quality, and scope.

For more information on monitoring and controlling cost, refer to PMBOK *Guide* section 7.4.2.

Note that you need to monitor more than just the tasks, the schedule, and the budget. The level of communication and cooperation between team members and the quality of the work being performed are also obviously important aspects of the project. In addition, you must monitor the use and availability of equipment. For example, you may be responsible for the usage of computer equipment on a large project. You also want to make sure the equipment doesn't suddenly disappear because no one was paying attention. An inventory of the equipment (for example, computers) can assist in the check-out and check-in process as team members start and finish.

On a large, complex project, the effort required for monitoring and control may take more time than you actually spend working on the project deliverables. This is okay. It is your job as project manager to be the chief integrator to bring the project to a successful conclusion. If you find yourself doing a lot of the work, that should be a red flag for you. Perhaps your budget will allow you to hire a project administrator who can handle the details of updating the plan—with your oversight and approval, of course. On smaller projects, the degree of monitoring and control should be much less time-consuming, and you can probably handle doing a fair amount of the actual work.

Using a simple scorecard with the colors of a stoplight, such as the one shown in the following table, can be a useful yet simple way to show the status of the project. Most people's eyes will immediately spot the red and yellow areas and not focus on green, which means everything is on track. However, be aware that some people are color blind and may not be able to see the status if you only use colors without additional words or symbols. The value of the colors is to focus attention on the areas where there may be potential trouble.

Project Scorecard

Cost	Yellow	Danger of a cost overrun in the development of the customer GUI
Schedule	Green	No significant problems in the schedule for the project
	Yellow	The vendor who is building the remote control device is running a little behind but believes they can catch up
Quality	Green	Peer review set for May to test the technical interfaces
Best practices	Green	Reviewed "Critical Success Factors for Projects" to remind ourselves of what to do
Functional issues	Red	Meeting to discuss billing structure with Accounting was cancelled and not rescheduled
	Green	New customer input decision for credit to be concluded next week
	Green	Ron to chair database working group
	Yellow	Lisa to chair group reviewing data streaming requirements document, but her travel schedule makes the timing difficult
	Green	Andrea working rollout issues with Marketing
Communication	Green	Project team to review and respond to Marketing queries
	Green	Project team to send out documentation that will be refined within the steering committee before the GUI is approved
	Green	Project group to provide complete list of known issues for the steering committee to resolve
	Green	Charles to obtain more information from vendors on their quality assurance plans
Risk	Green	None

Red = High Risk, Yellow = Marginal Risk, Green = Minimal Risk

The use of the appropriate level of reporting can help minimize the time spent monitoring activities on both small and large projects. Keep your reports simple and concise. In addition, the use of appropriate project management software that is adapted to your project needs can help reduce the time required to understand the impact of current activities and changes in the project plan.

For more information on monitoring and controlling the schedule, refer to *PMBOK Guide* section 6.4.2.

What Monitoring Should Accomplish

The tasks, milestones, and budget you documented in your project plan are the starting point for project coordination and control. These tasks and milestones form the checkpoints you should use to monitor progress. Whether formal or informal, project monitoring should serve one or more of the following basic functions:

- Communicating project status and changes to other project team members

- Managing the expectations of stakeholders (clients or customers) about the status of the project

- Providing the justification for making project adjustments

- Documenting current project plans compared to the original project plan (called the *baseline plan* in project management circles)

Consistency is very important in the monitoring and control process. You must monitor the project from start to finish because problems can occur anywhere along the way.

Inexperienced project managers may start out full of energy and monitor everything during the first few weeks. Then, when things seem to be going okay, the monitoring begins to disappear. These managers often end up with a big mess at the end of the project because they failed to keep track of progress and problems. Don't let this happen to you! Maintain your zeal throughout the project.

NOTES FROM THE FIELD

As you can probably gather from all the earlier chapters and this one, project managers have a lot of details to track. Some people are detail oriented and can handle all these details quite well. That is to say that for them, keeping a lot of details in their head is easier than it is for others. I am not one of those lucky people. That is why I need a good plan to follow. It is invaluable for me so I can pay attention to all the details during the execution of the project. If I didn't have a good plan, I am quite sure that the details would fall through the cracks and provide me with a lot of stress.

Using Earned Value Analysis to Determine Project Status

Earned value analysis (EVA) is an industry standard for doing the following:

- Measuring a project's progress
- Forecasting its completion date and final cost
- Providing schedule and budget variances along the way

The basic concept is that as project activities are completed, they will "earn value." EVA integrates three measures to provide a consistent, numerical indicator so you can evaluate where you are versus where you should be:

1. **Planned value (PV), also referred to as budgeted cost of work scheduled (BCWS):** Planned cost of the total amount of work scheduled to be performed by the milestone date

2. **Actual cost (AC), also referred to as actual cost of work performed (ACWP):** Cost incurred to accomplish the work that has been done to date

3. **Earned value (EV), also referred to as budgeted cost of work performed (BCWP):** The planned (not actual) cost to complete the work that has been done

Before you can calculate EVA, you need to have the right elements in your project plan to make EVA work. That includes having done your WBS, as described in Chapter 9, by using deliverables and work packages to define the activities to be completed by the project team. And each of those work packages and deliverables has a cost associated with it.

Let's imagine that you have a project that is scheduled to last eight weeks and cost $200,000. At the end of six weeks (75 percent of the allotted time), the project is only 50 percent complete, and you have spent $180,000. You can perform the following simple calculations can help you to manage your budget and schedule:

- **Schedule variance** or **SV** (EV minus PV) compares the amount of work performed (EV) during a given period of time to that scheduled to be performed (PV). A negative number (variance) means your project is behind schedule. If the number is positive, the project is ahead of schedule. In the example, the equation would be $100,000 (what we have completed) minus $150,000 (what we should have completed) = -$50,000. You are behind schedule.

- **Cost variance** or **CV** (EV minus AC) compares the budgeted cost of work performed (EV) with actual cost of that work (AC). A positive number (variance) means the project is under budget. If the number is negative, the project is over budget. In the example, to complete half the work, you should have spent $100,000; instead, you've spent $180,000. The equation would be $100,000 (what you had budgeted to spend) minus $180,000 (what you actually spent) = -$80,000.

With either calculation, you can see this project is in trouble. The biggest question now will be, how much more money and time will it take to complete? Many project management software packages can help you calculate this earned value data for you if you have the data entered into the program correctly.

For additional technical details on earned value, refer to *PMBOK Guide* **section 7.1.2.**

While the input and manipulation of data can create a considerable amount of work, and quantifying the work can be difficult at times, there is definite value in using EVA to control your project. It can help eliminate the guesswork in measuring performance, and forecasting and can also help eliminate some of the "fuzzy" measures used in controlling a project. Although calculating EVA is optional in most industry projects, it is often mandatory for any projects for the federal government.

Using Gantt Charts to Control Your Project

Gantt charts (see Chapter 10) usually display information in two ways: the left side displays it as a table and the right side as a chart. The table portion displays information about the project's tasks, such as when they start and end, how long they are, and what resources are assigned to them. The chart portion displays each task graphically, most often as a task bar. The bar's position on the timeline, and its length, indicates when that task begins and ends. In addition, the position of one task bar in relation to another indicates whether the tasks follow one after the other or are overlapping.

The best use of a Gantt chart is to see how activities are progressing over time. You can track progress by comparing planned and actual start and finish dates and by checking the completion percentage of each task. Although you can't see them in this chart, the bars are represented in different colors to indicate various aspects of the project status. Black represents the original plan, blue indicates the float available for the activity, and red indicates where the activity has slipped and taken more time than anticipated.

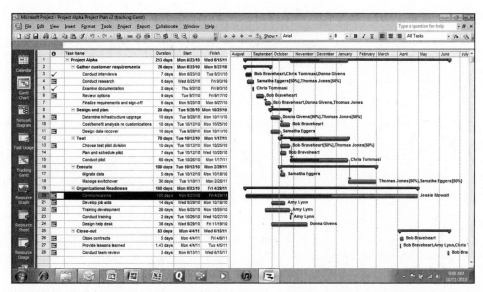

Using program software, such as Microsoft Project, can help you track your project. This tracking Gantt chart compares the project plan with the current status of the project.

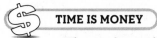 **TIME IS MONEY**

When working with outside vendors, suppliers, and agencies, strike up friendships with their support personnel. That way, if things start running off the rails for any reason, your friends can alert you before your project misses a milestone.

90-Percent-Done Syndrome

Many people are optimistic about their ability to make up for lost time. Others simply attempt to look good on paper. For these reasons, the phrase "90 percent done" on a project status report usually indicates a big problem. What is hiding behind that unfinished 10 percent that no one wants to admit? Why does it seem that 90 percent of the effort only takes 30 percent of the time, and the last 10 percent takes 200 percent of the original schedule?

If you see that 90 percent or some other large percentage of a complex task is completed very quickly but then the work only inches up to 91 and 92 percent over the next couple of status reports, you need to figure out what is really going on by talking to the project team members in an environment of support and understanding.

Use these guidelines to get to the root of the 90-percent-done syndrome:

- Investigate the scope of the remaining work through meetings or one-on-one sessions with key project members. Are there technical difficulties that the team doesn't want anyone to know about? Should the task be broken down into smaller, more measurable work packages?

- Consider whether the remaining 10 percent of the work is really predictable. Creative tasks, such as inventions or coming up with ideas, are often difficult to schedule. In the development of a new technology and in other high-creativity situations, the break-through required to complete a project may not happen as scheduled. Creative tasks need to be more realistically assessed. You can't schedule spontaneity, so don't try. Just be honest about the creative blocks, and document the schedule changes accordingly.

- Help the team be honest in its assessment of project status by encouraging open communication and by pointing out the problems with being too optimistic about risky endeavors. Team members may be giving you the estimates they think you want to see, not the real ones. Reward yourself and the team for honesty and effort rather than false statements of accomplishment or unrealistic commitments to impossible dreams.

The Project Review Meeting as a Control Process

Analyzing reports from your office chair will never be enough to help you guide your project to completion. Resolving conflicts, problems, and staffing issues is almost impossible using just reports, so meetings with people are always a necessary component of project control.

The project review meeting is an opportunity for key team members, not just managers and supervisors, to get together to resolve issues. It's also a time to discuss the current project status and to forecast performance toward meeting future milestones. Project review meetings are often held at the completion of a major milestone or before or after a key phase of the project. Some project review meetings are held on a periodic basis in place of formal reports. For example, a short subproject, such as the training design for new customer relationship management (CRM) system users, is best handled with brief reports and regular meetings because the project is of a short duration. Some projects may have less frequent meetings at certain stages and then more frequent meetings when more coordination is required.

If a project meeting is necessary to resolve issues, have one now, not later. It's best to take action as soon as you are aware of a problem instead of waiting for a regularly scheduled meeting. Make the meeting short and focused on the single issue that you just became aware of and then adjourn. Long, drawn-out meetings that wander into other issues can dampen enthusiasm and obfuscate the problem. At the end of three hours, no one cares anymore.

The Project Audit

The most formal type of project monitoring (and the process project managers most fear) is the audit. You may choose to use a different name, as the term *audit* strikes fear or anger in some people because of internal audits that they have experienced in the past. Sometimes audits are required as a part of the contract; sometimes they are necessary because the project is really off track and the source of the problem remains a mystery. The goal of a project audit is to get an accurate picture of the quality of work, current expenditures, and schedule of the project. (These are the goals of all monitoring activities, so the audit is really no different from putting together a big status report.)

In most cases, objective outsiders perform an audit by reviewing progress, costs, and current plans. After discussions with team members, reviews of reports, and direct observations, the objective auditors (who usually work for the customer or the government) report their conclusions on the current status of the project to the project manager or to executive management. They often make strong recommendations, giving better ways things should be done to keep a large project under control.

If your project ever gets audited, you'll be okay if you've followed all the tips for monitoring and tracking progress covered in this chapter. If you've done a good job of communicating and monitoring, the audit shouldn't reveal any surprises, but if it does, take them to heart and take action. Just because you didn't discover the problem is no reason to ignore the suggested solution.

Monitoring and Controlling the Budget

Reports and meetings are great for tracking schedules and performance, but budgets and cash outlays require special monitoring techniques. The way the budget tracking is set up depends on the accounting systems already in place in your company. As you make expenditures or sign contracts with vendors, establish a formal tracking method to measure your actual commitments.

In most companies, if you rely on expenditure reports from the accounting department to provide the financial status of your project, you'll likely go over budget or think you have more money than you actually do. Money is often spent in the form of contracts or agreements long before it is accounted for in the billing and invoice cycles of the corporation. Accounting reports typically deal with invoices that have been "paid to date." Unfortunately, they don't usually report on invoices that have not been paid or have yet to be billed. Think of it the same way you would your checking account. You need to account for outstanding checks before you can get a true picture of the balance you really have in the bank.

For this reason, you must track actual expenditures to date in addition to reviewing the accounting reports. Ultimately, your expenditures and the accounting department documentation should match, but it might take as long as 90 days for the two systems to be reconciled. Most of the available project management software packages will allow you to track expenditures as well as tasks and people.

You and each person on your project team who will be making financial commitments to vendors or suppliers must account for all monetary commitments as they occur. At a minimum, all expenditures should appear on the formal status reports. For larger projects, you may want to have someone with accounting skills on the project staff who can assist you in tracking and auditing the project expenditures.

When you get reports from accounting that don't match your budget file, you will have the documentation necessary to reconcile the differences. If you don't have such a file, you'll be at the mercy of your accountant or finance officer (not a desirable condition).

 TIME IS MONEY

When you collect data from your team, collect information on all aspects of the project at one time (tasks, budget, quality, and issues). If you keep going back to people for additional information, you'll irritate them and diminish productivity.

Integrating Everything

The project team is your best source of ideas for keeping the project on track. After you have complete input from your team, you can analyze the project status and decide on new actions to take (if any) to keep the project moving toward a successful conclusion. This includes two steps. The first step involves—you guessed it—updating the project plan to reflect the current status. The second step is a review with the stakeholders and team to gain consensus on the revisions to the plan. I discuss this second step in detail in Chapter 22; for now, let's tackle updating the project plan and the related documents.

Your plan documents—including the charter, product specifications, blueprints, budget, and schedule—are the most important control tools you can use. They allow you to present the work that's been agreed to and to communicate necessary changes.

For more information on integration management to control work, refer to *PMBOK Guide* **section 4.4.2.**

If you're comfortable with your cross-checking of project tasks, schedules, and budgets after gathering data on the current status of the project, compare the reality with the approved plan and other project documents as appropriate (such as comparing the charter and product specifications to better predict what's going to happen from here on out). For large projects, this is most easily done with computerized tools. Plugging in the status data may predict required changes to the schedule, budget, and critical path. (Computerized project management tools allow you to see comparisons of the old versus the new by highlighting changed paths, dates, tasks, and budget variances.)

After you have used the new data to forecast a new schedule and budget, look for the problems causing the variances. If your critical path suddenly goes late, follow the lines back to see what tasks are late and who or what is responsible. If the critical path changes, it may or may not be a major flag. Again, study the flow to see what went wrong.

Tracking the budget is a matter of having good accounting practices in place that can give you timely figures on the committed costs and expenditures of the project. The process of comparing current to planned expenditures is similar to matching work completed to the planned task network. Graphs and spreadsheets are useful for demonstrating cost variances and projections. Good project management programs will offer a number of graphing techniques to allow you to visualize the budget through time.

 NOTES FROM THE FIELD

After building a great project plan, I had to manage a series of 10 projects that covered four states in the United States. Each project had different people working on the WBS activities, including some of the operations teams in the field. The amount of detail was staggering even for someone as experienced as I was at the time. However, I always felt in control because if someone called me to ask a question, I had an answer. There was a reason—because I had great team members submitting progress reports against the plan. As things changed, we changed the plan and the schedule. I could have only done that with an up-to-date plan and meaningful progress reports. It provided my stakeholders with a lot of confidence because their questions were answered in a timely fashion and it appeared that the project was well organized. And we delivered on time!

Review Questions

- Am I clear on why I need to keep my plan up to date and use it to monitor the project?

- Do I understand the details I should be tracking?

- Can I use earned value analysis as a tool for monitoring the type of projects I manage?

- Do I need some training on the use of a project management software package to help me keep track of all the details, or can I use a spreadsheet?

- Do I recognize the 90-percent-done problem and understand how I will make sure I don't fall into the trap?

The Least You Need to Know

- Control requires knowledge of the project status. Since the status is constantly changing, you'll need to monitor the project and compare it to the plan in some way regularly.

- If you keep the plan and other key project documentation up to date to reflect changes and adjustments, you can more accurately determine your status.

- Use important project methods like EVA to help you understand the status of your project.

- If a project is 90 percent done but the last 10 percent seems to be taking too much time to complete, investigate why that is happening and what steps you and the project team can take to make that last bit more manageable.

- Use project audits to help you maintain control.

- Monitoring the budget takes time and effort, but it's part of good project management.

Preparing Operations for Success

Very often in projects, project managers forget that the final product or deliverables from their projects will ultimately be transferred into the everyday operations within the company. In other words, the product moves from being a project to being the operating procedure, tool, or equipment people will use every day to help them do their job. While many tasks must be completed before handing the project deliverables over to the operations group, one of the most important is preparing the operations group to be ready to receive those deliverables.

In this chapter, I discuss why it is important to focus on these preparations and when the project manager should begin to concentrate on this aspect of preparation.

In This Chapter

- Recognizing the five requirements for operations integration
- Developing a training plan
- Warning signs that operations are not ready
- Dealing with resistance to change
- Developing a leadership plan

Five Requirements for Operations Integration

If you go back to the very beginning of the book, you will see that the high-level purpose of any project is to improve the performance of the business. We have all witnessed, or perhaps even been part of a project, that delivered what it was supposed to deliver but was considered a failure. How can that be? If you analyzed most of the projects where that has happened, I would be willing to bet that the root cause of the failure centered on operations not being ready to receive the deliverables. In the mind of the users, it did not solve the problem that caused the project to be sanctioned in the first place.

In developing the plan for *operations integration,* you must meet these five requirements if you are to succeed:

1. Create and communicate the conclusion.

2. Have the skills to use the deliverables.

3. Create incentives.

4. Help users make the transition.

5. Let stakeholders know the schedule.

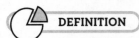

DEFINITION

Operations integration means that people are using the product or service (delivered by the project) exactly the way it was intended in the business case.

The following table shows what can happen when all of the requirements aren't met.

Requirement	Requirement	Requirement	Requirement	Requirement	Result
Create and communicate the conclusion	Have the skills to use the deliverable	Create incentives	Help users make the transition	Let stakeholders know the schedule	Operations ready to receive the deliverables
X	Have the skills to use the deliverable	Create incentives	Help users make the transition	Let stakeholders know the schedule	Confusion; lack of interest
Create and communicate the conclusion	X	Create incentives	Help users make the transition	Let stakeholders know the schedule	Old ways of work continue
Create and communicate the conclusion	Have the skills to use the deliverable	X	Help users make the transition	Let stakeholders know the schedule	Disregard for the deliverables and lack of motivation
Create and communicate the conclusion	Have the skills to use the deliverable	Create incentives	X	Let stakeholders know the schedule	Frustration, anger, and disappointment
Create and communicate the conclusion	Have the skills to use the deliverable	Create incentives	Help users make the transition	X	Wasted effort and lack of orderly progress

Let's look at each requirement to see why it is important and then discuss ways to implement that requirement for success.

For information on a change management plan for stakeholders, refer to *PMBOK Guide* section 13.4.1.1.

Create and Communicate the Conclusion

You must create a vision for what the workplace will look like after the deliverables are in place. Some people have dubbed this conclusion as "a day in the life," and that might work, but what you are really trying to do is paint them a vivid picture of how they will use the deliverables from the project in completing their everyday work. The communication must not just say "you'll be able to work faster"; it must also explain why and how they will be able to work faster. And it must borrow from the case for change you built (described in Chapter 7) to answer the question, "Why are we doing this?" If this requirement is not met, you will create confusion and lack of interest within operations.

Have the Skills to Use the Deliverable

You'll need to explain to people how they will develop the knowledge and skills necessary to use the project deliverable effectively. Skills training should focus on "what you do" and not "what you need to know." Much of the resistance to change that project managers face when handing over their project is that the operations group is worried they will not be properly prepared, and therefore will look foolish or incompetent. Very few people, regardless of their mindset, are going to let someone make them look foolish without putting up a fight. You will need to explain, in detail, the training (discussed later in this chapter) they will get and assure them repeatedly that they will be ready when the project is ready. If you don't meet this requirement, the old ways of working will continue.

Create Incentives

When you prepare to transition the project into operations, you'll likely need to provide some incentives for the users to try it. Companies have done this for years when they develop a new product or service; they give a substantial discount or sometimes even give a free sample, just to get people to try it. For example, the project manager for a new sales software program for the sales reps to use worked with management in sales and marketing to create a contest with a cruise as the grand prize. Not every project will be able to use that tactic, but it is worth considering.

Some people are called *early adopters*. These are people who like the latest products and will readily try out a new item. As you plan for the transition, try to identify these people and begin to pull them into the process of handing the project deliverable over to operations. Usually they will not need incentives because of their eagerness to try a new product. In the IT world, this is called *user acceptance testing*. This tactic may have application beyond the introduction of new software.

TIME IS MONEY

When he was preparing for a new campaign, the great French general Napoleon Bonaparte knew that his generals would fall into three groups. The first group would follow him anywhere at any time. The second group would always tell him the campaign was a bad idea. The third group would listen to his idea and then give their approval or rejection. As you expect, Napoleon focused on the third group. You should, too, when attempting to overcome resistance to change.

One effective tactic that many project managers have used is to have a lunchtime demonstration of the new product. To entice people to attend the session, the project manager might provide free soft drinks and cookies. It's amazing how many people will attend if they get free food! At other times, when the budget would allow, you can provide a full lunch (free, of course) for the influential users/operators whom you want to support the implementation. Again, it's the idea of an incentive for coming and seeing! If you fail to meet this requirement, operations is likely to disregard the deliverables and have a lack of motivation to actually use it.

Brainstorm with your team and the business people in your working committee to determine the right incentives to stimulate participation and ultimately buy-in.

For more information on incentives, refer to *PMBOK Guide* **section 13.3.2.2.**

Help Users Make the Transition

It is very important for people to have the right help in making the transition. One obvious form of help is the training you will provide. If you follow the suggestions for developing a training plan outlined later in this chapter, you'll be training people to use the project deliverable in their actual job. That will help tremendously in building confidence among the target audience.

Also provide extra help, such as a hotline, for people to use in the first weeks to get information they might need if they forget how to do something in the interval between their training and when you actually roll out the deliverable. And depending on the geographic locations, you might even have experts wandering around the floor or worksite on the first few days so people can easily call someone over to their workstation if they need some immediate help. If you fail to meet this requirement, operations will likely be frustrated, disappointed or angry—none of which is good!

Let Stakeholders Know the Schedule

Most people are very aware of the fact that something will be happening to them. Knowing when these events will unfold is some comfort. They want to know when the following will happen:

- They will get their training

- They will start using the project deliverable

- The old way of doing things goes away and the changes go into effect

Giving stakeholders enough detail to help them know when various events will happen will give them the security that there will be no surprises. Failure to meet this requirement will usually result in wasted effort.

Developing the Training Plan

Often project managers take a superficial look at training and only ask the question, "What will people need to *know* to make the project deliverable work?" If they ask the training professionals within their organization, they will typically get the same sort of answer because many of those trainers come from an educational background. However, training should instead focus on the question, "What will people need to *be able to do* to make the use of the project deliverables successful?" Focusing on *doing* rather than *knowing* is a critical difference because it changes the paradigm from a learning solution to a job-focused solution. If people only need to *know* something, then it probably belongs in the communication plan, not the training plan.

Basically, people *do* work, hence the focus on *doing* rather than knowing. There will be process changes, and there may be new equipment, tools, or systems. Developing the training plan should incorporate information from the process changes as well as any technical training in the use of a project deliverable, such as a software application.

Work with a key stakeholder group in the working committee for approval of the training plan by looking at the following two types of training:

- **Product training** focuses on the technical function and features of the new project deliverables.

- **Job-focused training** focuses on "how" individuals will use the project deliverables within their workflow and demonstrates how to use the deliverable to do their specific work assignments.

For example, if the project was installing new customer information database, let's look at how it might apply to the customer service people after the database is installed and ready for use.

If you consider product training, it would focus on giving the employees the ability to do the following:

- Navigate the screens to find the customer's name and address

- Input data correctly when they are taking an order

- Create searches for billing information if the customer has questions about a bill

- Display and print reports

Now these are very useful and helpful abilities, but they may not really help the employees become the kind of customer-focused people that the company wants for the future, nor will they help the company in achieving the business case.

Therefore, you must concentrate on job-focused training. Now the project team will be helping train the employees to do the following:

- Navigate the screens to help a customer solve a problem by being able to access that customer's needed information

- Input data accurately to place the customer's order in the right priority category so the correct discounts and incentives are applied during billing

- Create searches for information so marketing and sales representatives and product development people can begin to assess and predict buying trends

- Display and print reports that allow customer service representatives to recommend other products or services a particular customer might be interested in purchasing

If the training plan is developed correctly, people will feel confident they know what they are doing, and the resistance to change will drop dramatically.

Signs That Operations Is Not Ready

Some warning signs may suggest that operations may not be ready for the project deliverables. In other words, you and the project team are nearly ready to turn things over to operations, but they are not ready to receive it. If this is the case, you will begin to see telltale signals. If you notice any of these, take corrective actions to try to alleviate the problem:

- Key people or groups are not aware of the project or do not seem to support it in actions or words.

- Training is not well attended by some groups, which means their management is probably not providing the support you need.

- Incentives that you have provided are not producing the results you had hoped for and may need to be adjusted.

- Key people or groups are not aware of the timeline for the implementation.

If any of these signs occur, you'll need to confer with the working committee and develop some remedial plans to address them. The worst thing you can do is ignore the problem. Try to determine why people are not on board and plan for corrective action as quickly as possible. Your working committee is the best source for uncovering that information. Why? Remember who is on that committee—people who represent the needs and concerns of the group. People within the company are much more likely to talk with them about their concerns or reservations than the project manager or project team.

 NOTES FROM THE FIELD

As you can probably guess by now, I am a fan of including a working committee on your projects. It is especially true in preparing operations for the project deliverables. However, constantly monitor the working committee members to make sure they are communicating with everyone, not just to a small, select group. This is especially true in designing the training required to get users ready. The group resisting change will have real ammunition if they aren't being consulted. And don't be under the illusion that the stakeholders will blame the working committee member!

Overcoming Resistance to Change

Many people naturally resist change in their lives, whether it's moving to a new house or city, finding another job, or any other situation where they must give up the tried-and-true for the unknown. People may be resistant to the changes your project deliverables will bring for a variety of reasons, including the following:

- Fear

- Feelings of powerlessness

- Simple discomfort

- Absence of self-interest

Any of these emotions can cause people to refuse to accept the changes that the project will bring. You will need to build actions and communications to help them address the root cause and gradually bring them into a mindset that accepts the project.

Fear

For some people, when they hear about changes that a project will cause, they immediately assume a worst-case scenario. This is particularly true if they have previously been subjected to poorly implemented projects. They believe that their reaction is normal until proven otherwise.

Others may fear a reduction in the workforce based on the implementation of the project: "They aren't going to need all of us after the change, and I'm the one who will go!" Indeed, a reduction may happen as the result of a project, and if that is the case, you must communicate it clearly. Work with the management team to send the right messages regarding any reduction in force that may occur. If a reduction is not part of the plan after implementation, then you must also communicate frequently since people probably will not believe it initially. They may think management is hiding the "true" intent, so don't be surprised. And don't give up!

Some people may fear they won't be personally competitive in the new operating environment. You must give them a clear idea of how you will prepare each and every person to handle his job confidently and competently as you transition into operations. Obviously, training will be a centerpiece of that effort, but so will the use of job aids, a help desk they can call when they have questions, and any other elements you have planned to prepare people correctly. Make sure everybody understands the new environment.

Another common fear is that mistakes will be punished because the company has spent a lot of money on this change. Some might fear the first one to make a mistake will be fired. Hopefully, that is not the case; however, this has indeed happened in some organizations, but not when you have the type of extensive planning and preparation I am talking about. You will need to communicate how mistakes will be handled and the real level of tolerance that management will have as the transition to operations proceeds. And then you must hold both management and employees to the approach you have communicated.

Feelings of Powerlessness

Often, resistance occurs because there is a general feeling that people's ideas are not valued. They will state, "I told them the problem the first time the idea came up. I told them how to make it work, and they didn't listen." Again, the working committee will be very helpful for these people. They should solicit ideas and feedback from them before decisions are made and then follow up with them after decisions have been made. In this situation, you may need to help the working committee with the messages they deliver to make sure all of the messages are clear and consistent.

Other people tend to view themselves as outsiders and feel management only cares about a certain privileged few. The best way to handle this is to communicate the plans so they see how things will happen and when. Usually they will realize that everyone is being impacted and the plan appears organized and comprehensive. That will reduce the anxiety and give them confidence that management is not "playing favorites" as the project moves to operations.

RISK MANAGEMENT

You may hear the cry "It's not fair!" from people who believe the project is just "one more change" inflicted on the workers who are carrying the company. To address this type of concern, you should work with key members of the working committee and use the case for change and communication plan as your basis for addressing this problem. In my experience, this is usually more a perception problem than anything else.

Simple Discomfort

Let's face it, some people are just happy with the status quo. They take the attitude of, "If it's not broken, don't fix it!" That is not unusual. Many of us like things the way they are and consider the future a foreign place we would just as soon not visit! The good news is that if you have painted a strong picture for them and clearly explained how the job will work in the future, when it finally happens, it will likely be a nonevent, and they might even look forward to the change!

Absence of Self-Interest

Usually, people who are driven by self-interest (and aren't we all, to some extent?) don't understand the perceived benefits when the project moves to operations. They are basically asking, "What's in it for me?" or thinking, "I'm putting more into this than I will get out of it!" Strong communications must constantly reinforce the benefits that operations will reap from the successful implementation. Now remember, because people are looking at their self-interest, they may not be persuaded by the benefits the company will accrue. In that case, you must show individuals how they also benefit. Some people may also believe that the benefits of the project are long term or will be achieved by others before they personally receive any benefit. "I'm suffering now for 'maybe' benefits in the future" is another common complaint of this group.

You will need to communicate how this project will help them in both the short term and the long term. Much of the information will probably come from the business case, but put the case into everyday language that will help people understand the benefits to them personally. The only way to do that effectively will be to do a careful audience analysis prior to developing your communication plan for these people and get the working committee actively involved in selling the benefits.

As you work to handle the resistance to the changes your project will deliver, you will need effective leadership from operations. As you analyze the sources of the resistance, remember the power base for messages I discussed in Chapter 19. At times, you may need an authority figure like a vice president or a respected person who is known for his technical knowledge of the business to explain what is going on, and why, to those who are resistant. Be sure to pick the right person to deliver the message that the change is coming and they need to be ready. But remember, it is your project that is going into operations. You will usually need to develop the content of the message for the person who will deliver it. Don't expect the vice president or working committee chairman to do it!

Creating a Leadership Plan

At certain times, and in certain situations, only management can communicate and overcome resistance to change. For example, if the new way of working is *not* optional, only management— and specifically, senior management—can make that type of statement. Ultimately, a person's boss is the one each person feels accountable to, and they need to hear a statement like that from that person. Just like a training plan, you need to determine which actions or activities and create a leadership or management plan. Finally, after you have developed the detailed activities where you need senior management involved, give them plenty of advanced notice and explain clearly and concisely why you need them to handle this activity or message. My experience has been that they will embrace the opportunity and provide the leadership you seek. And don't forget to include these activities in the overall project plan!

 WORDS FROM THE WISE

Executives are like joggers. If you stop a jogger, he goes on running on the spot. If you drag an executive away from his business, he goes on running on the spot, pawing the ground, talking business. He never stops hurtling onwards, making decisions and executing them.

—Jean Baudrillard, philosopher and developer of the theory of hyper-reality

Review Questions

- Do I understand each of the five requirements for operations integration?

- Does my training plan address what users need to do and not what they need to know?

- Do I recognize the symptoms that signal that operations is not ready for the project to deliver?

- Do I understand how to overcome resistance to change?

- Have I identified activities that only management can do and added them to my project plan?

The Least You Need to Know

- Resistance to change will occur if you don't fulfill the five requirements for operations integrations.
- You will need to prepare a training plan for your project deliverables.
- Deal with resistance to change as soon as you begin to see it.
- Watch for warning signs that operations is not ready to receive your deliverables.
- Develop a leadership plan for those activities or messages which only senior management can deliver.

Changes, Changes, and More Changes

One of the most difficult challenges for any project manager comes when the scope of the project changes. Although many factors cause change, two reasons are most common. One cause of change would be to overcome a technical problem not foreseen when the original project scope was developed; a second cause for a change in scope would be a shift in the business drivers for the project.

Remember from Chapter 1 that the reason for the project in the first place is to solve a business problem or to enable the organization to perform at a higher level. So it's reasonable to expect that over the course of a large project that will take 18 to 24 months to complete, the business requirements for producing that higher performance may change—and with that, your project scope will probably change, too!

In This Chapter

- Developing a process to deal with changes
- Estimating the impact of change
- Balancing a project
- Understanding the trade-offs and the options for change
- Communicating with the sponsor when problems arise
- Creating an issues log

Some changes are under your control. For example, you might be able to shorten a schedule because you learn faster ways to do things as you proceed through the steps of the work plan. On the other hand, if the vendor who was manufacturing components required for the new processing plant closes because of a strike, you'll have to change the schedule, like it or not. In both cases, you'll have to anticipate the impact of the change and adjust your project plan accordingly. Because change is inevitable, managing the impact of change is a key aspect in controlling your project.

A very common change is a change in requirements when you are already in the execution phase of a project. Recognizing that changes impact the schedule, cost, and quality, you must balance those factors as you manage the change; this chapter shows you how.

Developing a Process for Integrated Change Control

During the planning phase, you and your team will need to develop a *change control system* that you will follow, and will expect the stakeholders to follow, when a request for a scope change occurs. To handle these requests by using a process is particularly important because the process will be an important part of managing the expectations of various stakeholder groups.

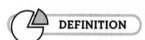 **DEFINITION**

The Project Management Institute (PMI) defines a **change control system** as "a set of procedures that describes how modifications to the project deliverables and documentation are managed and controlled."

What Might a Change Process Look Like?

The answer to this question is not as simple as it may seem. When the project manager begins to assess the impact of a change, the first consideration is to do a quick assessment of how difficult the change may be. The simple changing of the color of the background on a screen may not be too difficult as opposed to a more dramatic shift in the scope of the project. In either case, the process should begin with a formal request.

You should then follow that request with a review of the impact on the project—its schedule, cost, and quality. Depending on how big the impact is on first assessment, you need to make your first decision about who to put on the evaluation of the change request. You should pick people who are able to devote some time to the evaluation without impacting the overall project schedule. However, these people also have to have had enough experience and knowledge to provide a reasonably accurate assessment. Also, if the change is technical in nature, the person should understand any technical risks involved in making a change.

The next step is to develop a high-level cost/benefit analysis. You construct this analysis against the original scope requirements and specifications. Remember, the reason organizations invest in a project is the increased performance results they expect to achieve.

Finally, a decision needs to be made as to whether this request requires an authorization beyond the decision-making authority of the project manager. In most cases of scope change, the answer is obvious. If your team decides that the impact will make a serious change to the cost, schedule, or quality of the project, then the decision is something that you should definitely take to the steering committee. However, don't surprise them. This is where managing stakeholder expectations comes into play. If you believe that a decision may be elevated to the steering committee, then immediately brief your project sponsor on the situation. Let her know that you may be coming to them for a decision. Give the sponsor a rough idea of the nature of the request and reasons you think it will require their approval. You can then encourage the sponsor to begin networking with the steering committee members to let them know what's going on. The key is to make sure they know that the project will make a request and provide them with alternatives to consider.

By using this process, you, as the project manager, will be able to engage the right people and arrive at a decision that may not have been what the stakeholder had hoped for, but they should be prepared to accept the decision.

RISK MANAGEMENT

It is not the project manager's job to prevent change. It is the project manager's job to assess the impact of the change and to make a decision (or ask the steering committee to make one) based on her analysis.

Managing scope change and monitoring and controlling the project go hand in hand. As you monitor your project over time, you'll get feedback on the general issues, problems, and other factors that may be affecting your progress (positively or negatively) in completing the project. Lots of things enter the picture as the project proceeds; some are desirable, others are unpredictable, and once in a while, one can be disastrous. (I was working on a project at a major airport and was almost finished when 9/11 occurred. No one could have predicted that event, and needless to say, it had a dramatic effect on my project.) The good ideas and the unpredictable problems will all result in the same thing: the need to change the project plan in some way.

Through a project review process, new ideas and new ways of doing things can be evaluated and decisions can be made.

The Rules of Change Control

Now that you've accepted the inevitability of change, these four suggestions will help you when changes occur:

1. During the planning phase, establish a decision-making process regarding changes that are requested. Be sure to follow that process during the execution of the project.

2. Consider establishing a change control board that is a subset of your working committee or governance board. Use them to evaluate changes that have an impact on the stakeholders and the project. They may also be able handle the politics of changes within the company.

3. Establish emergency decision-making authority in case things need to be done too quickly for even the sponsor or a change control board to meet and discuss a change. This is particularly important at times in the year when many people may be on vacation and unavailable.

4. Maintain a change control log within a spreadsheet to track all change requests and the decisions that were made. This log can capture vital information needed to complete the lessons learned during the close-out phase (see Chapter 24).

 NOTES FROM THE FIELD

> There's always someone associated with your project who "knows" how to do things better than you're doing them. Sometimes you need to be assertive and keep this person from getting in your way. Establish a clear process for suggesting and reviewing changes so people offer constructive advice. And if you fail at a project because of outside interference, guess who will get the blame? I bet it won't be the person with all those "good" ideas.

Use the change control log to track information, including the tracking number that corresponds to the number on the work breakdown structure (WBS). You would normally keep a record like this in a spreadsheet or database application, not in written form.

PROJECT CHANGE REQUEST	
☐ **APPROVED** ASSIGNED CHANGE REQUEST NUMBER:_____ [1] ☐ **REJECTED**	
DATE:_____ DATE:_____	
Change Authorization Decision Required (Date/Time):	
Project Name:	Category of Change:
Customer:	Decision Maker:
Project Sponsor:	Project Manager:
Description of Change Requested: *(Attach any additional documentation required to access necessity for change)*	
Justification for Change: *(Include the reasons for the change as well as the consequences if the change is rejected)*	
Cost Impact:	Schedule Impact:
Other Impacted, Re-planning Activity Required *(Attach Supporting Documentation)*;	
Submitted By:	*Printed Name*		*Signature and Date*
Project Sponsor:	*Approval Signature & Date (if req'd)*	Project Manager:	*Approval Signature and Date*

---

[1] See Change Log for next available sequence number.

The project change request form has several key items to consider. First is the impact of the change so that later on you can track how the impact was assessed to see how correct you were. Second, it tracks who authorized the change. That may be important if someone questions a change later.

Understanding and Estimating the Impact of Changes

If you want to stay in control and help your project evolve in the right direction, a well-documented project plan is your first line of defense in managing change. If you want the results you expect as opposed to the consequences that just happen, you need to keep your plan up to date—period. With a plan in hand, you can quickly assess the impact a change will have on the project's budget, schedule, and resources. You can also use the plan and your current status analysis to show why a new or different requirement may have an impact that means the project will take longer to complete or require more money than budgeted.

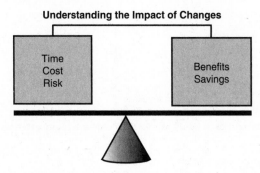

Understanding the Impact of Changes

Any changes to the project need to balance the time, cost, and risk against potential benefits and savings. Obviously, the best changes tilt the balance to benefits and savings.

As you review your plan, you'll see that really only six major components in any project can be changed. They are the same components you used to create your project plan in the first place:

- The business reason the project was undertaken in the first place, as articulated in the business case that you translated into project goals and objectives

- The people who work on the project

- The money (budget) you have to spend on the project

- The material and technical resources you have available to support your project

- The time you have available to complete the project

- The quality requirements that were acceptable for the finished deliverables

Any change in your project plan will affect one or more of these project components. Most changes will affect all six in some way.

The Balancing Act

Balancing a project—or managing changes in the project plan—can take place at three levels of authority, depending on the severity or immediacy of the change needed:

- *Project-level balancing* involves making adjustments to keep the project within its approved cost, schedule, and quality outcomes. The project manager and core team members should have enough authority to make these decisions.

- *Business-case balancing* is necessary when a project cannot achieve its approved cost, schedule, and quality goals. When this becomes obvious through project monitoring, the business case for the project must be reevaluated. Maybe the project will be useless if it doesn't come in on time. Maybe there isn't enough money (or profit) left in the project to make it worthwhile. Business case changes are beyond the scope of the project manager's authority alone and must involve the review and approval team of the sponsor and the steering committee.

- *Enterprise-level balancing* is required when a company has to make decisions about projects because the business climate or regulatory requirements have changed. This could result in a project being cancelled (terminated) or postponed. This is primarily a business management decision that is well beyond the scope of the project manager, although you may be involved in the process.

RISK MANAGEMENT

It's important to always get formal approval for revisions from the powers that be. Even if the disruption is minimal, managers and stakeholders should be fully cognizant of changes. For changes that impact delivery dates or the budget, written correspondence should accompany your request. Remember, if they're not in writing, agreements are easily forgotten.

After the changes are decided upon, document these changes on the original plan, date them, and communicate them as you would a new project plan. On large projects, the documentation of the changes is often called *configuration management,* and it can require a full-time staff in the "project office" responsible for controlling the different versions of the project plan.

After the new plan is approved, inform all team members of the changes to their tasks and delivery dates. Make sure that all team members are aware of exactly what you will expect of them and how the changes will impact the project. You'll also need to let team members know how the effect of the changes will be measured so that things don't end up going on just like before. Do this measuring through ongoing monitoring, reports, and communication. (And yes, you might need to change some of your project reports or procedures to make sure you get the new information you need.)

In balancing a project where changes impact its time, cost, or quality objectives, here are the basic things you can do:

Reduce the scope of the tasks. Sometimes the best way to get a project done is to scratch some of the work from the list. This can turn an impossible list of tasks into a doable (and scoped-down) project. Before promising to do less as a way of dealing with change, however, make sure the downsized project is really worth doing. Also make sure the stakeholders agree to the downsizing. If they don't, you'll need to negotiate what you really need—more time or resources or a bigger budget—to get the project done right.

Increase productivity by using in-house experts. Some people are simply more productive than others. By reassigning people, you may still be able to meet your original cost and schedule performance. Be sure there isn't a better way to make the staff more productive, such as training people or prudently using new technologies.

Use outside resources. Assign part of the project to an external firm that can manage and complete it within your original guidelines (outsourcing). This moves the work to outside experts who will hopefully be more productive. However, this may create more risks in terms of lost in-house control and the gamble that the outside experts will actually do what they say they can.

Crash the schedule. This involves compressing the tasks on the critical path to reduce the time required to meet the desired finish date. You'll need to produce a cost/schedule/trade-off analysis, which can help analyze the cost of reducing the schedule. Sometimes the increases in cost to get things done faster will outweigh the need for speed.

Adjust the return on investment (ROI) requirements for the project. A reduced ROI for the project can make a project successful by lowering the bar. If the project won't bring in enough money to meet the business case, however, this is a bad idea. A decision to reduce profit is clearly the territory of the company executives, not the project manager.

Adjust the project goals. This is like playing on thin ice. For example, it may be appropriate to reduce some of the functionality or scope of the project end results, but to reduce the performance characteristics (quality) of the project is not usually a good idea. Remove some of the functionality only when it doesn't affect the performance of the product overall.

 RISK MANAGEMENT

People can get frustrated with endless rounds of picky changes. To avoid this frustration, limit the self-induced changes to those that are truly necessary and important.

Comparing Changes with Trade-Off Analysis

Trade-off analysis is one method of dealing with change that lets you evaluate the impact of various alternatives: "We can do this if we skip that. Which is more important?" Analyzing trade-offs is also a way to understand the pressure change is placing on the project. Understanding trade-offs clarifies the changes that will affect later tasks and milestones. Here are some considerations for understanding the impact of various options (or trade-offs) when implementing a change to a project:

- Determine the underlying rationale for the change. Are the changes motivated by rational thinking or a political agenda? Does the change really make sense?

- Are the project goals still appropriate? Will the change also affect the eventual outcome of the project?

- Do the options affect the likelihood of completing the project successfully? You should have already reviewed how the various options impact schedules, budgets, and team member availability. When changes increase the risk of failure, this problem needs to be carefully analyzed and then clearly communicated to all involved.

- Analyze the options at all levels. Try to hold the budget and objectives constant, and then evaluate how you can accommodate the changes. Look for alternatives, tasks that can be deleted or shortened, or dollars that can be moved around in the project. This is usually an exercise with your team leads. Be patient when trying to come up with alternatives; don't always jump on the first ideas. Only after looking at all options should you ask for more money or more time.

Changing the Charter When the Changes Are Approved

Back in Chapter 7, I discussed developing the charter for the project. If a change in scope is approved, you need to go back and revise the charter. You will probably need to adjust the following:

- Goals and objectives

- Approval requirements

- Benefits and risks

You may also need to rewrite the scope statement to accurately reflect the new project deliverables.

I would recommend that, just like the earlier charter, you get this revised charter signed by the sponsor and any other key stakeholders that signed the original document. You want it to be crystal clear that this change was "signed off" and approved.

Communicating a Scope Change

A variety of people need the information about a scope change—whether or not they approved that change. Review your stakeholder analysis and remember the power base the message should come from. No matter who ultimately sends the communication, they need to clearly explain the process the business used to make the decision and explain the rationale for the choice.

To ensure that you are communicating to the right people, keep these three steps in mind:

1. **Inform your project team.** Sometimes changes will occur, and you need to make sure that all team members understand the nature of the change and will support the change. Make certain they are on board before you do anything else. Nothing can destroy the reputation of the project more than having project team members openly, or covertly, grumbling about a change.

2. **Go to your communication plan and see which stakeholders are impacted by the scope change.** Then follow the same format for communicating the scope change. Start with examining what information they will need and when, and then decide who is the right person to deliver the message and what medium to use. You probably should start with the project sponsor and the working committee. They should have already sanctioned the change, but it is a smart tactic to remind them of that formally in the communication. You can handle small changes through email or the regular project updates you already have in place; however, large changes should be handled in a richer forum, such as a town hall meeting.

3. **Log the change into your change log.** Notice in the project change request form shown earlier in this chapter that the authorization is noted in the log. Later, when you conduct your lessons learned for the project, having that information will be helpful in writing your final report.

When a change has been requested, even before it has been accepted or rejected, conflicts may occur. People will have legitimate differences of opinion on the wisdom of the change. In that light, a project manager must understand how to handle those types of situations.

Many people have studied conflicts and how managers resolve them. These studies have identified five general ways to resolve conflicts, all appropriate at one time or another:

Withdrawing means that the manager retreats (withdraws) from the disagreement. This is often an option if the conflict is petty, of inconsequential impact to the project, and not worth spending time to figure out.

Smoothing is used to emphasize areas of agreement to help minimize or avoid areas of disagreement. This is the preferred method when people can identify areas of agreement and the conflict is relatively unimportant. However, this is a weak approach; chances are the conflict will flare up again even though sparring parties shake hands and make up. Use it to get the project moving until you can find a better solution.

Compromising involves creating a negotiated solution that brings some source of satisfaction to each party in the conflict. Compromises are best made after each side has had time to cool down if the conflict has escalated to the anger and hostility stage. The best compromise makes each party feel as though she "won." A well-constructed compromise will hold the project together. A poor or weak one will come apart in the future, so be ready for it. The solution to a collapsed compromise is usually another compromise. This works best when people have a give-and-take attitude and a shared focus on the priorities of the project. (The delicate art of negotiation is described in Chapter 23.)

Forcing is used when someone exerts her position of power to resolve a conflict. This is usually done at the expense of someone else, and I do not recommend it unless all other methods have failed to resolve the conflict.

Confronting is not quite as strong as forcing, but it is the most utilized form of conflict resolution. The goal of a confrontation, if handled professionally, is to get people to face their conflicts directly, thereby resolving the problem by working through the issues in the spirit of problem solving.

All these things require that you update your plan (including the charter) for the project. As I've emphasized, updating the plan means making changes to the goals, tasks, workflow, schedule, budget, or people and getting them approved by the appropriate stakeholders. Be prepared for change. It's not a question of what to do *if* there is an issue; it's what to do *when* there is an issue.

Alerting Your Sponsor to Problems

Sometimes, problems will be the cause of a change in the scope for a project. Talking with the sponsor, usually a senior manager, about problems is always difficult for project managers. However, if you will follow this approach, I think you can feel more confident in the discussion.

1. Never surprise your sponsor with a problem. Remember in Chapter 6 about the politics in senior management—there must be a perception that they are in control. Give her a "heads-up" as soon as you suspect a problem and arrange a time to brief her more fully on the issues.

2. If you have the escalation process in place that I suggested earlier, follow that process now. For example, if the process included giving the working committee three tries at solving a business problem first, remind the sponsor that you have tried and the working committee was not able to agree on a solution.

3. Determine how to best frame the problem. Remember that framing is a way of describing the situation in such a way that it encourages a certain perception and discourages others. That might include defining the problem from each point of view and the risks of each potential solution. If the sponsor will need to communicate the issue to the rest of the leadership team, you may offer to help build the message.

4. If it is appropriate in your company, recommend the solution you believe is the best for preserving the business case.

5. If a decision needs to be made (for example, it is an issue that more than one functional group must agree on), make sure the sponsor knows how time-sensitive the decision might be. It will often take time to manage the politics in these situations. However, the sponsor must know if there is some deadline out there that, if missed, will impact the overall project delivery schedule.

I have used this approach in many projects, and it works for me; I am confident it will work for you.

 NOTES FROM THE FIELD

There is an old saying that "you can't please everyone." And that couldn't be more true than making decisions during a project. So what to do? I think you have to weight your decisions toward the key stakeholders. That may create a risk with the stakeholders who didn't get their way, but you manage that risk just like you would any other. And if you have a strong relationship with your sponsor, ask her opinion. You will have your strongest defense from unhappy stakeholders if your key stakeholders and your sponsor support you when conflicts occur.

Creating an Issues Log

Whenever conflicts or issues arise, an issues log is a great tool for the project manager. An issue may be a difference of opinion on how to solve a technical problem that the project must deal with. Smart, honorable people may have legitimate differences of opinion on the way to solve the problem. In that light, an issues log makes a great deal of sense because it forces everyone to be as objective as possible. This log contains detailed information about the conflict or issue and includes the following elements:

- A description of the issue or conflict

- The person assigned to work it through

- The impact the issue has on the project

- The individual who authorized the accepted solution

- The date on which the issue was successfully resolved

Always keep track of any issues that arise during the course of the project. Then use the issues log to make sure you have addressed all the conflicts (note that doesn't mean they are solved to everyone's satisfaction). You can also use the log at project close-out as part of the lessons learned. Following is a sample issues log.

Issues Log

Issue	Impact	Assigned	Due Date	Resolution
Coding language	High	Bob Braveheart	4/15	ABOP chosen
Union request	Medium	Julia Robins	5/02	In progress
Software acceptance	High	Ben Samuels	5/10	Accepted as tested

For more information on an issues log, refer to *PMBOK Guide* section 13.3.3.1.

Changes in projects are always difficult, and nothing will ever change that. As a project manager, your job is not to prevent changes; it is to manage them the same way you manage the project—carefully and thoughtfully. If you use a methodical approach as I've described in this chapter to analyze the change and provide people with the right information, they will usually make rational decisions (note I said *usually*—we are dealing with human beings, after all!). What makes a difference is that you approach these changes in a calm and collected fashion that gives everyone confidence that you have it under control.

Review Questions

- Do I have a clear process in mind to manage change requests?

- Do I have the people who will be able to assess the impact of the change on the budget, schedule, and quality?

- Is there a decision-making process in place to approve various change requests?

- Do I understand how to communicate change requests whether they are approved or not?

- Do I have an issues log in place, and have I decided on who should have access to it?

The Least You Need to Know

- Changes are a natural and expected aspect of any project, but changes made through a defined process will be easier to control.

- Be sure to balance the project when changes create situations that impact workload and schedule problems.

- When you must consider a change for whatever reason, always do an impact analysis and understand the trade-offs and options available.

- Requests or the need for change will almost always cause some friction. Be prepared for it and use the techniques for managing conflict so it won't adversely impact your project.

- Create an issues log to capture all the issues and how you solved them. It will be a great resource for you later on.

Quality: Delivering the Best

The issue of quality will always surface as you attempt to balance the four main elements of your project: time, cost, quality, and scope. You've spent a lot of time on monitoring and controlling your schedule and costs (see Chapter 20), so now it's time to work on assessing and ensuring the quality of the project's deliverables. In reading this chapter, keep in mind that even though I refer to the "product" of the project as a deliverable, in reality, it can mean a service as well as a physical good.

What Exactly Does Quality Mean in a Project?

In its simplest form, the definition of *quality* is "conformance to requirements." Remember when I talked about developing the requirements in Chapter 1? That's the starting place for developing your quality plan. During your quest for quality, you need to identify which quality standards are relevant to your project and determine how to satisfy them.

In This Chapter

- The meaning of quality in a project
- Planning for quality
- Using peer and technical reviews
- Useful tools and techniques to ensure the quality of a project
- Controlling quality during the project

Often, a project team may confuse *quality* with *grade* and end up hurting the project overall. For example, a software product may have high quality because it does what it is supposed to do with few problems. However, it may have a low grade because it has very few appealing features. On the other hand, we have all had software that had not only a ton of features but also so many "bugs" that we wanted to throw it away. That product would be defined as having high grade (a lot of features), but low quality (too many problems).

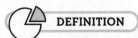

DEFINITION

Quality is defined by the Project Management Institute (PMI) as the "degree to which a set of inherent characteristics [of the finished project] fulfills requirements." **Grade** is "a category or rank used to distinguish items that have the same functional use (e.g., hammers) but do not share the same requirements for quality (e.g., different hammers may need to withstand different amounts of force)."

Determining the right balance between the quality and the grade is the work of the project manager along with the project team.

Planning for Quality Is the Starting Point

When you begin to plan for the quality of the product your project will produce, first go to the charter and review the scope of the project because quality actually starts with the scope. Let's look at what can happen when the project manager and the working committee believe they have agreed on the scope of the project for a new customer database.

The project manager and the working committee found they had some difficulty in agreeing on what would not be included in the project. The project manager believed that the project did not need to include a record of items returned by customers for any variety of reasons (for example, wrong product, wrong number of units delivered) because the company had another system in place to capture that information. However, the working committee believed that was essential information to be captured and was part of the scope of the project. After meeting three times to resolve the problem with no success, they took their concerns to the sponsor. After each laid out their arguments, the sponsor shared the information with the leadership team. The leadership team debated and came back with a decision to include returned items within the scope of the project.

Now imagine what would have happened if the project had moved forward for several months with no progress on capturing returned items within the customer database! Several key stakeholders could have been upset all because the project started with different assumptions.

When you begin to plan for quality, a key consideration will be the criteria that the key stake-holders will use to accept the final deliverables. These familiar examples illustrate the point:

- **Major functions.** Are all the required functions built into the database?

- **Appearance.** Is the appearance consistent with the other software we offer the employees?

- **Accuracy of information.** Are the customer's bills accurate in both customer information and billing information?

- **Reliability.** Is the database up and running every time our sales staff wants to place or track an order?

- **Security.** Have we built security into the system so unauthorized people can't access the system without the proper permission? Have we built security into the system so our customers' information is secure?

There are many more than these. The key will be to understand what the operations team will use as criteria for judging the quality of your project team's work.

Just as important as how you will plan for quality, it is vital that the activities you identify as important must be added to your project plan. If quality activities or tasks are not on the plan, chances are quite high that you will forget them.

You will also need to review other aspects of the project to gauge the impact on quality. For example, you may need to review the procurement process for selecting vendors who will supply you with products or services to be sure the quality requirements for the vendors you choose will meet your project requirements. This will also help you control the quality of the vendors' work during the course of the project.

For more on starting a quality plan, refer to *PMBOK Guide* **section 8.1.1.1.**

The Project Peer Review

Another strategy for managing quality is to gather some of the sharper minds both inside and outside the company (probably no more than about 10) for a peer review. Such reviews usually last from one day to a maximum of one week for a large, complicated project. The objective of the peer review is to ask knowledgeable people to review your project from a technical and business standpoint and to alert you to any risks or problems you and the project team may be overlooking in delivering a quality product or products. You know it's funny, but if you work on something day after day for quite a while, the whole team can begin to make the same assumptions that turn into oversights.

In a project, you might consider asking users of the final product for their input on the project at various milestones. This approach has the added benefit of getting them engaged in the project. If credible users have done peer reviews to ensure the quality of the project deliverables, it will go a long way in convincing people that the project is valuable. People from vendor companies (with whom you already have nondisclosure agreements) might be asked to participate in the peer review. Consulting firms might also offer valuable insights; just make sure you have nondisclosure agreements with them. If you are using an outside consulting firm, make it clear that the review is not an opportunity for them to sell work for their firm.

You can then take the outcome of the peer review and make adjustments to the project plan.

Doing Technical Reviews Along the Way

Technical reviews are similar to peer reviews, except they are only focused on the technical aspects of the project. You would want subject matter experts or technical specialists to participate in this type of review. And you may want to break them up into smaller teams. For example, one group may only be looking at engineering aspects of the plant design or construction. Similarly, another group may be looking at the equipment and the data it provides for operating the plant after commissioning.

Look at your project plan and schedule technical reviews at key milestones so you ensure the quality of the final deliverables and reduce any chance of rework when the project should be in the close-out phase.

Quality Planning Tools and Techniques

You can use several tools and techniques to plan the quality of your project's deliverables. The following are the more common ones:

Cost/benefit analyses: One of the most useful techniques is to do a *cost/benefit analysis* as part of the planning for a project. As you work to balance time, cost, scope, and quality, you will need to weigh different factors and come up with alternatives to satisfy your stakeholders. For instance, to determine which features to include in a customer relationship management (CRM) screen menu, the project manager or a member of the project team will do a cost/benefit analysis of the features.

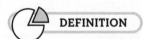

DEFINITION

A **cost/benefit analysis** is an estimate of the costs and benefits of various alternatives and then the use of financial measures, such as return on investment (ROI) or payback period, to determine which of the alternatives is the most desirable.

Other features may be optional. For example, the project manager may have two options for backing up customer information. One option might be to conduct the backup daily, and a second option might be to only do a backup weekly. The project manager will need to show the steering committee how these two alternatives might affect the cost for the project by discussing the options with them, providing them with the cost/benefit analysis, and letting them make the decision.

Benchmarking: This can also be a very useful tool in quality planning. This involves comparing your project plan or practices to those of other projects to generate ideas for improvement or to provide a sound standard you can use to measure your project's performance. You may want to benchmark against other projects within your organization if they are available, or you may want to use standards developed by the Project Management Institute (PMI). Either way, it should help you plan and execute your quality process within your project.

Cause-and-effect diagrams: Also called *Ishikawa diagrams* or *fishbone diagrams,* these can help identify how a problem may be solved by showing the linkage between various factors. The basic idea is to find the cause of a problem and separate that from the effect it is having (similar to a doctor noting a high fever—the symptom or effect—and the cause—an infection or a virus). As you measure the progress of your project, any potential quality problems should begin to show up, and you will need to take corrective action. Cause-and-effect diagrams can give you and your team a visual linkage between factors to see whether the problem lies with manufacturing, people, a technical specification, and so on. Also, you will need to collect data that helps do the following:

- Define the problem using what has been observed or reported

- Identify where the problem is occurring

- See any patterns for when the problem is occurring

- Determine how often the problem occurs

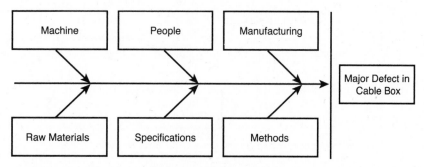

Cause-and-effect diagrams can help the project team to uncover problems by showing how various parts link together.

Finally, system or process flow charts can illustrate how information flows during a process or throughout an organization. The project team can also use them to help show where quality problems might occur so they can plan to prevent them. The pictorial representation can help people see what is happening and when. As a result, detecting the source of a problem or potential problem may be easier to identify.

As you use these tools, you and your project team should develop a quality management plan that explains the following:

- How you will implement your plan

- What operating guidelines you will use to measure quality

- Which checklists you will be using to verify that you have implemented your plan

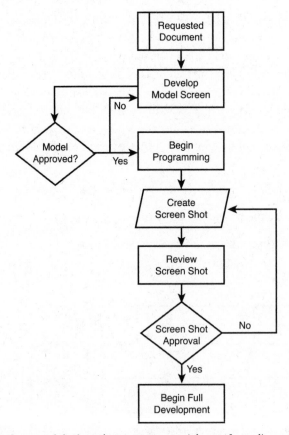

Flow charts can help the project team spot potential areas for quality problems.

To learn more technical information about quality tools, refer to *PMBOK Guide* **section 8.1.2.3.**

There are a variety of ways to ensure that the project will meet the quality requirements set out in the quality management plan, and these tools are a great start. For example, doing benchmarking to see how a successful project operated is an easy way to ensure your project team will know how to succeed. All the quality tools are also helpful in keeping the quality of your project deliverables on track. You may decide to use a Design of Experiments (DOE) which is a statistical method for identifying which factors are influencing specific options for a product or a process under development. You can then determine the number and types of tests to enter into your project plan.

 WORDS FROM THE WISE

Good project management in an organization is, in itself, a quality management process.

—Lynn Crawford, DBA, University of Technology, Sydney, Australia

Quality Control: It's All About Results

In quality control, as project manager, you and your project team are monitoring very specific project results to ensure they meet the requirements of the project. Some organizations have a quality control department; if yours does, get them involved early on in the project so they can help with quality planning. Or maybe you have a quality expert on your team; if so, also involve him in the planning process. If you don't have that expertise, don't fret; there are still some things you can do.

One of the most common methods of quality control is simple inspection. For example, if you were the project manager for a cable company, you might want to assign a team member to visually inspect and test the cable boxes the manufacturer is producing for the company. The purpose is to make sure the boxes conform to the requirements established in the quality management plan. It's far better to learn of some mistakes *before* the customer gets those faulty boxes!

If there are too many boxes to inspect individually or you are short on time, you can conduct a statistical sampling. This means that instead of inspecting all the cable boxes, the team member will look at a certain percentage of them—say, every tenth cable box being made. Or maybe he will look at 3 boxes in each large container of 25. A number of books on the market give detailed approaches to sampling and the evidence that it works. This sampling can also reduce the cost of conducting quality inspections, usually a primary consideration in cost-conscious projects!

After you've inspected the product, you can use a Pareto diagram to put the information you have collected into a usable format for quality control. A Pareto diagram is basically a histogram that shows how many results were generated by an identifiable cause. It will show you where the problems are and help you and your team establish priorities for tackling any defects.

It involves collecting data and types of problems from the various sources. In the following figure of a Pareto diagram for the cable company, the sources of problems are the video signal, audio signal, remote control, power cable, and cable connection. The Pareto diagram is the source of the famous 80/20 rule that says that 80 percent of your problems will come from 20 percent of the sources. You are trying to evaluate where the greatest source of problems is occurring and take corrective action. In this case, the video component seems to be the greatest source of problems, so it becomes the highest priority for corrective action.

Using checklists and the whole suite of available quality tools will aid you tremendously in getting the results you and stakeholders want.

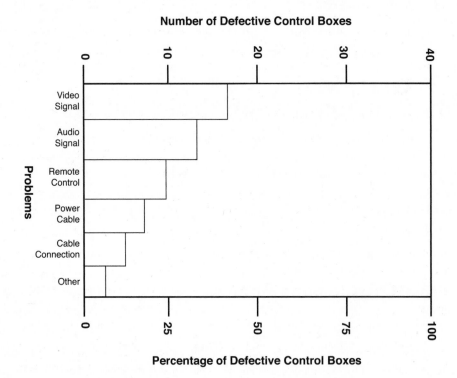

Pareto diagrams can help the project team set priorities.

For more information on quality control measurements and checklists, refer to *PMBOK Guide* sections 8.2.1.4.and 8.3.1.3.

TIME IS MONEY

Focusing on quality is something that every project manager agrees to in spirit. We all want to produce a quality deliverable. However good our intentions are, as project managers we have to consciously manage. Unlike the schedule or the budget, the quality of our work can seem more intangible. That is why it is often more difficult to manage. Collecting data and using tools to analyze the data takes our good intentions and turns them into actionable items. Conducting peer and technical reviews keeps us, and our team, oriented toward quality because no one wants to be called out on poor quality. But if the quality begins to slip, we have data and feedback that helps us correct the issue before it gets to the end and the stakeholder users are the ones who complain because of the poor quality of our product. Build quality into the project plan and then execute those activities, and you—and your user stakeholders—will be very pleased with the results!

Review Questions

- Am I clear on the relationship between the scope of the project and quality?

- Do I appreciate that I must include quality management activities in my project plan?

- Can I see where a peer review and a technical review would improve the overall quality of my project?

- Can I see how I might apply the quality tools to manage quality in project execution?

The Least You Need to Know

- Focus on quality, not on grade.
- Plan for quality right from the beginning.
- Use peer reviews and technical reviews as a way to ensure quality assurance.
- Use tools such as cost/benefit analyses, benchmarking, and cause-and-effect diagrams to help you ensure the project will meet the quality requirements.
- Remember that quality control is all about results.

The Close-Out Phase

Just as predictable as sunrise and sunset, there comes a time when all good things must come to an end. Likewise, your project must move through the close-out phase so that you can wrap up the details, pay the bills, evaluate what you and your team learned, and move on to the next project with a sense of satisfaction. That's what the chapters in this part are all about—showing you the steps to bring a project to a proper conclusion as carefully as when you started.

Many companies—even those that are pretty good at project management—fail to give the close-out phase enough attention. Everyone is in a hurry to either get on with the next project or return to their day job. Doing a proper job on the close-out phase will help everyone—and the company—get even better by discussing and documenting what you have learned. It should be part of the continuous improvement process for everyone, but especially for you as a project manager.

Closing Out the Project

After you've successfully completed your project, the close-out phase is a time of celebration and accomplishment. Not every project ends gracefully, but all projects should have a distinct ending. Without a proper closing, some projects seem to just drift into operations without any formal recognition that the project completed its mission.

In this chapter, I'll show you how to close out any project—especially those that finish successfully, but also those that die prematurely and the more annoying ones in which team members never seem to want to let go! Closure is important because it's the point at which, while wiping your sweaty brow with relief, you can say to yourself, "It's over." (And regardless of the outcome, break out the chilled champagne—you deserve it!)

In This Chapter

- Life after the project ends
- Reasons to close out a project
- The steps for closing a project
- Evaluating the lessons learned
- Conducting an after-implementation review
- Releasing the workforce

Is There Life After Project Termination?

As the end approaches, some project members get nervous, while others are glad that the end is in sight. The nervous ones may wonder what their next assignment will be. Particularly if they are contractors, they may wonder whether there will be a next assignment at all. Unfortunately, this morale problem occurs with the worst possible timing—when a project is almost complete. The problem runs deeper than just the risk of unemployment or a new assignment in another part of the company. It means the end of budding friendships, interesting after-hours socializing with other team members, and the other good times that accompany a well-run project. Your people will miss it. You will, too—really.

 WORDS FROM THE WISE

When projects veer off course or no longer meet strategic needs, companies must know when and how to let go.

—Dr. Xiaojin Wang, PMP, Yuman University, Kumming, China

Why Is a Close-Out Phase Necessary?

There are several good reasons for a formal close-out to a project. Some involve people issues, and others involve you personally learning from the experience and recording what you've learned. You need to acknowledge people for goals they have achieved and for them to feel the work is complete. Because you as a project manager need to evolve your skills for managing projects, analyze the techniques, processes, and procedures used on a project so you can adapt and improve them in the future. These are the most fundamental and underlying reasons to formally close a project. You may also want to hold similar closing, acknowledgement, and review meetings at the close of major milestones or phases in a longer project as well.

 NOTES FROM THE FIELD

For a wide variety of reasons, project close-outs often never happen. I suppose it is understandable that people—including the project manager—want to move on to other project, or their day job, now that the execution phase is finished and the deliverables are handed over to operations. However, I would ask you to try to avoid that trap and follow the guidance outlined in this chapter.

In the interest of continuous improvement, you can't really learn from each project without a hard look at the project and what went wrong and what the team did well. Now you have information that allows you to do even better next time!

Preparing for the Final Shutdown

Make the following tasks part of the final termination process for most projects, as they are necessary to bring them to the final closure and include them in the project plan:

Meet with key stakeholders identified at the beginning of the project to get their final approval of the project deliverables. They are the reason for the project existing in the first place, and their approval signals the project's completion. For larger projects, you may want to request a formal document acknowledging the completion of the project by the project sponsor or customer.

Transfer responsibilities to other people if required. For example, the end results of some projects are inputs for operations (remember Chapter 21?) or new projects to be managed by other people. In the example I have often used in the book about a customer database project, after the project is finished, the company's sales and marketing group will take formal control of the business processes related to the database. The team members for development of the billing database will finish and turn over the maintenance of the database to the information systems department. The team members who were responsible for answering customers' questions during the pilot test will turn over the ongoing responsibility to customer relations to handle future questions. These activities are all part of the transition of the product into operations.

Work with others, such as human resources, to identify where to reassign people from the project. You may return people to their functional areas, assign them to new projects, or both. Follow the human resource plan you developed earlier for rolling people off the project.

Complete the final accounting of the project. This includes totaling the costs, paying all the bills, and closing the books on the project.

Gather data regarding the results of the project, and identify recommendations for the future. If you have been using a project diary, as suggested in Chapter 18, this is not as daunting a task as you might think. This information will be useful in developing the final report, which is described in Chapter 25.

 TIME IS MONEY

Once you are certain you have delivered everything according to the charter and scope statement, schedule a review session with the sponsor. You will want to summarize the information and get confirmation that you have, indeed, completed the project in the eyes of the sponsor. After that briefing, I would recommend that you schedule a review with other key stakeholders to ensure they concur with the sponsor that you have finished according to the charter and scope statement. If there are any holdouts, you will be able to identify them at that point and make any adjustments or corrections before you start releasing key team members.

For more details on providing feedback to team members, refer to *PMBOK Guide* **section 9.4.2.2.**

Projects that aren't closed formally may continue to consume resources required elsewhere. Most projects should end as soon as you have achieved the goals.

Closing a Small or Large Project

For small projects, the formal closing can be a simple matter of having a meeting with the team and the stakeholders to acknowledge attainment of the project goals and writing a brief final report on the project. The closing meeting should focus only on the accomplishments of the completed project so people feel satisfied with the work performed.

For large projects, the closing phase can be a time of stress and anxiety. Team members may have developed friendships and a sense of family. Some team members will be going their separate ways, adding to the apprehension. Termination of a long project with a close-knit team is always difficult and can be complicated. However, you can reduce the anxiety if you acknowledge the team members for their current accomplishments and then give new assignments and challenges as soon as possible. It's also a good idea to have a formal celebration to close down the project.

Because some people fear leaving the security of an established project team or changing roles after the project is complete, it can be difficult to get the final details of a large project completed. People may continue to work on insignificant tasks. Remember your work authorization system! If they are working on work packages you haven't given them, you need to stop that work—gently, of course.

As a project manager, it is your responsibility to see that the project ends by helping the people involved move forward into new challenges and opportunities. To reduce the stress associated with project close-out, remind your team members of the overall goals they have achieved and the fact that the stakeholders consider the project completed. Emphasize the importance of the project to the business and their contribution in meeting the project objectives. Then remind them of new goals and objectives they have yet to achieve on other projects and assignments.

In addition to having a formal meeting or even a party to acknowledge project completion, many projects involve other formal close-out tasks, some of which I mentioned earlier.

The closing tasks for a large project are not always clear-cut. When such a project is almost complete, often some small details need to be resolved. The project manager must decide when a project is "finished" so it can move into the termination phase. Don't drag out the close-out phase and cleanup details to keep the project alive. Get on with it, and turn the final details over to the operations group to finish.

These wrap-up details usually take the form of what is called a *punch list*. A punch list includes tasks or activities that still need to be completed but are not significant enough to keep the project team working on them. These punch list items are the responsibility of operations to complete. Make sure the sponsor is aware of the punch list even if you don't review it with her in detail. That process transfers responsibility in the sponsor's mind to operations.

For many projects, large or small, a checklist is useful in determining the requirements for termination. Later in the chapter I provide an example of a termination checklist for a complex product development project to demonstrate the kinds of tasks that might be required to terminate a large project. Of course, the checklist you develop may include entirely different elements that require shutdown, but my example should give you the basic idea of what to consider.

Writing Out Your Lessons Learned

Closure is also the point at which management evaluates your success in meeting the goals and your skills as a project manager. In project management circles, this is part of a process called *lessons learned*. Was your project a big success? Where could you have done a better job? What did you learn that would be helpful in the next project? Writing down the specifics will help you and your team capture the information you need regarding lessons learned during the project. All of the following questions apply to each focus area.

Focus Areas: Project Management, Communications, Schedule and Budget, Training, Quality, Issues, Human Resources, Support Templates

- How did we do overall? _____
- What did we do well? _____
- What did we do poorly? _____
- What should we improve? _____
- What did we learn that we can use on future projects?_____

  _____

- What else did we learn? _____

  _____

- Recommended actions: _____

  _____

Write out what you and your team learned during the project, what worked well, and what you would do differently if you had to do it all over again. These types of reports can be very helpful for you in the future, but they can also help other project managers who may read your report as they tackle a similar project in the future. At least they won't make the same mistakes you did; they can find some of their own!

Some of this information will be captured in the final report that I describe in the next chapter.

For more details on lessons learned and key stakeholders, refer to *PMBOK Guide* **section 13.3.3.5.**

Some Additional Details for Project Shutdown

The cleanest closure of a project comes when all the work is done and team members already have other work or have returned to their permanent jobs. The easiest project to close down is the small one in which tangible (visible) results demonstrate completion to one and all.

On the other hand, closing down the project of, for example, building a large refinery in Houston is much more complex. Not only are there multiple subplans, but for the uninitiated project manager, reaching the state of completion may seem impossible. Yes, the plant itself may be up, but all the little details may seem endless. In addition, some work may linger on. After completion, repairs may be on the project manager's shoulders as necessary. In a sense, the project continues rather than winding down in a planned and predictable process. Although 99.8 percent of the work is complete, remnants of the team must address that other .2 percent or hire outsiders if former team members are no longer available.

To shut down a project, here are some additional details on the steps to take toward an orderly closure. Each of these are part of the completion of any project. The additional steps to project termination are as follows:

1. **Decision to close out.** Make sure that operations has accepted the project and you are finished.

2. **Task list.** Make a list of small tasks that need to be accomplished and get them taken care of—what I called a *punch list* earlier.

3. **Meetings.** Hold individual meetings with team members and team managers who have reported to you. Thank them for their contribution, and take notes on what they thought of the project's highlights and lowlights and your leadership (take a deep breath first). I usually try to focus on a few things they did well and a couple of items they could improve on. You will see more about how to evaluate the team in the next chapter.

4. **Communication.** Instruct all team members in writing as to when their participation in the project will end (use your company's policy if it is different). This puts pressure on the stragglers who need a little more time to complete their role. If you suspect that more time is needed, set the end date several weeks into the future and give weekly reminders of the drop-dead date. For real problem people, visit them daily to assess their progress and remind them of the date.

5. **More communication.** Notify outside suppliers and vendors that the project will cease to exist in an appropriate number of days or weeks. Since the project is ending, tell them you will not accept bills received 30 days after the termination date. (Be flexible on this one. It's really a tactic to get the bills coming in the door from vendors with tardy billing practices.) It also saves you interest charges, and really prompt payment may knock a percentage off the total project bill. If possible, check purchase orders to see what's outstanding.

6. **Even more communication.** Inform managers of "borrowed" employees, temporary agencies, and contractors in writing that the project's end date is near. This provides the managers time to find other opportunities for these people or to move them back into their usual job responsibilities.

7. **Closing the books.** Assuming you are working with a finance department, once a project is complete, finance must close the books so wayward bills aren't charged against a non-existent budget. Most companies assign code numbers to accounts for projects. Assuming your project receives one or more codes, have finance render the codes invalid. That way, you can review any invoices that pop up for legitimacy prior to payment or rejection.

8. **The celebration.** After a project is (successfully) completed, hold a team celebration. (One of my customers was so excited about the success of the project that he took the whole project team to Las Vegas for the weekend!) Awards may be in order for team members who performed above and beyond the line of duty. This event is not only fun, it marks the official end of the project in everyone's mind. If the project was not as successful as it could have been but not because of team failure, still hold such an event, even if the occasion is somewhat more subdued.

9. **Dispersal of other resources.** Take an inventory of supplies and equipment. Return borrowed and rented equipment, send back unused supplies for credit where possible, and haul off trash to the recycler or landfill. If the project was large and ends up owning a lot of surplus equipment, an auction on eBay can be the ticket to parting with 12 printers or 48 slightly dated computers. Money from such an event can go into the organization's general fund, be distributed to team members in the form of profit sharing, or be donated to charity.

10. **Handing over the keys.** Transfer responsibilities to the operations team.

Checklist for Closing a Large Project					
	NEEDED?		REQUIRED DATE	RESPONSIBLE PERSON	NOTES
DESCRIPTION	YES	NO			
Identify Remaining Work	☐	☐			
Closing/Termination Plan	☐	☐			
Personal Evaluations	☐	☐			
Close-Out Work Orders	☐	☐			
Audit Final Changes	☐	☐			
Pay All Vendors	☐	☐			
Close-Out Books/Audit	☐	☐			
Final Delivery Instructions	☐	☐			
Customer Training	☐	☐			
Notify Purchasing of Completion	☐	☐			
Equipment Redeployed	☐	☐			
Materials Returned to Inventory	☐	☐			
Staff Reassigned	☐	☐			
Close-Down Procedures	☐	☐			
Engineering Documentation	☐	☐			
Final Staff Meeting(s)	☐	☐			
Final Report and Review Meeting	☐	☐			

This checklist for closing a project may not include everything you need to remember, but it should help you consider all the items that are important.

 TIME IS MONEY

When you were first developing the budget for the project, it would probably not have been appropriate to earmark money for a celebration at the end of the project. However, as you approach the conclusion of the project, meet with your sponsor and begin to plan how to celebrate the success of the project. It will require money and time, so you'll need to determine if you are the right person to handle the details or if you need to delegate that to someone else. The scale of the celebration is probably proportional to the value to the company and the difficulty of completion. Just make sure it is nice and shows the company's appreciation for a job well done. Too often in business, people don't believe in a pat on the back because they expect people to do a good job. And while that is true, the successful completion of a project that will improve the performance of the company is definitely something to celebrate.

The After-Implementation Review

A common practice among experienced project managers, particularly on large projects, is to conduct an after-implementation review. A meeting is scheduled, usually between three to six months after the project is closed out, with the key team members and some of the stakeholders. The review is a discussion about what has happened since the project was turned over to operations. Often getting a little distance from the project will help everyone gain some insights on what went well and what they would do differently in the future. Also, any problems or surprises that occur will happen in those first few months, and that information can help in crafting your lessons learned.

Three Ways to Release a Workforce

While some might have other ideas, there are generally three ways to release team members in the project management biz: inclusion, integration, or extinction.

Inclusion is a happy ending of sorts. Your project proved successful, and upon nearing completion, was absorbed into the organization. Again, it may become a part of the company or be run as a separate function. In the happiest scenario, many of the original team members keep their jobs and continue to contribute. However, it may be that not all staff members are offered a position because they are deemed unsuitable for the postcompletion phase of the project. Some team members may choose to leave anyway because, while they found the project phase exciting, the thought of running day-to-day operations makes them yawn.

Integration is the most common technique for dissolving a project workforce. Team members are reintegrated into the departments from which they were borrowed. On a long project, integration becomes complex because management may have been forced to fill slots held by the team members. Now they must find a new position for each returning team member that is satisfactory to the employee and the head count. That is why keeping stakeholders informed is important because they will need time to handle an integration.

Extinction of a project and everything and everyone related to it is an all-too-common route to unload personnel. This is obviously the least desirable outcome and one you should avoid if possible. Once a project is closed down, the people are simply let go.

 TIME IS MONEY

Leave good documentation for your successors. When you consider almost any project, you'll understand why this is a good idea. Given current job tenure across the nation, it's entirely possible that the people who worked on the project may not work there five years later.

Give It Up!

At the end of a project, especially a major one that has absorbed six or more months of your life, get ready for a letdown period. It's like postpartum blues. You've spent nine months devoting your energies to a specific project (a baby). You've been so focused on that one goal that, once it is successfully achieved, you feel lost, directionless, and sad. You feel these emotions even though you know what your next project will be (raising the baby). Think how much more difficult it would be to cope if you didn't have the prospect of a new project and had to adjust to your former everyday routine.

Suddenly, you are no longer the head of a project with team members constantly seeking your advice and decisions. Instead, you return to civilian life with your normal job duties and responsibilities. You may have a period of letdown in which the project stays on your mind. You may keep thinking of improved ways to accomplish some tasks, or ideas may come to you that might have better met the project's goals. Your "symptoms" may indeed be real. But if it's your skill and desire, freelance project managers do well and make good incomes depending on their experience and success. This could be you! Be encouraged: there's always another project to manage somewhere.

Here's a simple checklist that can help you do the project close-out and move on:

Project Close-Out Phase

- A. Document project lessons learned.

- B. Schedule after-implementation review.

- C. Provide performance feedback.

- D. Close out contracts (as needed).

- E. Complete administrative close-out.

- F. Deliver project plan memorandum to decision authority.

Right now you should have a celebration. Your project is done—except for the final report, which you learn how to write in the next chapter. You didn't think you'd get away without another report, did you?

Get your team together. Revel in your accomplishments. Then move on to the next project.

For more on the various items related to closing a project, refer to *PMBOK Guide* section A1.8.

Review Questions

- Am I clear on the importance of a methodical close-out of my project?

- Have I scheduled a meeting with my sponsor and key stakeholders to review the project?

- Do I understand the importance of creating a punch list for operations?

- Have I identified the data I need to collect for the lessons learned and the final report?

- Have I scheduled an after-implementation review for the project?

- Do I have a plan for releasing the project team members?

- Do I have a checklist of what needs to be completed?

The Least You Need to Know

- Dissolving a project takes time and deliberate effort on your part.
- A key success factor for growing as a project manager is to conduct a "lessons learned" process.
- Closing down a project is a process that follows a predetermined series of steps.
- Conduct an after-implementation review as part of closing out a larger project.
- After a project is finished, team members will be included in the operations component of the project, reintegrated into the organization, or terminated.

The Final Evaluation

Now that your project is closed out, you may think you're finally done. But there's one more important step—the final project evaluation. The purpose of this step is to appraise your actions: what you did well and what you could have done better. Only through a final project evaluation will you learn how to better manage your next project.

Evaluating Your Project

Through an effective *postmortem*, you can efficiently apply lessons learned from this project to the next one. The final evaluation should happen whether the project achieved its goals or fell short of the target.

Small leftover tasks, such as tasks or activities on the punch list, shouldn't delay the final evaluation. Large leftover tasks indicate a project that's incomplete, however, making it too early to analyze results even if the scheduled completion date has come and gone.

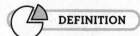

DEFINITION

The term **postmortem** is borrowed from the medical field. When applied to a project, it means a close examination of all parts of the project to determine its successes and its failures.

The final evaluation has three components: project assessment, a final written report, and team member performance reviews. A final meeting of the core team is often in order as well because this will assist you in evaluating the project and producing input for the report. The team's technical expertise and experiences may provide data you hadn't previously considered.

For more on the content that might be included in a project report, refer to *PMBOK Guide* section A1.7.8.

Meeting with Core Team Members and the Working Committee

Before you formally evaluate your completed or closed-down project, you need input from your core team (generally those you nominated as team leaders or subject matter experts). Ask for a brief written report, or provide them with a simple questionnaire to complete. Then schedule an informal meeting with key players and ask their opinions about the project and what they would do better next time. Take notes so you remember comments and confirm that you value their input.

The first question to ask when evaluating a project is whether the desired results were accomplished. You then need to consider the project from start to finish in order to understand what worked and what didn't. Look closely at problems you captured in your issues log and how you and your team coped with them. Picking up the pieces and successfully gluing them back together is an art, so consider when you did this well and when you could have done better.

After you meet with your core team members, have a similar session with the key members of the working committee. If you have utilized them well during the course of the project, they will have important insights and a different perspective on the successes and shortcomings of the project and the team. Capturing their ideas and incorporating them into the final report will be important.

Comparing Goals to Achievements

Project evaluation has no hard-and-fast rules. Essentially, you match your achievements to the project's goals. If what you produce lines up clearly with well-defined requirements, chances are you've succeeded. If you have met the requirements only partway, your project may be considered a success by some and a failure by others. The toughest evaluation is one in which the scope was fuzzy to begin with. That's why it's so important to clearly define a project's scope during the planning phase (see Chapter 7).

To evaluate your project's success, make a list of the project's accomplishments and place it next to the requirements outlined in the charter. Study each list, checking off requirements as you consider your list of accomplishments. This is the best way to evaluate your project—using actual data.

With the exception of the smallest projects (and sometimes even for those), management will mandate a final report at the close of the project. The final report for a megaproject is more formal and obviously longer than for a small, simple project. As previously mentioned, reports are necessary for both successfully completed projects and those that are canceled. On a successful project, the final report may precipitate bonuses for the team members and their project manager. If the project went belly-up, the report serves to document the problems and to help others avoid the quicksand you and your team slipped into. The report can also explain why a project problem wasn't necessarily your fault.

Writing the Final Report

The final report is both a history of the project and a final evaluation of performance. While the final report for a small project may be no more than a two-page memo, the report for a large project may be 10 or 20 pages in length. If you kept a project diary (see Chapter 18) and the various logs suggested in this book, producing the final report should be relatively easy.

The reality of the final report is really twofold:

1. You are attempting to report on the project and the results achieved against the goals.

2. You are creating a marketing tool that highlights the value created by the team.

Often you will be underwhelmed at the final response to the completion of your project. However, if you can create a financial analysis with net present value (NPV) using assumptions given to you by the users themselves, you will have a powerful marketing tool for additional projects. Managers in companies will gladly imitate success and decide "I want some of that, too." I talked about framing the communications in Chapter 19 and I want to remind you to frame your final report in a way that encourages a perception of success.

In the project report for a simple project, cover all the topics included in the final report for a large project, only in less detail. Consider these topics in the final report:

- An overview of the project (primarily schedule and budget), including revisions to the original project plan

- A summary of the business case for the project

- A summary of major accomplishments

- An analysis of achievements compared to the business case objectives for the project

- Final financial accounting and an explanation of variances from the budget

- An analysis of the quality of work performed on behalf of the project against the expectations of the stakeholders

- An evaluation of administrative and management performance

- The team's performance (keep this section confidential when it applies to specific individuals and their performance)

- Special acknowledgments to team members

- Total number of approved changes and the impact of those changes to the accomplishment of the business case

- Issues or tasks that require further investigation

- Recommendations for future projects of this type

- A scheduled date for the after-implementation review

In addition, the following elements are appropriate to include in the final reports for more complex projects:

- A summary of performance issues, conflicts, and resolutions from the issues log (see Chapter 22), the risk log (see Chapter 8), and the change control log (see Chapter 22)

- The results of each phase of the project, including actual versus forecast dates and the budget versus actual expenses (budget use, additions, and so on require thorough documentation)

- A description of ongoing activities related to transitioning the project to operations that will require further project team member participation (if any)

- Recommendations for changes to future projects so they will run more smoothly

- An in-depth analysis of reporting procedures and recommendations for improvements

- An analysis of the project management process as a whole

In each section of a final report for a project, analyze the procedures used in the project. Acknowledge things that worked. Explain things that didn't work. Make recommendations for improvements in future implementations of the project methodology, and include clear examples and rationales for the changes. All core team members should either contribute to the report or review its contents for accuracy before it is finalized. You can have others write and submit their relevant portions of the final report and then, after editing, add your own comments as an overview to cement the document.

Packaging Options for the Report

Everyone involved in the project, from your management to the project stakeholders, should review your final report. You may want to break it into five sections, as outlined here:

- **The executive summary.** This one- to two-page document summarizes the report's content for people who need a quick briefing and don't have time or are unable to digest the entire document.

- **The report, part A.** This section contains information that can be disseminated to all team members, managers, and other interested stakeholders. It includes a detailed review of the project and an assessment of the project's success in meeting the business case for the project.

- **The report, part B.** This section includes information for management only or that may be confidential in nature. Confidential reports are the most difficult to manage. They may contain information not appropriate for team members' eyes, such as salaries, bonus recommendations, team-member performance, and recommendations for using the results of the project. It can also include the financial reports for the project.

- **The project plan.** Include the project's overall plan along with copies of the goal information. If they fit and make you look good, include the original baseline plan and the final plan so readers can see how you met the scheduled dates.

- **Miscellaneous components.** If tangible proof of a project's success is possible, such as the opening of a new store or facility, include photos in this section, referenced from report parts A and B.

RISK MANAGEMENT

Keep all financial documents very secure. In CIA terms, a portion of a report may be "for your eyes only," while the rest is available for distribution. If you find yourself in the awkward situation of not knowing what to release and how to keep it secure, get advice from your sponsor who is already privy to the report's contents.

The Political Impact of Final Reports

In a politically sensitive organization, a negative report can cause problems. Remember from Chapter 6 on stakeholders, the environment, at the highest levels, is all about politics. Before you state emphatically that a particular vice president was the major roadblock to successfully completing the project, you had better be in line for another job or an unemployment check.

As was strongly (if wrongly) suspected of the Warren report on the slaying of President Kennedy, for political reasons there were two versions of the report: one for the public and another for high-level government officials and operatives. You may consider this tactic for presenting information to your management. However, as many people have learned the hard way, written communications have a way of circulating beyond the intended audience. You may want to provide a verbal report on the difficult VP to your sponsor, but I would discourage you from writing two distinct reports.

WORDS FROM THE WISE

Honest criticism is hard to take, particularly from a relative, a friend, an acquaintance, or a stranger.

—Franklin P. Jones, American author and humorist

Who Accomplished What and How Well?

Since your project involved people, you'll likely be called upon to evaluate the performance of team members. This may be limited to core team members or may apply to all team members and even outside vendors, consultants, and suppliers. The evaluations can be used for anything ranging from promotions to new assignments to layoffs. In a project in which a team member's contribution is made before the project terminates, hold a review when the team member departs rather than waiting for project closure. Why? Because on any really large project, the time between an individual rolling off the project and the actual time for the review may be a considerable amount of time. It may be hard to remember exactly what points you want to emphasize if too much time has passed.

Many companies have standard evaluation procedures that must be followed, and the human resources department may also insert itself into the evaluation process. Chances are, HR will provide standard evaluation forms for both you and the employee to fill out.

The basic criteria I have used for appraising team member performance may include the following:

- Quality of work

- Cost consciousness

- Timeliness

- Creativity (for example, in solving technical problems)

- Administrative performance (for example, submitting timesheets)

- Ability to work as part of a team

- Attitude

- Communication skills

- Technical ability

- Recommendations for improvement

- Consistency in meeting deadlines

As a rule of thumb, I would not necessarily cover all of these points with each individual. I would choose three or four where the individual did quite well and then one or two, at the most, where I think the person could improve in the future. When giving a performance review in person, try for a relaxed atmosphere away from other team members. For stellar performers, this is a good time to hand out any bonus checks (if appropriate), with the agreement that the team member will keep it quiet so as not to make other members unhappy.

The Bottom Line and You

In addition to the formal review of a project, every project manager needs to do some personal soul-searching to understand why a particular project went well or why it went poorly. After the project has been completed for a while and the emotion is gone, stand back and look at the project and your own management skills as objectively and dispassionately as possible. What did you do well? What could you have done better? What do you still need to learn? These observations—if acted on and taken seriously—will help you prosper, develop, and improve as a project manager. A good time to complete this exercise is after the after-implementation review discussed in the previous chapter.

At this point, I have exposed you to the complete process of project management. You have learned how to complete project management calculations and develop diagrams, reports, and communications that will help you plan, monitor, and control your project to a successful conclusion. Congratulations! And good luck in your role as project manager!

Review Questions

- Have I gathered the information I need to write the final report?

- Am I confident that I understand how formal it needs to be, or should I consult with my sponsor?

- Do I understand how the final report is a marketing document as well as a project document?

- Have I prepared to meet with key members of the project team to evaluate their performance on the project?

- Have I scheduled an after-implementation review (see Chapter 24) to provide input into the final report?

The Least You Need to Know

- After a project ends, take stock of what went right and what went wrong.
- On most projects, management requires a final report to inform all participants and stakeholders of the project's results.
- Always evaluate the success of the project by comparing it to the business case.
- Review performance formally or informally (depending on the organization) when team members depart the project or when the project is completed.

Building an Organization

How can you know what the right organization is for your project team? How do you get people to move where you want them to go? Who should lead the work, and who should follow orders? This appendix looks at some of the pros, cons, and alternatives to help you organize your players for maximum impact.

No Easy Task, but Someone Has to Organize These People

The most important aspect of organizing your team will be to make sure that everyone understands three things:

- The reason you chose each of them for the team; what he or she had to offer that you required

- The clear role and responsibility each person is fulfilling on the project

- The standards you will hold them accountable for in completing the work with high quality

Structuring a project organization means more than just choosing team members and committing outside vendors to specific tasks. To function effectively, your project team members require clear reporting responsibilities and a road map to their location in the project. On top of this, your core team may require ancillary support such as administrative assistants, computer installers, technical help, and others who are trained, ready, available, and prepared for secondary but vital duties.

Turning all these people into a viable project team involves cementing relationships, making the right resources available in a timely manner to the right people, implementing reporting relationships, and establishing a schedule that works. Many people may believe this is fairly straightforward, but it is hard work and can be complicated.

The Human Drama: Personality, Politics, and Corporate Culture

To help you understand ways to organize the people in your project, compare your project team to the cast members in a play or a movie. You have the producers and backers of the project (managers and other stakeholders), the director (the project manager), the main actors (the team leaders who play a key role throughout all or most of the project), the bit players (people who do one important task and then disappear from the scene), and the cameo players (the important people, such as consultants or advisors, who may add value to the project but don't necessarily stick around through the entire play). You also have the special-effects folks and the production crew, who have special skills but aren't as visible as other members of the cast. Just like in the acting world, you may have prima donnas and stars on your project team, and these people may require special care and attention.

Give Them a Script

One of the first considerations in developing your team is the same for actors in a play. They need a script to work from. Your script is your project plan. The members of your team need to see how the role they play helps the production (the project) be successful. Without that, they will make up lines, work on things that are not important, and possibly make some poor decisions. If you simply ask them to ad lib, just like actors, they won't do very well unless they are very experienced.

Avoid Casting Catastrophes

As you consider the organization of your cast, you'll need to develop some procedures to get things done. Lead players, bit players, and cameo players might possibly be directed (supervised) by assistant directors (other managers), and the production crew might work for lead crew or assistant producers.

Sometimes, after you have designed your ideal project organization, you'll find that the first choice for a team member in a particular role isn't even a possibility. For example, a person you would like to use in the project may not be available because of commitments to other, higher-priority projects. Or you may ask to use one person from a key function like accounting, but the manager from the group assigns a different person to your project. Thus, you may not get the experience you wanted in the cast and might have to adjust the schedule to accommodate for the less-experienced actor because it may take longer for him to learn his lines.

If you say you need a person with a particular skill for your project and the line manager (middle manager) assigns a person to you, you usually must accept this person's judgment unless you can make a good case for someone with whom you have more direct experience. If you find out later that the assigned person lacks the required skills, you can negotiate or look at other alternatives.

Project managers often need to make these kinds of concessions to other managers to get people for a project. It's like signing up Sean Penn to star in your movie and then finding out that Vince Vaughn was assigned the role instead. Obviously, the script and direction will require some adaptations.

The Proud, the Few ... the Project Team

When talented actors work on a play together, they all share and support the same goal (to produce a successful play). To this end, the actors, great and small, generally follow the lead of the director, and each player does his or her best to fulfill the specific role assigned in each play. Even the stars must follow the rules of the game. People on your project team need to play their roles in the same way.

For the people working on your project to become a real team, some specific things need to happen with your coaching and leadership as project manager. Project members need to ...

- Realize they'll be working on activities that involve more than one person. Therefore, they'll need to communicate and cooperate with each other to get things done.

- Share common methods and tools for assessing and communicating the status of the project.

- Identify and solve problems together and then live with the results (together) and agree to support the common decision in public.

- Accept the fact that, if one person makes a mistake, the entire team suffers. Therefore, they need to help each other avoid as many mistakes as possible.

- Realize that new people will be joining and other people will be leaving the project as time goes on, but the overall team structure and project goals will remain the same until the project reaches fruition.

- Recognize that changes will occur, and they must be flexible enough to adjust.

When other functions or departments are involved, positive interaction between the project manager and these groups is also critical to creating a good team. The relationships among line, staff, vendor, customer, and project personnel must be tempered with mutual trust.

On Becoming a Team: The Basic Ways to Organize People

Even though infinite possible combinations of people are involved, you should structure the organization of a project in only a few basic ways. These include functional (or line) organizations, pure-project structures, matrix organizations, or mixed organizational structures. These structures may be distributed over multiple locations as well, making the organization more of a virtual team in cyberspace rather than a group of people in a defined location. And as you'd expect, each organization has its pros and cons.

The Functional Project Organization

On a project that uses people from the same functional group (like sales), you can use the existing line organization to manage the project. This organizational structure is appropriate when the project is clearly the responsibility of one department. Many small projects use the functional organization as the project organization. A functional project is assigned to the functional department or division in a company that has the most interest and technical ability to complete the project. Almost all tasks in a project organized as part of a functional organization will be completed within the one functional area. Existing managers in the department often double as project managers.

The advantages of using a functional organization to complete a project include the following:

- **Familiarity of the team.** The team members are already familiar with each other, and the skill levels of the staff are clearly understood.

- **Established administrative systems.** The general administrative policies and procedures are already understood by the team and cost centers.

- **Staff availability.** The staff is readily available to the project because the line managers control the staff assignments. Thus, few, if any, interdepartmental conflicts arise over the use of resources.

- **Scheduling efficiency.** The scheduling of staff can be highly efficient. As a staff member is required, the person can immediately be assigned to a task and then return to routine work without serious logistical interruptions.

- **Clear authority.** The lines of authority and communication are understood. Thus, the conflicts between project authority and line authority are minimized.

The disadvantages of using a functional organization include the following:

- **Project isolation.** The project may be completed in isolation from other parts of the company and may fail to realize larger strategic goals as a result. However, if new collaboration, networking, and web-based tools are employed, this isolation can be minimized.

- **Limited resources.** The project is limited to the technical resources within the department, which may not be adequate to complete the tasks required. Of course, you can hire outside vendors and consultants, but expertise within other departments of the company is not readily available. This may lead to inefficiencies or redundancies in the project organization.

- **Bureaucratic procedures.** In a functional organization, the project manager usually has very weak decision-making authority. There may be more levels of approval than really necessary for the project because of the established bureaucracy in the line organization. This may impede progress and slow decision making.

- **Lack of project focus.** The project may lack focus or priority in a functional organization because it is not the only work being done. Thus, routine departmental work may interfere with project work. In addition, motivation for project work may suffer because the project is considered "additional" or "optional" work as opposed to being a clear responsibility.

- **Department orientation.** The project may suffer from "department-think," which occurs when the priorities of the department become the project priorities, regardless of the actual goals for the project. Work outside the department's normal concerns is given little attention, and the finished project may not be complete or may suffer quality problems as a result.

The Pure-Project Organization

In a pure-project organization, a team or "task force" is put together to accomplish the project's goals. In such an organization, all the team members report to the project manager during the course of the project. The team members do not have responsibility to other managers or jobs during the course of their work on the project. When a team member's responsibility for the project is complete, that person returns to another job or is assigned to another project. Only one project and one job are assigned at a time.

In the direct version of the pure-project structure, every project team member reports directly to the project manager. This is especially appropriate for small projects with 15 or fewer people involved. In what is termed the indirect version of the pure-project structure (suitable for larger projects), the project manager may have assistant managers or supervisors to manage subprojects or functional areas within the project. As in an ordinary line organization, the supervisors and assistants report directly to the project manager, and the various functional teams within the project report to the second-level team leaders. Extremely large projects may have multiple management levels, just like a corporation.

Pure-project organizations are found in companies fulfilling large government projects or in some engineering-driven companies that produce predictable model updates for their products. Large construction projects often employ a pure-project organization as well. If work on a complex, priority project spans a year or more, a pure-project organization is often an advantage.

The advantages of the pure-project organization include the following:

- **Clear project authority.** The project manager has true line authority over the entire project. Thus, there is always a clear channel for resolving project conflicts and determining priorities. The unity of command in a pure-project organization results in each subordinate having one and only one direct boss, a clear advantage in most situations.

- **Simplified project communications.** Communication and decision making within the project are simplified because everyone reports to the same project manager and focuses on the attainment of the same project goals.

- **Access to special expertise.** If the company will complete similar projects on a cyclic basis, specific expertise in the components of the project will be developed over time. It simply becomes a matter of transferring the experts to the right project at the right time.

- **Project focus and priority.** The pure-project organization supports a total view of the project and a strong, separate identity on the part of the participants. This helps keeps the project focused and integrated.

However, there are distinct disadvantages to the pure-project approach, including the following:

- **Duplication of efforts.** If a company has multiple projects with important goals in progress at the same time, some efforts may be duplicated, making the overall cost of the projects higher than necessary.

- **Unclear loyalties and motivations.** Project members form strong attachments to the project and each other, which is good. When the project is terminated, however, the team must be disbanded, which leads to uncertainty and conflict. Team members fear layoffs or anticipate assignments in undesirable projects in the future. Thus, keeping technically qualified people happy over the long haul becomes a major challenge. Your staffing management plan should clearly address this problem if you use this model.

- **Intra-company rivalry.** Rivalry and competition may become strong between various projects in a company that uses pure-project organization for its major projects. This may result in a company that competes with itself instead of with the competition—an ugly state of affairs.

The Matrix Organization

Implementing project management techniques sets into motion a significant change in the culture of an organization. One of the more common results of using project management in business is the introduction of "matrix management," a situation in which people report to multiple managers—one on the project side and one on the functional side. Matrix management involves coordinating a web of relationships that comes about when people join the project team and are subject to the resulting multiple authority-responsibility-accountability relationships in the organization.

The matrix organization is an attempt to take advantage of the benefits of a pure-project organization while maintaining the advantages of the functional organization. It is rare to find pure-project or pure-functional organizations in business anymore. Matrix organizations are typical today, even when other project management tools aren't involved.

In a matrix organization, a clear project team that crosses functional boundaries is established. Thus, team members may come from various departments. A project manager for each project is clearly defined, and projects are managed as separate and focused activities. The project manager may report to a higher-level executive or to one of the functional managers with the most interest in the project. However, the specific team members still report to their functional departments and maintain responsibilities for routine departmental work in their functional areas. In addition, people may be assigned to multiple project teams with different responsibilities. Some of the problems of coordination that plague other project structures can be minimized because the most important personnel for a project work together as a defined team within the matrix project structure.

The management responsibilities in these projects are temporary; a supervisor on one project may be a worker on another project, depending on the skills required. If project managers in a matrix situation do not have good relationships with line managers in the organization, conflicts may arise over employees' work and priorities. Not everyone adapts well to the matrix structure for this and other related reasons.

The complexity that a matrix organization causes is clear: people have multiple managers, multiple priorities, and multiple role identities. Because of these complexities, before a company enters into a matrix organizational structure to complete a project, the enterprise should meet at least two of the following criteria:

- A need to share scarce or unique resources required in more than one project or functional area

- A requirement for management to provide high levels of information processing and communication to complete the project

- Pressure from the outside by customers or agencies to have one person or group centralize control of the project, even though other groups in the organization may carry out the project

In cases in which projects meet these criteria, the matrix organization has the following distinct advantages:

- **Clear project focus.** The project has clear focus and priority because it has its own separate organization and management. A matrix organization realizes most of the planning and control advantages of a pure-project structure.

- **Flexible staffing.** Staffing is relatively flexible in matrix organizations because resources from various line organizations are available without job reassignment. Scarce technical resources are available to a wide range of projects in a company that regularly employs matrix-organized projects.

- **Adaptability to management needs and skills.** The authority of the project manager can be expansive or limited, depending on the priority of the project. If a project manager has strong authority, with command authority over most of the project and is assigned to the project full time, this would be called a "strong matrix" structure. If a project manager has weak authority, is assigned only part time, and the line managers have a strong influence on project activities, this type of organization would be dubbed a "weak matrix" structure. A "balanced matrix" structure falls in between. Thus, the matrix organization can be adapted to a wide range of projects, some that need strong support from line managers and some that require independent management.

- **Staff development opportunities.** People can be given new challenges and responsibilities that are not as likely to be offered in a purely functional organization. People can gain exposure to new technical areas, develop management skills, and have new experiences that maintain their interest and motivation at work. Ultimately, these new experiences can lead to more effective employees with high degrees of independence and flexibility. And because people tend to be more responsible for the quality of their own work in project-oriented groups, overall corporate productivity can improve.

- **Adaptability to business changes.** Matrix organizations can adapt more quickly to changing technological and market conditions than traditional, purely functional organizations, largely because of the high people-to-people contact in these organizations. In addition, matrix-organized projects encourage entrepreneurship and creative thinking that crosses functional responsibilities.

To take advantage of the benefits of matrix management, you must understand and deal with the disadvantages and potential conflicts within a matrix organization. The more frequently reported problems in matrix-managed organizations include the following:

- **Built-in conflicts.** Conflicts between line management priorities and project management priorities are inevitable. The question of who is in charge affects both the project and routine departmental work. The division of authority and responsibility relationships in matrix organizations is inherently complex. Matrix organizations are no place for intractable, autocratic managers with narrow views of organizational responsibilities.

- **Resistance to termination.** As in pure-project organizations, team members may prefer their project roles to their line responsibilities, creating interesting motivational challenges for managers. Because the team members have unique identities and relationships in their project roles, matrix projects often resist termination.

- **Complex command and authority relationships.** There is no unity of command in a matrix organization, a clear violation of traditional management principles. The team member is often caught between conflicting demands of the line manager and the project manager. The discomfort and uncertainty of having more than one boss at the same time cannot be adequately described to someone who has never experienced the situation. Of course, if the two bosses are adequately trained and are open in their communications, many of these difficulties can be resolved or eliminated.

- **Complex employee recognition systems.** In a matrix organization, which manager should complete the employee's performance reviews or make recommendations for raises? If the reward responsibilities and authorities of the project manager and the line manager are not clearly identified, the employee may feel unrecognized. It is imperative that both line responsibilities and project responsibilities are accounted for in the employee's performance review process. Some form of reward system needs to be established for team members within the project; whether this is just public acknowledgment of a job well done or formal monetary rewards depends on the project and your budget.

The Mixed Organization

Some companies employ a mixture of functional, matrix, and pure-project organizations to accomplish enterprise goals. In companies with a wide range of projects, a Project Management Office (PMO) may be set up to help administer projects as well. The people in this office provide expertise and assistance in planning and tracking projects. In other companies, the PMO may become a division in its own right with full-time project managers and staff responsible for project-oriented activities.

When a project has more than one purpose, mixed organizational structures are usually the norm. The space shuttle missions are a perfect example. Getting the astronauts ready for a flight is one project. Building and installing a new robot arm is another. Although someone is responsible for coordinating all the projects and making sure they get done at the same time so the launch can happen as planned, the people are organized on a subproject basis. Each subproject requires a completely different set of team members and organizational structures.

Mixed organizations are not distinguishable from most matrix organizations because of the complexity of relationships, and most of the strengths and weaknesses of a matrix organization also apply to a mixed organizational structure. The unique problem in mixed organizations is one caused by the extreme flexibility in the way the organization adapts to project work. This leads to potential incompatibilities, confusion, conflicts, and duplications of effort if the managers are not adequately trained to deal with these complexities.

Which Structure Should You Use?

The organization you choose for most ordinary business projects will probably be an adaptation of a matrix or functional organization. No matter which organization you choose, always develop an organization chart that clearly shows who reports to whom so there are fewer mistakes or incorrect assumptions.

For example, a project manager may decide to use a strong matrix organization with a mixture of functional people from the company and consultants with skills and experience who are not available within the company.

Using a RACI Chart

Like a RASIC chart, a RACI chart is a special type of responsibility assignment matrix that helps all the project team members understand whom to work with on various decisions and issues as the project progresses. RACI is an acronym for the following:

- Responsible
- Accountable
- Consult
- Inform

Take a look at the following high-level RACI chart of sample project activities and people who are responsible for those activities.

Activity	Alan	Beth	Colleen	Duane	Ellie	Fred
Requirements	R		C		I	A
Design		I	C	R		A
Development	C	I	I	R	A	
Testing	C	R	I	I	I	A
Training	A	I	C	C	C	R

R = Responsible   A = Accountable   C = Consult   I = Inform

Matching the Organization to Fit the Project

Project size, project length, experience of the team members, location of the project, and factors unique to the project all have influence on the selection of a project organizational form. For example, on a small, short-term project for creating a new process for bringing new customers into Pinnacle Equipment, the organization of the project might be along functional lines that already exist with the involvement of a few outside resources and key vendors to complete specific tasks. On a larger project to design and build the next generation of customer relationship management (CRM), a matrix organization might be more appropriate because of the wide range of involvement and ongoing communication required across departments of manufacturing, marketing, engineering, and customer services.

Managing the Working Committee

Remember the working committee? Now you really need to get them working. If you remember, committee members come from different parts of the organization, and the committee's role is to provide feedback on the impact of project decisions and deliverables on their various departments.

Develop clear ties between working committee members and members of your project team. For example, in a project, the project manager will develop a working relationship between the business analysts working on the accounting portion of the project and the accountant sitting on the working committee. As the project team works the options around decisions, the business analysts should be talking regularly with the accounting representative about those options.

You may consider scheduling regular meetings of the working committee to give them status reports, but you will rarely excite people about going to a meeting where they hear only about the status of the project. Focus most of the WC meeting on working through issues that have an impact across the organization. For example, a project manager on a certain project has options around how to handle financial data that will impact sales (i.e.: commissions), accounting, invoicing, and accounts payable. He will have the WC consider the options and develop a recommendation for the project team. That will ensure the buy-in of the commercial side of the business after the project has been completed.

The Project Management Office (PMO)

It is widely believed that companies that implement Project Management Offices (PMOs) have a higher rate of overall success. Surprising (even shockingly), the Standish Group reports that companies with PMOs generally do not fare any better than those companies without PMOs. The author of the Standish survey thinks "in some cases, compliance and governance processes caused programs to run longer and be delayed … projects don't do well, so you add governance. Then they do worse and you add more governance without ever knowing what you get out of it."

A popular misconception of the PMO is that it should only be responsible for driving standards and what has been identified as best practices across a company for all projects. Actually, that turns a PMO into what could only be described as the Project Police. No wonder some people think that PMO stands for "Pile More On"—meaning bureaucracy! So let's look at how a PMO might work more effectively.

What Is the Purpose of a PMO?

The purpose of a PMO should be to drive the strategic goals of a company. The PMO is not involved in developing the strategy itself; it is the vehicle for achieving the goals the strategy has defined. Usually, multiple projects will be required to achieve a strategic goal. Seldom will one project do the trick. The business purpose for the PMO is to provide focus and oversight for related projects. Too often related projects can develop a narrow focus (which is very appropriate) but do not have the big-picture view of how a particular project might be connected to other projects. When the project is completed, the program will end, and the real effort to obtain the business benefits falls on the operations group to deliver.

Nature of Program Management and Projects

Program management is the coordination of multiple projects to deliver the strategic objectives and benefits. It involves assuring alignment in the projects to, hopefully, provide the return on the investment/cost and optimize the use of often limited resources.

Just as you learned about dependencies within the work breakdown structure (WBS), there are dependencies between and among projects within a program. The greatest responsibility of the program office can be to manage those interdependencies between projects and try to ensure that one project's problems don't spread to others. That may involve shifting people to handle project work that is falling behind from one project to another. Only a program manager would have that kind of visibility on resources—a project manager would only be concerned about their project—and rightfully so!

Joint Planning Within the Program

At the program level, projects often share people and other resources, and the PMO will assist in setting the right priorities when there are competing interests between projects. The decisions at the program level should always be focused on the decision, or decisions, that best serve the interests of the business in achieving the strategic objectives for the program. And that may mean pushing a project or two back in priority when resource constraints demand action.

There can also be joint planning for activities like risk identification and mitigation that is monitored and managed at the program level. Having all the project managers engaged in joint planning will help them understand the interdependencies among their projects. And it will highlight the importance of maintaining their schedule and milestones. As part of the risk planning and monitoring, it should be agreed by all the project managers within the program that if their projects start having difficulties, they will let the entire group know so a common solution can be developed.

Resolving Issues

Often, there are issues regarding scope, quality, schedule, and cost that occur when various projects are attempting to coordinate and deliver against a strategic goal. The PMO will usually assume the role, in conjunction with a Governance Board or Steering Committee, of governance for managing and resolving those issues. It may require key decisions on priorities, including the impact those decisions may have on individual projects and their ability to deliver on time and on budget. Each project manager should provide input on the options being considered and the impact on schedule, budget, and quality for his or her project. However, after the decision is made at the program level, the project manager's job is to carry out the decision to the best of their ability at the project level.

Global Programs

Finally, the PMO may be required to manage diverse projects that are occurring all over the world. Balancing culture, language, time zones, and other considerations can be a full-time job in itself. Here is where a set of global standards can be very important—particularly around such questions as the requirements for preparing for a stage gate review. However, a program manager should be aware that local variations may need to exist. The trick is to make it clear to each project how far they may vary from the standard and when they have crossed a line.

Relationship Among Projects, Programs, and Portfolios

In order to understand how all of these elements fit together, it might be helpful to review the definitions for each part of a PMO:

- **Projects** are defined by the Project Management Institute (PMI) as a temporary endeavor undertaken to create a unique product or service. In other words, it has a definite beginning and a definite end with a unique deliverable at the end. Ultimately, that is how you can distinguish between a project and ordinary work.

- **Programs** are comprised of multiple projects that are managed in a coordinated fashion to meet a strategic business goal that would not have been achieved if they had been managed separately. And programs often include work that is outside the scope of a discrete project or projects.

- A **portfolio** is defined as a collection of projects and programs—but may also include the ongoing support of the project deliverables after they enter the market—that are grouped together in order to meet the business objectives in an effective and efficient management fashion. The portfolio is the truest indicator of a company's goals, vision, and path forward because investment decisions and the attendant priorities are made at the portfolio level.

It should be obvious, but is worth stating that not all projects fit into a portfolio. For example, there may be a project to upgrade the software of the company to a newer version. That is clearly a project, but it may not have any higher strategic goal. It is simply a project that meets a specific need and nothing more grandiose than that.

The Role of a Program Manager

A program manager has a different role than a project manager. A program manager works with and interacts with project managers but is neither their supervisor nor their peer. The program manager is usually very experienced in project management and has usually managed very expensive and/or complicated and risky projects. That kind of experience allows the program manager to offer help and advice to project managers. Depending on the nature of the way a company might organize the PMO, the project managers may have a direct reporting relationship to the program manager just like a line manager in a functional part of the company such as accounting or sales.

What It Takes to Become a Program Manager

To become a program manager takes a special blend of knowledge, skills, and competencies to move in that direction. Look at the following chart and notice the path for progressing from project manager to program manager. There is a definite progression and road map for moving along the career path in project management.

Project Management Levels	Project Manager	Senior Project Manager	Program Manager
Typical nature of project in terms of overall risk, exposure, size, and complexity	Lead and manage low-risk projects	Lead and manage medium-risk projects	Recognized as an expert; lead high-risk projects
	Entry-level project manager	More experienced in project management	Strong customer relationship and management skills
	Have a greater understanding of the project life cycle	Manage projects with increasing complexity	Responsible for improvement of project management discipline
Project Skills			
Initiation	Fundamental	Advanced	Expert
Planning	Fundamental	Advanced	Expert
Scope, Time, Cost, and Quality Management	Fundamental	Advanced	Expert
Reporting Communications	Fundamental	Advanced	Expert

Project Management Levels	Project Manager	Senior Project Manager	Program Manager
Risk and Procurement Management	Fundamental	Advanced	Expert
Project Tools and Techniques	Fundamental	Advanced	Expert

Leadership

Leadership skills are very important in the PMO. Since there are multiple projects within the program, developing confidence and respect among the project managers is key to success. They will look to you to lead the direction of the projects, to establish communications around requirements and progress, and to work with them to make decisions.

People Skills

As a leader, you must utilize all the people skills you possess. That includes the following:

- Listening carefully
- Exhibiting empathy
- Communicating clearly
- Demonstrating fairness

That is not to say that your technical skills are not important (they are), but your people skills will be the ones that motivate people and encourage them during difficult times in a project or program.

These people skills are important, not only for the project managers and project teams within the program, but also in the broader spectrum of stakeholders.

External Factors

Outside influences can have a major impact on a PMO. These influences may come from a variety of sources, but their effect on the PMO will be tangible, so you must learn to recognize and manage them.

Internal and External Politics

Everyone knows that politics can play an important role in any project, let alone a program. Within the PMO, managing politics can be just as big a job as managing the project work. Just as there are competing interests to be managed within projects, there will be competing interests among the senior management staff that you will have to navigate carefully. If your sponsor has a sound grasp of the broader political spectrum, use that person's counsel wisely before you make any rash moves or decisions.

Changes in the Organization

Major changes in the organization, such as a widespread reorganization, might bring new stresses to a PMO. New stakeholders may appear on the scene and want to shift the direction of the program. The location of a division of the company might change and cause a distraction to the key people who are required to make a program successful. Working through these types of external factors can challenge any program manager. The best course of action is to meet with the sponsor and the Governance Board or Steering Committee to see whether the business requirements for the PMO to deliver have changed. If things have changed, you need to recharter the program and understand the new requirements. The worst action is to assume everything is status quo and move on.

Alterations in the Situation

Often over the course of a program, the PMO may encounter a shift in government regulations that can have an immediate impact on the business goals for the PMO. Get the right stakeholders involved to understand the changes and determine how to modify the programs to meet the new requirements.

There may also be a shift in market conditions that can cause a program to slow down, speed up, or even be canceled. A strong PMO manager will do their best to keep up to date with any shifting market conditions and seek to understand the impact to either a particular project or the entire program.

Shifts in the Enterprise

During the course of a long program, there may well be a change in direction, particularly if the change is accompanied by a new CEO. These types of changes require the PMO to review all of the programs and projects to assess the impact of the change on the strategic goals for the programs.

In all of these situations, the best course of action for the PMO is to meet with the sponsor and the Governance Board or Steering Committee and work out the new strategic goals for the PMO to deliver. In most cases, everyone will want to take a wait-and-see stance. Find out whether the sponsor would recommend that position or just keep plowing ahead until the new direction is clear.

Web Resources for Project Managers

The following internet resources provide general information about project management or refer individuals to vendors who can provide special training programs for project managers. All of the organizations listed here have certified training practitioners they deem qualified to teach their methodology for managing projects.

Project Management Institute
Website: pmi.org

The Project Management Institute (PMI) is a not-for-profit organization dedicated to the advancement of project management methodology and the training of project managers. The quarterly *Project Management Journal,* published electronically by the PMI, includes timely articles about project management procedures, experiences, and techniques. The institute holds regular seminars and has local chapters all over the world where meetings are held for members. The PMI also offers various certification programs for people who want to verify and document their project management expertise—the Project Management Professional (PMP) and the Certified Associate in Project Management (CAPM) are the most common. As of this writing, the membership fee for an individual is $129 per year, and corporate memberships are available. A subscription to *Project Management Journal* and *PM Network* and a copy of the *Project Management Body of Knowledge (PMBOK) Guide* are included as part of the membership fee.

PRINCE2
Website: prince2.com

PRINCE2 (an acronym for Projects IN Controlled Environments) is a de facto process-based method for effective project management. Used extensively by the UK government, PRINCE2 is also widely recognized and utilized in the private sector. The PRINCE2 method is in the public domain and offers nonproprietorial best practice guidance on project management. PRINCE2 has an extensive ITIL (IT Infrastructure Library) available for members. The Office of Government Commerce offers two examinations for the professional certification in PRINCE2—the Foundation examination followed by the Practitioner certification.

International Project Management Association
Website: ipma.ch

This organization is based in Switzerland and provides information on project management activities and standards around the world. IPMA is a federation of over 55 member associations and is the world's first project management association. There are both corporate and individual memberships available. Individual memberships cost €100 per year.

Index

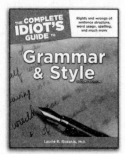

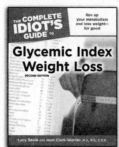
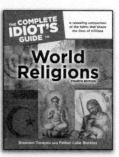

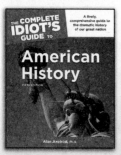

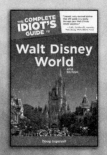